LIFE WITHOUT PAROLE

LIFE WITHOUT PAROLE

Living in Prison Today

FOURTH EDITION

Victor Hassine
Inmate AM4737

Edited by

Robert Johnson
American University

Ania Dobrzanska
The Moss Group, Inc.

Foreword by

John Irwin
San Francisco State University

New York   Oxford
OXFORD UNIVERSITY PRESS
2009

Oxford University Press, Inc., publishes works that further Oxford University's
objective of excellence in research, scholarship, and education.

Oxford   New York
Auckland   Cape Town   Dar es Salaam   Hong Kong   Karachi
Kuala Lumpur   Madrid   Melbourne   Mexico City   Nairobi
New Delhi   Shanghai   Taipei   Toronto

With offices in
Argentina   Austria   Brazil   Chile   Czech Republic   France   Greece
Guatemala   Hungary   Italy   Japan   Poland   Portugal   Singapore
South Korea   Switzerland   Thailand   Turkey   Ukraine   Vietnam

Published by Oxford University Press, Inc.
198 Madison Avenue, New York, New York 10016
http://www.oup.com

Oxford is a registered trademark of Oxford University Press

Library of Congress Cataloging-in-Publication Data

Hassine, Victor, 1955–
    Life without parole : living in prison today / Victor Hassine; edited by Robert
Johnson, Ania Dobrzanska; foreword by John Irwin.—4th ed.
        p. cm.
    Previously published: Los Angeles: Roxbury Pub. Co., c2004.
    ISBN 978-0-19-534113-3 (alk. paper)
    1. Prisoners—Pennsylvania—Case studies.   2. Hassine, Victor, 1955–
3. Life imprisonment—Pennsylvania—Case studies.   4. Prisons—
Pennsylvania—Case studies.   5. Graterford State Correctional Institution.
I. Title.
    HV9475.P2H37 2008
    365'.60922748—dc21   2007048885

Note: All author royalties are being donated to a nonprofit charity

Printing number: 9 8 7 6 5 4 3 2 1

Printed in the United States of America
on acid-free paper

In memory of Sam Hassine, April 20, 1933–March 7, 2006,
my father, my best friend, my strength, my heart.

CONTENTS

ABOUT THIS BOOK

I n 1981, law-school graduate Victor Hassine was sentenced to prison for life without parole for a capital offense. His updated book is an insightful look at conditions of confinement and prison life in America today, taking the reader on a guided tour of the prison experience. In powerful and poignant prose, Hassine conveys the changes in prison life that have come about as a result of the war on drugs, prison overcrowding, and demographic changes in inmate populations. Topics covered include rape, prison gangs, prison violence, AIDS, homosexuality, prison politics, the nature and evolution of prisons and the impact of prisons on the larger society of which they are a part.*

About the Fourth Edition

The first three editions of *Life Without Parole: Living in Prison Today* were enthusiastically received. The fourth edition features revisions of each and every chapter together with two new chapters that pave the way to a unique, insider's view of the evolution of prisons as living environments and as institutions of punishment. Every chapter also has a new introduction, which was either written or revised by Robert Johnson and Ania Dobrzanska.

New Chapters:

- Chapter 25: "A Hitchhiker's Guide to Prison, Part II: The Big House: What Goes 'Round Comes 'Round," walks the reader through the many prisons Hassine has lived in, comparing and contrasting them in terms of living conditions, social climate, administrative organization, and the experience of prison as punishment.

- Chapter 26: "A Hitchhiker's Guide to Prison, Part III: The Contemporary Prison: Yesterday, Today, and Tomorrow," presents

---

* **Editors' Note:** The names of many of the inmates and prison employees described in this book have been changed to protect their identity.

the mature reflections of a man who has seen all that prisons have to offer and helps us understand what tomorrow's prisons will have to offer.

Also available by the author and editors of this book is *The Crying Wall and Other Prison Stories,* a selection of fictional stories and poems about prison life. More information may be obtained by going to www.willotrees.com.

FOREWORD

John Irwin
San Francisco State University

Victor Hassine's *Life Without Parole* takes its place among a rather large array of descriptions of prison life written by prisoners. Some of these were written in the last century, but the majority of them came about in the last three decades, for the obvious reason that prisoners are becoming more and more literate. Some of the best of these are *In the Belly of the Beast* by Jack Abbott, *A Sense of Freedom* by Jimmy Boyle (a British prisoner), *Tales from the Joint* by K. Hawkeye Gross, and *The Big Huey* by Greg Newbold (a New Zealand prisoner).

I think Hassine's book is most like Gross's *Tales from the Joint* because both books were written by people who had little experience with the social worlds, mostly lower class, that supply prisons their inmates. *Life Without Parole*'s particular strength is that it is about a series of large, contemporary prisons. Until reading this book, I hadn't seen any good prisoner descriptions about prisons today, after the extreme overcrowding and the violence between prisoners that have changed conditions so significantly. Hassine has a sharp eye for contemporary prison violence because he came to prison as an outsider, unfamiliar with the patterns and values of the thieves, hustlers, drug addicts, state-raised convicts, and gang bangers who populate the prison. At times, perhaps, Hassine accepts too readily other prisoners' fairly standard explanations for the way things are, but he is intelligent and frequently sees things clearly from his very different perspective (he is a law-school graduate).

All in all, *Life Without Parole* is a very valuable work on the contemporary prison, produced by an intelligent individual who has experienced prison first-hand for an extended period.

ABOUT THE AUTHOR

Victor Hassine has been doing life without possibility of parole since 1980, the year he graduated from New York School Law. With others he filed a conditions of confinement lawsuit at Pennsylvania's Graterford prison, which resulted in $50 million of improvements there. Transferred to Western Penitentiary, he joined another lawsuit, resulting in $75 million in improvements. Many prizes from PEN's prison writing contest encouraged him in 1996 to publish *Life Without Parole: Living in Prison Today*, now in its fourth edition. In 2003 *The Journal of Applied Psychoanalytic Studies* published his essay of managing prison violence. Hassine is the major contributor to *The Crying Wall and Other Prison Stories* published in 2005.

TIME LINE

1955:   Born June 20.

1956:   Family exiled from Egypt for religious reasons.

1961:   Family immigrated to Trenton, New Jersey.

1966:   Became an American citizen.

1977:   Graduated from Dickinson College in Carlisle, Pennsylvania, majoring in political science and history.

1980:   June, graduated from New York Law School. November, arrested on an open charge of homicide.

1981:   Convicted of first-degree murder and sent to SCI-Graterford.

1985:   Helped to found the first prison synagogue.

1986:   Helped to found the first Jewish Post-Release House. Filed conditions of confinement suit in Federal Court against SCI-Graterford to abolish double-celling. September, assaulted by an inmate and transferred to SCI-Pittsburgh.

1987:   Filed conditions of confinement suit in Federal Court against SCI-Pittsburgh and Pennsylvania Department of Corrections.

1989:   January, assaulted by an inmate and recovered in outside hospital. April, transferred from Pittsburgh hospital to SCI-Camp Hill. August, transferred to SCI-Rockview.

1990: Received Pennsylvania Prison Society's Inmate of the Year Award.

1996: Published first edition of *Life Without Parole: Living in Prison Today.*

1998: Transferred to SCI-Albion

1999: Published second edition of *Life Without Parole: Living in Prison Today.*

2001: Transferred to SCI-Green Pennsylvania's super-max prison.

2004: Published third edition of *Life Without Parole: Living in Prison Today.* Transferred to SCI-Somerset

2006: Filed application for commutation of sentence—received recommendation of the Department of Corrections.

ABOUT THE EDITORS

Robert Johnson is a Professor of Justice, Law and Society at American University in Washington, D.C. His social science books include *Culture and Crisis in Confinement, Condemned To Die, Hard Time,* and *Death Work,* which received the Outstanding Book Award of the Academy of Criminal Justice Sciences. Johnson's creative writing includes two collections of original poems, *Poetic Justice,* which received the L.I.F.E. Award from Willo Trees Press, and *Burnt Offerings;* and two collections of short stories, *Justice Follies* and *The Crying Wall.* Johnson has testified or provided expert affidavits before state and federal courts, the U.S. Congress, and the European Commission of Human Rights. He is a Distinguished Alumnus of the Nelson A. Rockefeller College of Public Affairs and Policy, University at Albany, State University of New York.

Ania Dobrzanska, formerly a Grant Manager/Corrections Certification Specialist (CCP) at the American Correctional Association, joined The Moss Group, Inc., a Washington, D.C., criminal justice consulting firm, in October 2005. Her main duties involved work under cooperative agreement with the National Institute of Corrections assisting with implementation of the Prison Rape Elimination Act (PREA). She is a Certified Corrections Manager, a designation conferred by the American Correctional Association and has received a Commander-in-Chief's Coin of Excellence from Military Order of World Wars for putting together a Youth Leadership Conference for at-risk youth. Dobrzanska has published several articles in *Corrections Today* on issues of professionalism in corrections and leadership. She is coauthor of a chapter on the history of prisons in *Prisons: Today and Tomorrow,* a widely used text; and coauthor of an article on the adjustment of life-sentence prisoners published in *Corrections Compendium,* a peer-reviewed journal. Dobrzanska is also a published writer of fiction.

ACKNOWLEDGMENTS

*L*ife Without Parole is a living and breathing volume that thickens and matures as I continue to survive my prison odyssey. Because it became viable and quickened in previous editions, this fourth edition is equally indebted to all those who inspired, encouraged, supported and assisted in the writing, editing, and publishing of the first, second, and third editions. For that reason I feel obliged and honored to reprint the acknowledgments that appeared in the third edtion.

However, before recalling my indebtedness to those who made previous editions of this book possible, I would like to acknowledge those who have more recently helped breath new life into the fourth edition.

It is an unfortunate sign of our times that I dare not name the dedicated and decent corrections staff who, through example, professionalism, and refusal to abandon the possibility of reform, encouraged and inspired my contributions to this edition of *Life Without Parole*. Suffice it to note there is a unit manager and a team of librarians who represent the best in the field of corrections and to whom I am deeply grateful. Of course, I owe a mountain of thanks to my editors Dr. Robert Johnson and Ania Dobrzanska, without whom this new edition would not have been possible. Finally, a special thanks to Sherith Pankratz, senior editor, Leigh-Ann Todd-Enyame, editorial assistant, and all the others of the Oxford University Press team assigned to the production of *Life Without Parole*. I am honored to have the fourth edition included among the distinguished family of books published under the renowned Oxford label.

First and foremost is Anne Hartford, whose ennobling love encourages and perfects me so I am able to muster the great force needed to maintain a caring and reasoned vision over a desperate and angry one. Dr. Tom Bernard and Dr. Robert Johnson, my editors, who were able to gently tease out of me what I believe to be the most noteworthy and provocative edition to date. Superintendent Edward Brennan and Unit Manager Ronald Bryant of SCI-Albion defied the stern demands of a prevailing punitive/warehousing prison model to encourage and facilitate my writing. Claude Teweles, of Roxbury Publishing Company, for displaying the courage, vision, and patience to publish my controversial tome in the first three editions. Finally, there is Anton Diether, master wordsmith, who chiseled my words into their fullest and most meaningful voice.

I owe a lifetime of gratitude to a great many people who supported me, cared about me, believed in me, and encouraged me during these difficult prison years and while I was writing this book. You can't do time in prison alone and still expect to come out of it sane. I needed a lot of help from people on the outside to constantly remind me that I was still a worthwhile part of the American quilt.

I would like to start by thanking my father, mother, and brother who in many ways did this time with me so I would never have to feel completely alone. I hope the publication of this book will give them that sense of pride that I have not been able to offer since my incarceration. But for them I would have long ago lost this struggle to retain my dignity.

From Graterford Penitentiary I would like to thank Larry Karlin for being the devoted friend I could always count on to be in my corner; Ted Klugman (Tefka), who was the first one to encourage me to write about my prison experiences and who introduced me to the Fortune Society and the Pen Prison Writing Contest; Phil and Frida Zelt, Catherine Sion, Itka Zigmantovitch, and many other prison volunteers who showed me friendship, kindness, and concern, which in turn gave me the strength and inspiration to write this book; Angus Love, the best, most honest, and committed lawyer I know, without whose dedication Pennsylvania prisons would be much worse places to be; and Irv Hommer, the radio talk-show host who showed me in no uncertain terms that many people out there really do care.

From Western Penitentiary I would like to thank Meyer and Sandra Tattelman, Sam Steinberg, and Rabbi Epstein—Jewish volunteers who managed to inspire hope in the most hopeless prison imaginable; Ken Davenport who, with the assistance of Nelson "Peepers" Mikesel, helped me to file and successfully litigate my conditions of confinement lawsuit against Western Penitentiary; Ed Feinstein, the lawyer whose skill and talent kept me many times from harm's way; and Bob Koehler, my college fraternity brother (Phi Alpha), who has stayed with me all these years.

From Rockview Penitentiary I would like to thank Rita Foderaro, a dear friend who believed in my talent and encouraged people to read my work; and two staff members, Mr. Sefchick and Mr. Davys, who provided me with the encouragement and support to write this book.

Many thanks to former Pennsylvania Commissioner of Corrections, David Owens, who tried diligently to change the Pennsylvania prison system for the better; former Commissioner of Corrections

Joseph D. Lehman who gave not only his permission but his support for the writing of this book; the Pennsylvania Prison Society for having the courage and perseverance to demand a human face on the Pennsylvania Department of Corrections; the Fortune Society of New York for promoting the annual PEN American Prison Writing Competition, which was directly responsible for my decision to express myself through the written word.

Finally, a special thanks to the Superintendent of the State Correctional Institution at Rockview, Dr. Joseph F. Mazurkiewicz, for working so hard and unyieldingly to keep his prison safe and clean for its inmates. If I had been sent to Dr. Mazurkiewicz's prison fifteen years ago to serve my time, I probably would not have had very much to write about.

And a very special thanks to editors Thomas J. Bernard, Richard McCleary, and Richard A. Wright for their patience and dedication to making the second edition possible. Lastly, my deepest gratitude to Sherry Truesdell of Truesdell Word Processing Services for her professionalism, honesty, and dependability.

PRISON

Prison
life poisoning
punishment
for people of poverty

Prison
lash of rebuke
wielded like a whip
on the working wounded

Prison
dark black
dungeon of despair
denizen of the dispossessed

Prison
waste dump
for wasted lives,
house of refuge
for human refuse,
warehouse for
worn out,
used up
cast off
careworn creatures
now humbled and discarded.

Prison
time out
of sight,
time out
of mind,
for those
who don't
toe the line.

—*Robert Johnson*

Poetic Justice: Reflections on the Big House, the Death House, and the American Way of Justice. Northwoods Press; Conservatory of American Letters (2004:30). Reprinted with permission.

PART I

PRISON LIFE

EDITORS' NOTE

Victor Hassine, like all prisoners, is a man with two lives—the life he led before prison and the life he leads in prison. His life as a civilian ended in 1981 at the gates of the State Correctional Institution at Graterford. His second life, which began in June of that year, is the focus of the next several chapters. One day, Hassine may be granted a third life if he is released from prison and allowed to join the free world. For now, that is but a distant hope, since life-sentence prisoners in Pennsylvania are ineligible for parole.

Most of us think of prisons and prisoners in stereotypical terms. Before he became a convict, Hassine was no exception. He expected to do his time in the rigid Big House made famous in James Cagney movies, a place of rules, lines, and totalitarian order. He knew that "country club prisons" were mythical creations of the media, though he harbored hopes that such places might exist. What he found was a "prison in turmoil," to quote John Irwin (*Prisons in Turmoil*).

In the early 1980s, many American prisons were overcrowded and under-managed. Gangs had proliferated, and chaos and violence were remarkably common. In some institutions, officers could barely protect themselves, let alone protect the prisoners. To enter such a place, particularly as a first offender, was to enter a nightmare. Hassine introduces you to his nightmare. Put yourself in his prison-issue shoes and imagine your daily life unfolding in a world so alien that it might be called *Planet Prison*, where violence rules and justice is often little more than the law of the jungle.

How I Became a Convict

EDITORS' NOTE

Criminologists explore the nature of crime, probing the interplay of biological and social forces. Neither nature nor nurture works alone. Criminals are not "born," in the sense that their criminality is inevitable from birth. By the same token, criminals are not purely products of their environments, however bleak such places might be. Many people transcend high-crime environments and bring something to the world other than a "blank slate" on which a society or culture inscribes its values. Certainly, no one is born a convict. Just as certainly, though, the kind of prison to which an inmate is exposed will shape the meaning of the term convict for that person.

Victor Hassine entered a brutal and violent prison. Not all prisons are like Graterford, though many were at one time or another in their history. His coming of age in Graterford tells a story that applies to many prisons and prisoners, a regrettable reality from the point of view of public policy. If people adapt themselves to a savage jungle like Graterford, what kind of citizens will they become if and when they are ever released?

On entering Graterford, Hassine seems to step back in time. The place is reminiscent of a dungeon, dark, dank, and dangerous. The inhabitants seem scarred and deformed. Like primitives marooned in the past, they seem less than human. Yet, Hassine is wise enough to know that he must become a part of that world; and that, in time, a new generation of inmates may one day see him as a primitive creature of the prison world, a sobering thought.

In no uncertain terms, Hassine's initial experience is lonely, frightening, and degrading. First impressions, he tells us, are hard to manage but matter greatly, perhaps following a man for the remainder of his confinement. Prison officials offer little comfort and do not seem to be in control. The place is wild, the inmates unrestrained. Classification, like security, is an empty gesture. Staff members play-act at being in charge, but instead focus only on their own safety and filling out forms. Hassine must adapt on his own—choose friends, develop a routine, carve out a way of life, and get through the day. That he adapts as well as he does is a credit to his resourcefulness. That he can take us with him on this journey is a tribute to his skill as an observer of the human condition.

I have heard Graterford called "The Farm," "The Camp," "The Fort," and "Dodge City," but I have never heard it called safe. When I was in the county jail awaiting trial, I saw grown men cry because their counselors told them they were being transferred to Graterford.

Graterford State Prison, Pennsylvania's largest and most violent penal institution, was built in the early 1930s to hold all of the state's most violent prisoners. On June 14, 1981, while it could not contain all eight thousand or more of the state's most wanted, it certainly had enough room to hold me. Its steel-reinforced concrete wall measures four feet thick by thirty-two feet tall and encloses over sixty-five acres of land. Originally designed to hold eight separate cellblocks within its perimeter, Graterford ended up with only five. However these cellblocks are huge constructions, each containing four hundred cells.

Everything inside appears as huge and massive as the wall itself. Each housing unit is a rectangular structure, measuring about 45 feet wide by three stories tall by 820 feet long (over twice the length of a football field), perpendicularly attached to a quarter-mile-long main corridor that measures about 20 feet wide by two stories high.

I knew none of this as I sat handcuffed and shackled in the back seat of the sheriff's car, waiting to be taken inside to begin serving my life-without-parole sentence. All I could see was a blur of dirty, grainy whiteness from the giant wall that dominated the landscape before me. It made me feel very small and insignificant, and very frightened.

As I looked up in awe at the wall, the sheriff was saying something my mind couldn't process. I was distracted by fragmented recollections racing through my head—of my arrest, trial, the crowd of strangers who attended my sentencing, and my mother crying as I was led away for transport to this monster before me, opening it arms to me. These memories—uninvited, troubling—added to my fear, making it almost unbearable.

A giant steel gate rose up to allow the sheriff's car to drive into Graterford's cavernous sallyport area, a fortified enclosure designed to control traffic. Once the gate fell shut, I was immediately hustled out of the car by some very large, serious-looking corrections officers. I knew I would have to submit to a cavity search, but it wasn't the strip search that dominated my memory of this event. It was the *noise*.

Since concrete and steel do not absorb sound, the clamor and voices from within just bounced around, crashing into each other to create a hollow, booming echo that never ended. It sounded as if someone had put a microphone inside a crowded locker room with the volume pumped up, broadcasting the noise all around the sallyport. It was this deafening background noise that would lull me to sleep at night and greet me in the morning for the next five years. Though I have been out of Graterford for many years now, its constant din still echoes in my ears.

The prison guards finished their search and escorted me up Graterford's main corridor, a dim, gloomy, 20-foot-wide by over 1,500-foot-long stretch. They seemed distant, remote, almost unreal. Aside from their size, which was substantial, what was most striking about my escorts was their impenetrable air of routine and indifference. They were about to feed me to a pride of hungry lions as casually as if they were walking me through a part. The lack of natural light and the damp, dungeon-like air in this place was oppressive. As I took one tentative step after another, I promised myself never to take bright and sunny places for granted again. Having just left the courthouse hours before, I was so disoriented that I lost track of how far I had been walking.

Things changed dramatically and irrevocably once I reached the central corridor gate that separated the administrative section from the prison proper. This was the first time I saw the faces, shapes, and shadows of the men who would become my future friends, enemies, and neighbors. One man was staring menacingly at me, while another, displaying a row of broken and missing teeth, shot me an evil smile. Others seemed to stare right through me as if I had no physical form. They stared at me and I stared back, as scared as I had ever been in my entire life.

Once inside, I was walked through a gauntlet of desperate men. Their hot smell in the muggy corridor was as foul as their appearance. Most of them were wearing their "Graterford Tan," an ashen gray pallor. The discoloration of these distorted human forms represented the prison landscape. At Graterford you work, eat, sleep, and idle indoors. You never have to go outdoors unless you wanted to risk the sometimes deadly yard. Many inmates served their time like cave dwellers, never leaving Graterford's concrete and steel shelter.

My first impression was that most of these men brandished their scars and deformities like badges of honor. None of them seemed to have a full set of front teeth. Many bore prominently displayed tattoos of skulls or demons. They all seemed either too tall or too small, but none seemed right. Eyes were buggy, beady, squinted, or staring, but none were caring. Heads were too big, too small, pointed, swollen, or oblong, some with jutting foreheads, twisted noses, massive jaws, and gnarled hands. But none seemed human.

One could argue whether it was the look of these men that led them to prison or whether it was the prison that gave them their look. What tales of suffering their bodies told seemed to be of no concern to them. They were content to wear their scars openly like a warning, the way farmers use scarecrows to keep menacing birds away. Today I feel pity and compassion for those who have had to suffer so much pain and tragedy in one lifetime. But on that hot June day, all I wanted was to get away from these ugly creatures as quickly as possible. Just looking at them made me fear for my life. There was no pity or compassion in my heart then, because their grotesque faces, bizarre dress, and tattoos made me forget they were human.

Now when I watch a new arrival walking "the gauntlet of desperate men," I can always sense his hopelessness. I know my staring is as horrifying to him as it was for me on my first day, and I know what I must look like to him.

GETTING CLASSIFIED

Toward the end of the main corridor I was shepherded into the shadowy expanse of yet another corridor. This led to the clothing room, a cold, damp place equipped with a tile-walled shower and an adjoining room where endless rows of mothballed clothes hung on racks like mismatched goods in a thrift shop. The eerie stillness and strong scent of old clothes made me feel as if I'd entered an embalming room. I shivered involuntarily.

My escort guard ordered me to "get naked" and surrender my personal effects to an inmate dressed in brown prison garb. I was still wearing my nice suit and tie from the courthouse. I hesitated, reluctant to surrender my clothes, my last ties to freedom. "Take your shit off," shouted the guard, "we aint' got all day!" I hurriedly stripped down, and handed the silent inmate the last vestiges of my social identity. He tossed them impatiently into an old cardboard box. After the guard conducted another "bend-over-and-stretch-'em" search, I was given delousing shampoo and ordered to shower.

The water was cold, the tiles on the floor gummy with dirt. As I stood naked and shivering after my shower, I was assigned two pairs of navy blue pants, two blue shirts, three T-shirts, three pairs of boxer shorts, three pairs of socks, a blue winter coat, a blue summer jacket, two graying white towels, and a pair of brown shoes. Everything but the shoes and socks had "AM4737" boldly stamped in black. This number was my new identity, as permanent as the ink in which it was written.

I dressed slowly, tentatively. Once I had dressed, I was taken to be fingerprinted and photographed, then escorted to E-Block, officially known as the Eastern Diagnostic and Classification Center (EDCC). Though Graterford had five cellblocks, only A- through D-Blocks were considered part of the prison. E-Block was treated as a separate facility, which inmates and staff called "Quarantine." Because all new receptions, or new inmates, to Quarantine were issued blue prison uniforms, they were labeled "Blues." The general population inmates who wore brown uniforms were referred to as "Browns." Contact between Blues and Browns was strictly forbidden. Who was being quarantined from whom, I wondered idly.

Soon I found myself before the E-Block sergeant's desk, wearing my new blue uniform, cradling my belongings, and waiting for whatever came next. The sergeant walked me to a room full of bedding. There another inmate in brown dropped a rolled-up mattress on my shoulder. Few words were spoken.

Inside it were stuffed a blanket, pillow, metal cup, plastic knife, fork, and spoon, a pack of rolling tobacco, soap, toothbrush, toothpaste, and a disposable razor.

Awkwardly balancing the mattress roll on my shoulder with one arm and carrying my prison-issued clothes with the other, I followed the sergeant down a flight of stairs to my cell on one of the bottom ranges. The moment I twisted my body and cargo sideways into the dark, narrow cell, the sergeant slid the door shut and disappeared from sight.

The next two days were spent in the prison's infirmary for shots and a complete medical examination. While it was a doctor who examined me, it was an inmate who drew my blood and wrote down my medical history. Because the infirmary was also used by Browns from general population, a guard followed me and the other receptions everywhere we went. This constant surveillance had me wondering why we were so heavily guarded.

I later learned that any exposure of Browns to Blues was closely watched by the staff. One reason was that, since they had more liberties than the new arrivals, Browns often tried to barter privileges with Blues. For example, a pack of cigarettes could buy extra phone time or a library pass; and for a pack a day, you could rent a TV or a radio. Also, some Browns would sexually exploit weaker Blues. Almost all of them were point men for prison gangs, who reported back on the new prospects among Blues for possible gang membership or future victimization.

After I completed the medical examination process, there were about two weeks of idleness. During this period all I could do was eat, sleep, and spend a couple of hours in a small and crowded mud-flattened yard. Boredom and monotony ruled my waking hours and greatly increased the value of the dreamless sleep that each night would rescue me, however briefly, from this torture. Finally I was taken to an examination room on the block for a series of written psychological and literacy tests. There was no supervision in this room, and the testing process took about two days.

Two months of more idleness followed as I waited to be interviewed by my counselor. There were over four hundred inmates on E-Block and many fights. It seemed as if every time the block was let out into the yard, a fight would break out somewhere. From my experience, when convicts are let loose after being locked up for long periods of time, aggressive behavior is an immediate and natural consequence.

To occupy time, people played cards and worked out. It was during these idle days in classification that longstanding friendships and alliances were made, and when inmates distinguished the weak from the strong—predators from victims.

The first impressions I made on others during classification have stayed with me in prison ever since. Because I was not a career criminal, I was initially viewed as a "square john": a middle-class outsider with no experience of the social world of inmates. To both my advantage and disadvantage, I was seeing everything through the eyes of a foreigner, making many foolish mistakes yet gaining just as many unique insights into their world.

When I was finally called in for my interview, the counselor examined my test results and asked me a minimum of questions about my conviction and sentence. The interview took only ten to fifteen minutes.

Two weeks later, I was summoned to appear before the classification committee. Sitting before a counselor, the block sergeant, and a major of the guards, I was asked what prison I wanted to go to and why. I could only suggest Graterford because I didn't think other prisons would be any better or worse. Then I waited outside while they reviewed my file. Within a few minutes, I was called back and informed that I had been classified to Graterford. Just before I left, the major added in a pleasant voice, "You'll be working for me."

At the time I didn't consider the significance of my job assignment. I was too relieved to know that the tortuous classification ordeal was finally over. A few days later, I traded in my blues for browns and moved off Quarantine into the general population.

To me and most of the others, as I later discovered, classification was a total waste of time. While different prisons in Pennsylvania purportedly provided different types of rehabilitation programs meant to serve the needs of various kinds of offenders, in reality it seemed that only three considerations were used to determine a convict's ultimate destination: (1) race, (2) hometown, and (3) availability of cell space. At the time, most of the minority inmates in the state were classified to Graterford or Western Penitentiary. The other seven prisons consisted of mostly white inmates under an all-white civilian staff.

From the inmate point of view, the testing was an utter sham. For one thing, the written tests were given to everyone without even determining who could read or write. The written tests I took were in an unsupervised room with about thirty other men, most of whom just picked answers at random or copied them from someone else.

Because the officials seemed flippant about the tests, inmates tended to see their results only as a tool of manipulation. Under this assumption, many men had developed theories on how to answer the test questions. Some felt it was best to copy from the brightest men to improve their chances at getting a clerk's job over kitchen or laundry duty. Others felt they should give lunatic answers so they could be medically released from work altogether. Still others gave no answers at all and faked illiteracy. Such men reasoned that they could enroll in school and appear to do extremely well, thereby fooling the parole board into believing they had worked hard to make a positive change in their lives. All these connivances were based on the inmates' understanding that they were being conned as much as they were doing the conning.

GETTING DUG IN

Inmates serving long sentences preferred to lock at Graterford because, even though it was violent, it afforded them the most personal liberty. This was because the more violent a prison is, the more reluctant guards are to enforce petty rules for fear of being assaulted.

Once I was classified to Graterford, I had to move my belongings, along with my mattress, blanket, and pillow, to B-Block. This was a working block, reserved only for those inmates who had been assigned a job. My assignment turned out to be a fortuitous clerical job in the major of the guards' office. All my belongings were fit into a single shopping bag that I carried in one hand, while my rolled-up mattress was once again toted on my shoulder. I walked down the long main corridor to B-Block, my new home. Though it mirrored the design of E-Block, it was considerably less crowded and noisy. Comparatively, this hell seemed more like heaven to me.

The first thing I noticed was that the men on B-Block were much older than most of those on the classification block. These were the "Old Heads" of the prison, inmates who had done a long stretch. When I arrived at my assigned cell, I quickly signed in at the block sergeant's desk and requested cleaning supplies. Then I spent the morning scrubbing down every inch of my cell. By noon count I was able to lie down on my bed, smoke a cigarette, and consider what I was going to do next.

My cell measured about six feet by twelve with a ten-foot high ceiling, from which dangled a single light bulb with a drawstring switch. For furniture, I had a flat, hard steel bed and a steel desk and chair that had been assembled as one unit. The mandatory toilet afforded a sink directly above it with a steel medicine cabinet above that. High over the toilet was a rusty radiator that served as my only source of heat in the winter. Finally, I had a flimsy wooden foot locker with a hasp that could be locked with a commissary-bought combination lock. (A commissary is a prison store, a bit like a corner market in a poor neighborhood.)

My cell entrance was a solid steel sliding door with a fixed glass window on the top quarter. On the opposite wall was a window that could be manually opened and closed, just a little. The concrete walls were painted a dingy off-white and adorned with graffiti and cigarette stains.

Despite the grim accommodations, this was home. I was due to report to work the next morning, and I could feel myself getting dug in. In prison it doesn't take much to make a man happy: food, some quiet, a good book, a job, and enough heat in the winter. That day I was happy just to be able to lie on that hard bed with a seventy-watt light bulb glaring in my face. I felt the worst was over. I could now begin to serve my time.

ESCAPE FROM REALITY

Like most first-time arrivals to Graterford, I was only preoccupied with survival and how to avoid becoming the victim of violence. This sudden refocusing of attention led me to change my habits, my personality, and even my values. With these changes came a new way of viewing the world as a place of unrelenting fear.

If I made eye contact with a stranger, I would feel threatened. An unexpected smile could mean trouble. A man in uniform was not a friend. Being kind was a weakness. Viciousness and recklessness were to be respected and admired. Oddly enough, these changes were in some way comforting. In the struggle to survive, it was easier to distrust everyone than to believe in their inherent goodness.

Danger became a determining factor of the changes in my attitude and personality. When there was general movement in the prison, for example, the main corridor would fill with hundreds of inmates in transit. This made the corridor an extremely dangerous place to be. I was more likely to see a stabbing than a guard on duty.

The cellblocks were just as insecure. A guard at one end of a cell-block could not identify anyone at the other end; the distance of seven hundred feet was just too great. Because of their fear of being assaulted where no one could see them, many block guards never patrolled the inner perimeter and spent most of their time avoiding conflicts at all cost, even turning the other way. I was on my own.

By the time I had settled in, however, I found myself feeling safe enough to think beyond the moment. This was something I had not been able to do since my arrest. Unfortunately, this new sense of security brought with it the "sleeping phase." I began to sleep twelve to fourteen hours a day. My whole life consisted of eating, working, and sleeping. I never dreamed. I only tried to stay unconscious for as long as I possibly could. I would imagine I was clinically depressed, though no one thought to examine or treat me, and I couldn't think of anything except getting through the day.

Though I had no way of knowing it at the time, I had entered a very common prison-adjustment phase. So common, in fact, that walking in on a newcomer while he sleeps is the most practiced technique of cell thieves and rapists. In Graterford, a man who spends too much time in bed sends the same signal as that of a bleeding fish in shark-infested waters.

"You can't be sleeping all the time," cautioned my chess partner one day, waking me to play a game. "You can't sleep away your sentence. In here, you have to stay awake to stay alive."

He was right, and I knew it. So I resolved to keep myself busy. I took up reading and painting as hobbies. I was allowed to buy almost as many books, magazines, and newspapers as I wanted, as well as canvasses, brushes, and paints. Self-help was encouraged so long as you could pay for it yourself.

Soon I was reading everything I could get my hands on and painting well into the wee hours of the morning. My cell became crowded with books, magazines, canvasses, newspapers, and even an easel. I went so far as to rig up extra lighting, hung pictures, and bought throw rugs for the cement floor. I had successfully transformed my cell into a cluttered boarding-house room.

Like some literary critic and master artist, I was so deeply submerged in my hobbies that I became as obsessed as a man digging his way to freedom. But I was no literary critic and certainly no artist. I was just another lifer trying to escape the real world.

"You have to spend more time out of that cell, Victor," insisted my chess mate and only friend at that time. "It's not healthy to do a 'bit' [time] like that. Look at your cell, you have junk everywhere. You even have lights on your wall that look like they belong in a room somewhere else."

"I'm just getting dug in," I replied in defense, annoyed that my efforts at avoiding reality had been detected.

"This isn't getting dug in, this is foolishness. You're in a penitentiary—a tough one. You should never try to forget that. Never try to make yourself believe you're somewhere else. Do you know what a lit match could do to this cell?"

His words struck an unnerving chord. Only a few months earlier, I had watched a man whose cell across the way had been deliberately set on fire. He had screamed and banged helplessly on his locked door, flames dancing around him, biting at his flesh. Through his cell window, I could see billowing black smoke envelope his pleading, twisted, horrified face until he disappeared. It had taken some time before guards responded to his screams.

The very next day I gave away my books, magazines, newspapers, art supplies, and my easel. I knew I had to fight as hard for my safety as I did for my sanity. I still hear that man's screams sometimes, when I have trouble sleeping.

PRISON SLANG

As a child immigrant who neither spoke nor understood English, I once had to face the strange, intimidating world of the American school system. But I overcame my fear of the unfamiliar because of my strong desire to adapt to a community of classmates. I wanted desperately to belong and to speak their language.

Likewise, from the outset of my term in Graterford I once again found myself in a frightening world where I couldn't understand the language or the behavior of its inhabitants. I felt that same desperate urge to belong to a community of inmates in the strange, new world of the American penal system. Everyone in prison—staff and inmates alike—seemed to know each other not only personally but intimately. They laughed and interacted like siblings, even during exchanges of anger. This strong familiarity gave the population of Graterford the appearance of one big clan. I wanted to be accepted by this clan, to know its secrets, and to speak its language.

One of the first things I knew I had to do was to adapt myself to the pervasive use of jailhouse slang by both inmates and staff. The tenor of this prison lingo was generally vulgar and aggressive, expressed with self-important arrogance. Yet at the same time it exhibited an unbridled honesty that implied a certain unconditional tolerance for the opinions and beliefs of others.

The first column below provides some examples of prison slang that might be heard on any given day in Graterford. The second column is the nonslang English version. Because these examples are condensed, the slang is expressed in a somewhat exaggerated form. These are just brief samples from the vast repertoire of expressions used in prisons today.

Graterford Version	English Version
Three homeys played a tip and did a B & E on the humbug. Dudes were stick-up boys, not back-door boosters, so they weren't down with it. Turns out to be a fat take. They find the stash and it's full of gold, rocks, paper, and cash money.	Three neighborhood friends followed up on a tipster's information and committed a house burglary on a sudden impulse. These men were armed robbers and not burglars so they were not familiar with the business. As it turned out, they stole a lot of money. They found a cache full of gold, precious stones, negotiable checks, and cash.
After breaking down the tip man, the cutees get to breaking down the gapper, when one of the homeys throws shit into the game and pulls out a gat, talking about, "I ain't breaking down with no lames." He plucks one dude and goes to capping the other, but ain't nothing slow about home boy and he breaks camp.	After the man who tipped them off about the house was paid off, the three partners began to divide the money. One of them complicated matters by pulling a gun, saying, "I'm not sharing any money with losers." He killed one man, but the other one was faster and managed to get away.
Now cutee's fast but he's a trembler, he ain't got no ticker for this kind of drama. He gets to dry snitching to the police, talking about, "Officer, I heard some shooting at such and such a place and so and so might know something about it." Police bust the dude with the gapper and the gat. He ends up taking twelve in the box but pulls a life sentence with a nickel to a dime running wild.	While the man who escaped was fast, he was frightened and didn't have the courage to deal with this kind of situation. He went to the police and hinted about the shooter's acts by saying, "Officer, I heard some shooting at such and such a place and so and so might know something about it." The police ended up arresting the shooter with the money and the gun. He had a jury trial but was found guilty and received a life sentence with a five-to-ten-year sentence running consecutive to the life sentence.
Dude caught a bad break on a good score. If he'd broke down with his homeys, instead of pulling that slimy shit, he'd be living large.	The man had bad luck during a big robbery. If he had shared the money with his friends, instead of being underhanded, he would be living prosperously.

2

Things Missed

EDITORS' NOTE

Punishment is a central theme of the prison experience and, not surprisingly, a frequent topic of debate. Does punishment bring the community together in opposition to deviance—us against the criminal, reinforcing social bonds, as argued by Émile Durkheim, the first scholar to write about the sociology of crime. Does punishment deter the offender (specific deterrence) or others in the community (general deterrence)?

The first American prisons, built in the late eighteenth century, were designed to replace sanctions that were deemed inhumane—whipping, maiming, and hanging. When punishments were used, they were explicit and independent of imprisonment. For example, offenders would be whipped or placed in stocks and pillories. The punishments that Victor Hassine describes in this chapter, on the other hand, are implicit, part and parcel of the prison experience.

Readers may wonder whether the pains of modern imprisonment—the deprivation today's inmates suffer because they are removed from the free world, let alone the frustrations and dangers of everyday life in the prison community—are any better or worse than the explicit punishments of earlier times. Is a whipping or a mutilation worse than a lifetime of fear and loneliness? Prison is a world in which inmates are a kind of property of the institution, where a knifing victim might be punished for "possession" (in his bleeding body) of the weapon used to cut and wound him. We like to think that prisons are humane punishments. To examine this view, put yourself in Hassine's place and imagine that this is your world for the remainder of your natural life.

Reprimand and Warning

A warning from the Hearing Examiner not to do it again, "or else!"

Loss of Privilege

Suspension of privileges for a given period of time. These privileges include visiting, phone calls, commissary, yard, work, and television.

Cell Restriction

Confinement to one's cell except for meal times and two hours per day recreation on the block, and loss of job. All other privileges are left intact unless specifically suspended.

Double-lock Feed-in

Confined to one's cell except for two hours recreation on the block and three showers per week. Loss of job, all privileges suspended or curtailed, and three full meals in the cell.

Disciplinary Custody

The Hole, or "Siberia." Solitary confinement in the isolation unit (Restrictive Housing Unit, or RHU) with all privileges suspended or curtailed. Three full meals in the RHU cell, and two hours recreation per day.

O ne of the more subtle ways a prison punishes is by its neglect of a man's need for things, both the abstract (e.g., his freedom) and the tangible (e.g., his personal property). From the very start, I began missing both. Just when I would get accustomed to doing without old things, I would start to miss new things. Once I had gotten accustomed to doing without things, I would start to miss different free-world things. It was a selfish, childish, material missing that somehow kept me rooted in my pre-incarceration past by having me constantly remember and mourn those lost objects and things that had once represented the liberty I'd lost. It was almost as if prison life had created a newfound desire in me to miss something all the time.

At first, I missed the obvious: sex, love, family, and friends. This left me feeling sorry for myself. But it wasn't long before I stopped missing these things and started focusing on the next wave of things I no longer had: privacy, quiet, and peace of mind; intangibles that I have never stopped missing to this day. At least these things I could try to find in prison, or some version of them.

There are no trees in the great walled fortress of Graterford and very few shrubs. In fact, there isn't much of anything green that hasn't been painted green. Also, the prison is designed so that you can never get an unobstructed view of anything. Walls keep getting in the way.

Occasionally when I had to make trips outside the prison for court appearances or doctors' visits, I would sit in the prison van enraptured by the trees whizzing past. The brightness and the beautiful colors of everything around me made every outside trip an exciting experience. I know of several men who filed lawsuits or feigned illnesses just to get a moment, even so brief, out of the prison and see "some streets."

Well aware of this, the administration would try to make such trips as uncomfortable as possible. They would handcuff and shackle traveling inmates and strip-search every man coming and going, even though he never left the sight of an officer. They would make certain that an inmate wore ill-fitting clothes that were dirty, torn, and extremely uncomfortable. In the winter they had only summer clothes available and only winter garments in the summer. For a while they even required a man to be locked in his cell the day before making such a trip.

But no amount of discouragement worked. Inmates loved these trips because they reminded them of all the things they missed. Personally, I always came back from each trip remembering the trees, the beautiful women, and all the joys of the outside world. Longing for these things made me take a lot of risks in my efforts to reclaim even the most insignificant of things that I once had taken for granted.

HAVING IT MY WAY

My first misconduct at Graterford resulted from missing one of life's simplest pleasures: a fresh-cooked juicy hamburger. I had just come out of classification and started working the 12:00 to 8:00 PM shift as a clerk in the major of the guards' office, which was off the main corridor between E- and D-Block. One day a contraband sandwich merchant, or "swag man," walked into the office and offered me a ten-pound bag of frozen ground beef for a pack of cigarettes. I had no way of cooking it, but for another pack I could get a hot plate. I began to imagine myself biting into a hot, juicy burger grilled to perfection. I bought the contraband beef, which was a bargain considering that a pack of cigarettes at that time cost only fifty cents in the commissary.

A senior clerk helped me out by talking to an inmate kitchen worker, who quickly produced the heating element of an electric coffee urn and an aluminum cookie pan, both hidden in the lining of his oversized prison-issued coat. For only one more cigarette pack, he scrounged up hamburger buns, chopped onions, butter, sliced cheese, ketchup, mustard, and two bricks to hold the cookie pan over the heating element.

That evening when the meat had finally thawed, my coconspirators and I set up a makeshift grill in the major's bathroom. We fashioned burger patties and started frying the hamburgers as soon as movement in the main corridor had ended.

It was the onions that did us in. The aroma of sautéed onions in butter was so strong that it attracted a guard stationed some three hundred feet away. He followed the aroma to its origin and asked us for a burger. We were more than happy to share with him, and he was eating it as he left the office, which made us all sigh with relief.

A few minutes later, a Search Team raided us and confiscated everything. They had been tipped off when the previous guard offered one of them a bite of his tasty burger. When they asked him where he had gotten it, he simply told them. Apparently the members of the Search Team were not as impressed with our resourcefulness.

In the early 1980s, Graterford introduced the Search Team, or "A Team," as a special two-man guard squad whose sole function was to conduct cell searches and pat downs. Not even the block officers knew who or when they would strike. Whenever a Search Team entered a block, an inmate would call out, "Search Team up!" Inmates at the end of the block would immediately hide their contraband. Because it took so long for the team to make it down the long block, contraband was able to be moved constantly without detection.

Given that our hamburger caper took place in the major's office, however, we didn't have that advantage. We were all issued misconduct reports for the possession of contraband. Following a misconduct hearing, I was found guilty, removed from my job, and forced to pay for the food. I was also confined to my cell for sixty days, allowed out only two hours per day for recreation on the block. As shown at the beginning of this chapter, "cell restriction" is classified as a third-level punishment for misconduct.

My biggest mistake in this case was my naiveté. Until the Search Team had confiscated the burgers, I thought that such activity was merely business as usual at Graterford. I had only been in general population for about a month, and things developed with such effortless ease that I hadn't taken what I had done very seriously. For many years afterward, my prison handle became "Burger King," even though I had never gotten a chance to taste the object of my crime.

THE HOLE

Every prison attempts to gain a specific end in some way, be it deterrence, punishment, and/or rehabilitation. What makes a prison unnatural is the way it tries to achieve that end. For example, a prison imposes communal existence on loners and others who would normally segregate themselves from each other, such as blacks and whites.

And, despite the endless promulgation of rules, their enforcement is so arbitrary that inmates live in a constant state of uncertainty.

Disciplinary segregation, or the "Hole," serves no ultimate end but to deprive a man of *all* things except the bare necessities of survival. It is a highly contradictory experience for every inmate. To some it is punishment, to others it is safety, and to still others it is just another way to do time. Furthermore, solitary confinement is completely contrary to a prison's principle of imposed communal living.

From my own experiences in the Hole, the only thing that saved me from falling into the great abyss that separates the sane from the insane was the fact that I could read. For the illiterate, solitary confinement is a one-way ticket to madness.

While I was in the Hole, I discovered illiterate inmates who managed to alter their mental states enough to make the Hole their home, even convincing themselves that they preferred the "independence" of the Hole. Generally, they adapted to their environment in one of two ways: they totally threw themselves at the mercy of the guards to satisfy their hunger for conversation, or they communicated with other Hole residents by shouting from cell to cell for hours at a time. As I spent my time reading, I could hear their loud chatter as they tried to hang onto some last vestige of sanity.

One important thing that the Hole made me realize was how essential education should be to a prison system. I came to this conclusion because it seemed that only a literate inmate can truly know and understand the punishment attached to his wrongful acts.

At one point I had an opportunity to talk with an illiterate young man in the cell next to mine. He was doing disciplinary time for fighting. During most of his waking hours, he would sit on the floor next to the bars of his cell and talk to me or anyone else about everything and nothing. I knew he could not read so I understood what he was doing and tolerated his constant intrusion into my solitary world of reading.

One day he asked me what day it was and how many more days he had to go. The first thing I always did in the Hole was to keep some kind of a calendar, lest they forget to let me out on time. After some quick math, I told him he had only twenty-eight days left. He then asked when that would be. I didn't understand the question, until he explained that he wanted to know how many more Sundays he would have to do.

This young man's illiteracy was so profound that he had no concept of time. To him the number 28 was as remote as the number 1,000,000. So if he didn't understand the length of his disciplinary time, there was no way he could fully comprehend the time the courts had given him to serve his sentence in prison.

If a man's illiteracy prevented him from understanding relative lengths of time, then what other things couldn't he understand? How could he ever possibly be deterred if he can only fathom the consequences of his actions *after* he has experienced them? Literacy should be high on the critical list of missed things for such a man, especially if he doesn't even know what he's missing.

After my conversation with my young Hole neighbor, I didn't give it much more thought. I immersed myself back into my book, but only after I checked my pencil-marked calendar and thanked God for the few remaining days I had left. I also thanked God for allowing me to be literate enough to understand time, space, and the Hole.

THE INMATE'S DILEMMA

The foremost tangible things missed by inmates are their stolen personal possessions, particularly considering how little they're permitted to keep in their cells. At Graterford, there was always an epidemic of cell thefts.

Fortunately for me, everybody on B-Block where I lived had jobs. This meant that most of them made enough money to shop at the commissary every week. Some of them had manufacturing jobs in Correctional Industries, such as weaving, shoemaking, or tailoring and could make well over a one hundred dollars a month if they worked overtime. By prison standards this was considered to be a small fortune.

Total employment meant that there was not a major theft problem on B-Block at the time. This was a great relief to me, not because I didn't expect to get some of my things stolen, but because I didn't want to deal with the inevitability of catching some thief in the act.

In the life of an inmate, if you catch someone stealing from you, you're compelled to deal with it physically. This is not because you want to or you think it's the right thing to do, but because you absolutely must. If someone steals from you and you decide to report him to the guards, all that will happen is that the thief will go to the Hole for a while. Soon he'll be back in population and ready to seek revenge. Revenge in prison can take place years down the road. It generally occurs when you are vulnerable and the avenger happens to be around. This reality will leave you constantly looking over your shoulder. In additions involving the guards will get you the reputation as a "snitch," which means you will be physically challenged by inmates seeking to make a reputation or pass their own "snitch" label onto you.

If you choose to ignore the theft, the man will steal from you again and tell his friends, who in turn will also steal from you. Eventually, you will be challenged for more than just minor belongings. This "Inmate's Dilemma" is precisely why most men in prison hope they never have to deal with a sloppy cell thief. Unfortunately, many men who were caught stealing on the streets will just as easily get caught stealing in prison.

By 1982, there was no way an inmate could lock his own cell at Graterford. Cells were all locked or opened simultaneously at given intervals by the pulling of a single lever. At 6:00 AM, for example, all the cells on the block were levered open so each inmate could open and close his own cell during breakfast. Five minutes after last call for breakfast, the levers were pulled again to lock all the doors. If you returned late from breakfast, you would have to wait for all the cells to be levered open again before you could re-enter your cell. In case of an emergency, each guard had a key that could override the lever and let you in. But asking a guard to key you in was like asking for a key out of the prison.

This process of opening and closing all doors at once was repeated at 8:00 AM for work lines and yard line; then again at 11:00 AM for count; at noon for lunch; at 5:00 PM for count; at 6:00 PM for supper; at 6:30 PM for block out, yard out, or work lines; then finally at 9:00 PM for final count and lockdown. Every one of us religiously followed this schedule because we always wanted to be at our cells when they opened up. Otherwise, we stood the chance of losing everything of value.

To combat theft, I arranged a neighborhood-watch system with my neighbors to look out for my cell when I wasn't there and vice versa. But for the most part it was every man for himself. From time to time I would return to my cell and discover things missing. Any theft was an intrusion into "my space" and made me angry. My few personal belongings constituted my total worldly possessions so they were of great (probably inflated) personal value to me. I was also left frightened by the threat implied by someone taking something of obvious value to me.

Fortunately I have never had to face the Inmate's Dilemma, but many others have and the consequences were brutal. There is no walking away in Graterford—the walls see to that—so either the intruder or the victim ends up seriously hurt.

One example of a cell confrontation involved not a cell thief but a Peeping Tom. One of my cellblock neighbors was Dip, a cocky bodybuilder with an imposing physique. He was convinced that the mere sight of his impressive frame would deter anyone from ever messing with him. While other inmates ran to their cells when the levers were thrown to protect their belongings, Dip never bothered.

Then one day Dip returned to his cell from a shower, wearing only a towel around his nakedness. To his shock, he found an inmate hiding under his bed with an exposed erection, trying to watch him undress. Dip was so caught off guard that the intruder simply walked out, blowing him a kiss as he turned to run off the block. Once he had recovered his senses, Dip got very mad. He dressed himself for combat and stormed down the block to find the man who had challenged his manhood. The jeers and heckles of neighboring inmates only served to deepen his rage.

But the moment Dip stepped into the main corridor, the kiss blower was waiting with some friends. Dip was stabbed several times with homemade knifes. Lucky for him, his injuries were only "Graterford wounds," meaning that his vital parts were still intact. By the time guards had made it to the scene, the attackers were gone, one of their knives was left behind, and bleeding Dip was locked up—charged with possession of the weapon that had been used to stab him.

For the most part, the prison administration did nothing to curb cell thefts or invasion of cell privacy. Some guards also seemed to think that these thefts and intrusions were part of the punishment of prison. In due time, however, the administration's failure to provide adequate safety and security would have far-reaching consequences.

Throughout 1981 and 1982, inmates petitioned, begged, and even threatened in their efforts to convince the administration to provide some means by which inmates could lock their own cells. The administration rejected these requests, claiming that cells were secure enough. If the administration had conceded to such requests, it would have been a tacit admission that they did not have control over their own prison.

By 1982, Graterford's general population rose to over two thousand. Every cell in the general population blocks was occupied and in the classification block the new receptions were already being double-celled. There were not enough jobs to go around now, so many men sat idle on B-Block. This resulted in more theft, which in turn led to more fights and more stabbings.

THE DAY OF LOCKING CELLS

As thievery increased, gangs flourished. Some gangs were formed to steal, others to defend against burglaries and robberies. Since B-Block comprised mostly working inmates, the fighting was not as frequent. But D- and C-Blocks were virtual war zones. There were so many fights and retaliations that guards were getting injured in the melees.

Only then did the administration take action. Holes were drilled in the cell-door tracks so that any cell could be locked from the outside with a padlock, even when the master lever was opened. The commissary began selling padlocks that could fit in the hole. There was a general feeling of relief because now we could secure our belongings. It seemed less likely now that we would ever have to deal with the Inmate's Dilemma—or so we thought.

Once gangs form in a prison, they're hard to break up. When a group of cell thieves join together, no lock can stop them. Their incentive had increased now as well, especially since this new sense of security encouraged inmates to keep more valuable goods in their cells.

To get around the new cell locks, thieves simply changed their techniques. The problem that remained was that when the master lever was open and the inmate was inside his cell, he could not lock himself inside the cell. Instead of waiting until an inmate left his cell, a gang would simply rush into the cell while he was sleeping or using the commode. This resulted in even more fights and stabbings. Burglary is one thing, but strong-armed robbery demands an immediate and violent response. As the number of robberies and assaults surged, the new jailhouse wisdom was that you should always be awake and ready to fight when cells were opened, and that you should use the commode only when your cell was locked.

Some prisoners began fashioning weapons that could withstand a shakedown. For example, they would keep wooden floor brushes in their cells. Made of solid oak, these heavy brushes could knock a man unconscious. Because they were prison issue, they weren't considered contraband.

If a guard found one in your cell, all he could do was confiscate it or order you to return it to the block sergeant. Ironically, the heavy-duty combination locks sold in the commissary served as another shakedown-proof weapon. Placed in a sock, this weapon could be more effective than most homemade knives.

The ultimate defense against unwanted intruders was getting a hole drilled on the *inside* of your door. A bolt secured in this hole prevented the door from being opened, so you could now lock your cell from the inside as well as from the outside. The staff objected to this hole on the grounds that an inmate could barricade himself in his cell so it could only be opened with a cutting torch. If a guard saw a hole on the inside of your door, he might plug it up with metal solder, but it was easy enough to get another hole drilled.

A combination lock on the inside door-jamb hole rendered a man's cell fairly secure. The ability to keep more property without being restricted to their cells freed inmates from the routine of protecting their belongings. This meant more socialization, recreation, and work. It also meant the gangs would have to change their style of doing business once again. The treasures now accumulating in the cells were just too much to resist.

3

Playing the Opposites

EDITORS' NOTE

Writer Erving Goffman, in his well-known book, Asylums, *noted that inmates of mental hospitals must adapt to the stigma of institutionalization and the various pressures and stresses of institutional life. One such adjustment is "playing it cool," the strategy of telling staff members what they want to hear, while condemning and ridiculing them behind their backs. In the process of "putting one over" on the staff, patients reaffirm their autonomy and feelings of self-worth. Similar adjustments may be found among slaves and prison inmates.*

In this chapter, Victor Hassine describes a common prison adjustment strategy called "playing the opposites." Inmates who play the opposites routinely mislead or lie to staff members to get what they want. The truth alone is never enough. This game assumes that prison officials inevitably use their authority against the best interests of prisoners.

Playing the opposites has harmful consequences, because it confirms stereotypes held by prison officials that most inmates are deceitful, manipulative, and untrustworthy. To the extent that this strategy is in fact adaptive, it confirms inmates' stereotyping of staff as uncaring and deceptive in their own right. Inmates skilled in this ruse will almost certainly experience problems with authority figures when they are released from prison.

> "What we've got here is failure to communicate!"—Prison chain gang captain, played by Strother Martin, *Cool Hand Luke*, Warner Brothers, 1967.

Shortly after I arrived at Graterford, I discovered that my fellow inmates made a point of "playing the opposites." This game involves reverse psychology, where prisoners state the opposite of their actual feelings when asked by someone in authority to voice a preference or an opinion. A common occasion for playing the opposites is when an inmate is being interviewed by a counselor or employment officer for a job assignment. Naturally, some work details are favored over others, so experienced inmates will do whatever they can to secure a desirable job.

Some inmates will state their real job preferences and then try to influence assignments by summarizing their qualifications. This approach occasionally succeeds, but only if the convict possesses some unique skill currently in demand. As a general rule, inmates don't receive the jobs that they request. Consequently, a more savvy convict won't hint at his preference; instead, he misleads the staff member into believing that he would hate being assigned to a work detail that he secretly desires.

The conversation between an experienced convict and an employment officer might sound like this:

OFFICER: Okay, where do you want to work?

INMATE: I worked as a clerk in the library the last time I was here and I got burned. The job was too demanding and I couldn't get enough free time.

OFFICER: So are you saying you don't want a clerk's job?

INMATE: Yeah, I guess so. I don't think I could take working as a clerk anymore. I need something easier—you know, a no-brain job—so I can work on my legal papers and stuff like that.

OFFICER: So where do you want to be assigned?

INMATE: How about the kitchen? That's a pretty simple job and I get to eat real good. I think I'd like to work in the kitchen this time 'round. I got a couple of friends who work in the kitchen who can show me the ropes.

In this example, the inmate does his best to convince the employment officer that he really wants to be assigned to the kitchen detail, which is one of the worst jobs in any prison. The deception includes an explanation of why the inmate prefers this work detail even though he knows that the prison official would consider these as reasons *not* to assign the inmate to the kitchen. (The inmate makes himself seem lazy. Also, having friends who already work in the kitchen suggests a possible conspiracy to smuggle food out.) According to the strategy behind playing the opposites, if the inmate manages to convince the employment officer that he really wants a job in the kitchen, he will be assigned a clerk's job, if one is available.

You would think that the risk of a backfire would limit the use of playing the opposites, but, in fact, the game is popular among inmates. As for those who choose not to play, you can be certain they are careful not to let anyone know their real desires. Prisons seem to reward playing the opposites by punishing honesty.

When I first arrived at Graterford, I questioned the wisdom of this strategy. As a young man, I had been taught to "say what I mean, and mean what I say." More-experienced inmates would often try to explain to me how that philosophy simply doesn't work in prison, and that the best way for a prisoner to get what he wanted was to play the opposites. Thoughtful inmates told me that prison staff were trained not to care about inmates' personal preferences and were actually told to make prisoners as uncomfortable as possible. So when a prison administrator discovers an inmate's true preference, this knowledge will be used against him. Others simply said, "Who cares, all you need to know is that it works."

It was difficult for me to accept this conventional wisdom because I believed that corrections staff didn't have time to play petty mind games. I assumed that prison managers would treat inmates impartially. Impartial treatment would consider an individual's likes and dislikes, when balanced with particular job availability and other situational factors. It made no sense to me that staff members would maliciously try to maximize the discomfort of inmates.

CLARENCE AND THE PROGRAM REVIEW COMMITTEE

It was Clarence who convinced me there was more to playing the opposites than mere prison paranoia. Clarence was a drug dealer who had served most of his time and was now awaiting release from Graterford. He was memorable for his razor-sharp wit and pungent sarcasm.

One day, I found myself in a holding room seated next to Clarence, as we waited to speak to the members of the Program Review Committee (PRC) to request a reduction in disciplinary sanctions for infractions we had committed. At the time, anyone who had received a disciplinary sanction could petition the PRC for a reduction of the punishment. The PRC required petitioning inmates to explain why they deserved a reduction in sanctions. Every Thursday, fifty or more inmates would be summoned to the holding room to make a plea for mercy before a panel of three high-ranking prison administrators who called themselves the PRC.

The disciplinary sanction I had received was cell restriction, so I was seated in the waiting room wearing my regular prison uniform. Clarence had been caught trying to smuggle drugs into the institution on a furlough return. Because he had received a disciplinary sanction of six months in the Hole, he was seated next to me in handcuffs, wearing standard dress for the Hole (a prison-stripes jumpsuit).

The PRC always took its time, so someone could expect to wait for hours to plead for mercy. The waiting room was small and unventilated, stuffed with many hot and sweaty men. Waiting in that room was extremely oppressive. I wondered if the PRC had intentionally designed the conditions in the room as a means to discourage men from seeking leniency. Several men left the waiting room in frustration, choosing to abandon their plans to address the PRC rather than to melt.

Clarence was prison-wise and determined to see the process through. He devised a plan to coax more of the men into leaving the room by complaining about the unpleasant conditions. He guessed this would shorten his waiting time.

"Watch this," he said to me, just before he spoke loudly to everyone in the room. "Man, these people must think we're real suckers. They got us all crowded in here sweating and smelling like plantation slaves waiting for their master to give them a neck bone or some other bullshit. Man, fuck the PRC."

This immediately caused some grumbling among the other men, and before long two or three of them left the waiting room. "That makes it a little bit easier to breathe in here," he whispered to me. No doubt, Clarence knew the angles, and that's why I was puzzled by his desire to see the PRC. Certainly, he didn't expect to get a reduction of his time in the Hole, considering the seriousness of his offense.

"What are you here for?" Clarence asked me.

"I'm on cell restriction for stupid stuff. My lock was broken and the guard couldn't unlock it with his key so he wrote me up," I explained.

"That's petty shit! That guard must not like you," he offered.

"I guess not. But tell me, do you really think the PRC is going to cut you any slack?" I asked.

"Sure, sure they will. I bet I get a break before you do!" he eagerly wagered.

"You've got to be kidding! I've got a meatball case and you're in the Hole for smuggling drugs and you think they'll give you a break? You'll be lucky if they don't give you a new street charge!" I scoffed in disbelief.

"Laugh if you want to. But I know how these people work and you don't. See, you'll probably go in there and tell them that you've been a good boy and that the guard was picking on you and that you'll never do it again. Man, they don't want to hear that shit! That's all they hear all day long. You better not tell them that sorry stuff," he warned.

"Yeah, well what do you plan on telling them?" I asked.

"I'm going to get on my hands and knees and beg them, I mean really beg them, to keep me in the damn Hole until they let me go home. That's what I'm going to do," he answered smartly.

"And that's your big plan? You think they'll feel sorry for you and just let you go? Why don't you ask for your drugs back while you're at it?" I asked sarcastically.

"Real funny. I can understand where you're coming from. You think these people care about you. You're really going to be shocked when you find out they don't give a shit about you or me. They couldn't care less about us waiting in this nasty room or you staying locked in your cell twenty-four hours a day because some guard has a hard-on for you. That's the bottom line. When you understand that, you'll stop doing hard time. See, I know they really want to put a foot up my ass, so when I go in there I'm going to let them do that. I'm going to tell those people that I was bringing the drugs in for a big, mean mother-fucker in population and that if they let me out of the Hole, I'm going to get my ass kicked because I can't pay the dude back for the shit that was confiscated. I'm going to beg them not to let me out of the Hole. In fact, I'm going to ask for a transfer," he said with an impressive air of confidence.

"And that's your plan?" I asked.

"Yep, and if I were you, I'd figure out some reason to tell those people why you like it on cell restriction," he suggested.

We spoke together a little longer before the PRC finally escorted Clarence into the hearing room. About ten or fifteen minutes later I saw Clarence being taken back to the Hole. I remember thinking to myself that he was a fool to think that his scheme would work.

Eventually, the PRC called for me and I made my plea. As Clarence had predicted, I explained to the Committee that my infraction was a minor one. I noted that I had a history of good behavior and that I intended to obey all prison rules and regulations in the future. The PRC wasn't impressed and returned me to my cell to serve out the remainder of my restriction. I left the room angry, not for being turned down, but for having spent needless hours suffering in that hot and smelly holding room.

The next day, as I was reading in my cell, I heard a knock on the metal door. I looked up to see Clarence staring down at me. I couldn't believe it. The PRC had released him to the general population. His plan had worked!

"So I see you didn't take my advice," he said with a big grin. I was too stunned to respond. "Maybe this will teach you something about this place. These people don't care nothing about you and the sooner you realize that the better off you'll be." With that, he slowly walked away, whistling like a free man.

OF RABBITS AND INMATES

This wasn't the only incident in my prison experience to convince me that there is merit to playing the opposites, but it certainly was one of the most memorable. I've personally chosen not to play the game; when it comes to expressing my real preferences in prison, I generally remain silent. Still, because I recognize that playing the opposites is an effective tool for getting what you want from prison staff, I've advised inexperienced inmates of its benefits.

If it were simply a "prison thing," playing the opposites wouldn't be of much importance, other than reinforcing stereotypes of inmates as manipulative and dishonest. But the truth is that playing the opposites is an age-old strategy employed by all oppressed people.

I realized this after reading a collection of Uncle Remus stories, tales that were passed down orally by generations of black slaves in America. In one story, Br'er Fox (symbolizing the master) was trying to catch Br'er Rabbit (symbolizing the slave). Br'er Fox fashioned a trap for the rabbit by making a tarbaby (a doll covered with sticky tar) and leaving it out in a field. Br'er Rabbit, thinking the tarbaby was another animal, walked over to talk to it. Gradually, he became ensnared, hopelessly stuck to the doll. The gleeful fox ran out of hiding, gloating about the different ways he might choose to kill the rabbit. Playing along, Br'er Rabbit begged not to be thrown into a nearby brier-patch because, he explained, it would be unbearable to be torn to pieces in the thorns. Naturally, the malicious fox immediately tossed him into the briers. Waiting in the patch were Br'er Rabbit's friends, who freed him from the tarbaby. Hopping away, the clever rabbit ridiculed the fox for being so gullible.

This story reminded me of Clarence in the PRC waiting room. Apparently, playing the opposites is not only an adjustment to prison life but a survival tactic of the disadvantaged everywhere. It is a practice employed by all rabbits, slaves, and inmates to defend themselves against all foxes, masters, and prison staff. The most troubling aspect of this adjustment is that it encourages deceit as an acceptable means to an end. In prison, it is hard to know when an inmate is being truthful, or when he is playing the opposites. The longer a person remains in prison, the less likely it is that he will be able to share sincere feelings with anyone, a penalty of the ground rules of this game.

Staff are not exempt from the far-reaching effects of these lies. Some officials don't believe anything an inmate says, or they believe the opposite of whatever inmates tell them. In response, some inmates intentionally tell the truth in situations where they know they won't be trusted, perpetuating a cycle of deceit that makes communication almost impossible in prison.

So go the frustrating conversations between foxes and rabbits everywhere, trading an ounce of comic relief in the brier-patch for a pound of distrust, cynicism, and despair in the fields.

4

Prison Violence

EDITORS' NOTE

During Victor Hassine's time at Graterford, the prison had a problem with inmate violence, particularly group or gang violence. The sources of this problem were many, one being the decline in the power of prison officials to mete out severe punishments due to court decisions limiting their disciplinary and control procedures. Before the mid-1960s, the courts took a hands-off approach to prison management. Officials could practically make up rules as they went along, and inmates had virtually no rights. A troublesome inmate could be salted away in segregation for years at a time. When officials lost that totalitarian control, inmate groups and gangs emerged and became a considerable force in their own right.

Crowding was also a major problem. A crowded prison can be difficult to manage. Crowding is not the same as density, however. A densely populated prison only becomes crowded when the density of bodies interferes with adjustment, producing stress and frustration. A densely populated prison that offers an array of solid programs and recreational activities might well be a decent environment, whereas one that offers nothing constructive for the inmates to do might well be a riot waiting to happen.

Finally, the nature of the prison population is a vital factor. A densely packed prison of elderly inmates afforded recreational activities is one thing; a prison filled with angry, young urban males with no programs to speak of is quite another. Hassine describes a prison crowded with alienated refugees from the inner city with no future ahead of them. The rage is palpable, so violence comes as no surprise.

Readers should note that, by all accounts, things are different in Graterford today. Courts are once again less involved in prison management, giving officials a freer hand to enforce order. After the raids described in Appendix A, Graterford is essentially under the control of administrators rather than inmates. With the establishment of a super-max prison in Pennsylvania, where solitary confinement is regularly imposed on maladapted inmates, administrators have regained the upper hand. One might think of super-max prisons as descendants of the Big House, the last resort to deter prison misbehavior.

Rumor had it that Old Man Simpson had been beaten by the KKK as a young man and by white guards in prison. If you were white and walked within arms' reach, Old Man Simpson would punch you in the face without warning. He also had a habit of throwing hot coffee in any white man's face who stood too close to him in the breakfast line. Prison veterans always steered clear, but enjoyed watching him do his thing to newcomers.

But Old Man Simpson's acts of violence were mild compared to the random savagery spread by the new breed of young inmates who swept into the crowded main corridor of Graterford in the 1980s. They threw concentrated cleaning acid or bleach into men's faces, and formed prison gangs that stormed entire cellblocks, slashing prisoners' necks and faces with razor blades.

By 1984, Graterford's population exceeded 2,500. Gangs proliferated at a staggering rate, not only because of high unemployment inside the prison but because of the need for protection from the gangs' new money-making schemes.

If you couldn't rob a man's cell, you just robbed the man himself. On occasion you snatched an exposed wallet from a careless guard's pants or jacket pocket: Anyone and anything was fair game. Extortion became very lucrative. One of the favorite ways to deal with a resistant victim was to lock him in his cell and set the cell on fire. So if you were not aligned with a protection gang, it was only a matter of time before you would have to face the "Welcome Wagon" and be challenged to pay or to fight.

The Welcome Wagon visited me shortly after I arrived at Graterford. I was sitting in the movie theater. In those days, prison recreational staff didn't have videotapes, so they showed films in large auditoriums. It gets pretty dark there. I was watching the movie when suddenly I felt this sharp knife on my throat. The guy wasn't asking me for a match! Four or five inmates behind me started talking about how they wanted money and they wanted it quickly. I felt completely helpless, surrounded and isolated as I sat frozen in my seat. Somehow, I had the presence of mind to ask them how much they wanted and when, so I could have it dressed up and ready to go. That strategy bought me some time. About two days later, I met the Welcome Wagon again in the auditorium, but this time I was prepared to fight.

Once the movie had ended and most of the moving-going inmates had left the auditorium, the lights were turned on and I could see four of the extortionists cautiously inching toward me from different directions. I stood tense for battle in plain view in the center of the room with my back against a wall, daring them to come closer. I had a big deadly looking shank in each of my outstretched hands and my pockets were full of ground black pepper I could use as mace to temporarily blind anyone who tried to rush me. As I hoped, this bluff worked and the Welcome Wagon carefully retreated out of the auditorium, more than a little worried I might decide to go after them. After this, they left me alone, preferring easier game.

These were violent and deadly times at Graterford; times of random violence, murders, cell fires, paranoia, and knife carrying. According to the Department of Corrections' Monthly Morbidity Report in 1986–1987, Graterford accounted for the highest rate of assaults out of Pennsylvania's twelve state prisons: 392 assaults by inmates against inmates and 47 by inmates against staff, a total of 439.

While it seemed like total anarchy, it really wasn't. This was mob rule with a purpose, a throwback to a time long before civilized man developed modern social institutions. By now I began to realize how fragile civilization was and how easily modern man could be reduced to the savagery of his prehistoric ancestors. Although we had TVs, radios, clothes, and a wealth of commissary goods, behaviorally we had regressed thousands of years backward on the social evolutionary scale. The man (or men) with the biggest club ruled. The new order was now the law of the jungle.

Violence in Graterford had also become a form of escape for many inmates. In creating and maintaining a predatory environment, these men were able to avoid the reality of imprisonment by focusing all their attention on fighting one another. The more hostile the environment, the more they saw themselves as victims and the less responsible they felt for their own actions. This obsession with violence became as destructive as any narcotic addiction.

People caught up in this violent escapism never perceived it as their reaction to incarceration, any more than I could see the danger of oversleeping before it was pointed out to me. Sadly, the ones who ended up suffering the most were those who came to prison just to pay their debt to society—those who hoped one day to return to their lives in the mainstream. They suffered twice: once at the hands of the predatory inmates, and then again through the prison's system of punishment.

PRISON SUBCULTURES

One of the contributing factors to this upsurge of violence was the creation of new subcultures within the prison. These arose from the new types of inmates who had now extended the roster of victims and predators in the general population. People who in the past would never have been committed to an adult correction facility were now queuing up for their "three hots and a cot" in ever-increasing numbers.

Many of these were the mentally ill who had spilled out of state mental hospitals, which had been closed down in the seventies. These "nuts," as inmates simply called them, were pathetic and destructive. Their illnesses made punishment in the normal sense virtually impossible. Their helplessness often made them the favorite victims of predatory inmates. Worst of all, their special needs and peculiar behavior destroyed the stability of the prison system.

There were also growing numbers of the homeless as well as juvenile offenders committed as adults. But the largest group of new arrivals were young, minority drug dealers and users, most of them from inner-city ghettos.

When the homeless came to Graterford, they were just looking for a secure haven from the streets. They weren't interested in counselors, treatment, or discipline. They had no sense of their own criminality.

Juveniles suffered the most. They viewed prison as a surrogate parent and so expected to be protected and sheltered. What they got instead was victimization by adult inmates and indifferent bureaucrats.

Finally, the drug addicts and dealers saw Graterford as one more rehab center to dry them up and help them overcome their habit. Few thought of themselves as criminals because they perceived themselves as the victims of their own addictions.

Like me, all these newcomers sought to have their needs met. But Graterford, a maximum-security prison, could not identify these needs, let alone meet them. A prison confines, punishes, and sometimes deters. It is neither designed nor inclined to foster, cure, or rehabilitate.

In meeting only the basic needs of the new arrivals (food, shelter, clothing, and medical care), Graterford's resources were stretched beyond its limits. Additionally, many of the guards and treatment staff, who were accustomed to supplying inmates with only a minimum amount of services and a maximum amount of discipline, were embittered by the fact that these new arrivals were coming into the prison with expectations of treatment and care.

Soon, the mentally ill were commanding too much of the staff's attention. Drug addicts, many of them going through withdrawal, were doing anything they could to get high. Juveniles were being raped and causing havoc trying to attract some "parental" attention. Because of all this, instead of changing people, Graterford itself was changing. Because most of the new commitments came from blighted urban areas, the changes often reflected that environment.

NEW INMATES VERSUS OLD HEADS

Fear and violence had changed Graterford as profoundly as it had changed me. The new prison subcultures with their disrespect for authority, drug addiction, illiteracy, and welfare mentality had altered the institution's very character. All the evils of the decaying American inner city were being compressed into one overcrowded prison. Ironically, the violence that had long been a tool of control by the administration was now being used against it to send its prison system hurtling out of control. Much of the violence that invaded Graterford in the 1980s was actually imported from the streets by the social misfits who were now being called convicts. They were criminals before— the only change in their identity is that now they're incarcerated, lost their names, and were assigned numbers. For many of these newcomers, prison violence was simply life as usual.

Reacting to this new environment, the Old Heads would tell anyone who would listen about the "good old days." The typical Old Head had come to Graterford a decade or more earlier after spending most of his life behind bars. What puzzled me and others my age was how these seasoned prison elders would pine over the rigidly structured routine, solitude, mistreatment, and hard labor of those good old days. When asked about it, they would talk about times when the outside world was kept outside, when an inmate's natural enemies were the guards, and when men did extraordinary things to go home.

Now those good old days had become a bygone era. To the Old Heads, prison life today lacked the honor, quiet solitude, and routine that had once made incarceration more noble. Now the greatest threat to an inmate had become other inmates, particularly the "Young Bucks" who had infested the general population. With their ruthless and reckless selfishness, Young Bucks relentlessly challenged the established routine and order of both convicts and staff, so that the stability and relative peace Old Heads had established and now enjoyed were being replaced by chaos and mayhem.

An example of this new threat was the way debts were collected. Old Heads were always careful to whom they gave credit. If a debtor fell behind in payments, the debt was usually doubled and any of his belongings would be taken as collateral. Physical violence was employed only as a last resort.

In contrast, the Young Bucks would lend anything to anybody. Should a debtor be late in paying, even if it was a single pack of cigarettes, he would immediately be beaten and robbed. It seemed almost as if these compulsive youths were more interested in committing violence than in making money. This all too common practice of swift punishment for indebtedness disturbed the Old Heads' sense of fair play. "Working from the muscle" was to them unsound business, but the Young Bucks would have it no other way. To the Old Heads nothing in business was personal, but to the oung newcomers *everything* was personal.

What disturbed the Old Heads most was how these newcomers had so readily and completely accepted prison as their life. Everything they did, including using and dealing drugs, smuggling contraband, forming violent gangs, and embracing homosexuality, was undertaken to make themselves more comfortable *in* prison—not to get *out* of prison. Few of them challenged their convictions in court and still fewer contemplated escape. They were too busy enjoying themselves.

This confounded the Old Heads, who could not conceive of a life beyond the walls so oppressive that it would cause all these strong and able-bodied young men to forfeit their freedom so willingly. Nor could the Old Heads win in their losing battle against the new prison subculture of Young Bucks who fought for prison turf as if it were their birthright.

To illustrate this conflict between generations, one of my closest Old Head friends was released from prison the day after he had slapped a Young Buck in the prison yard because "he didn't know how to talk to a man." Some time after his release, my friend was shot to death in a bar by that same young man, who had recklessly sought revenge beyond the prison walls with no regard for the consequences. The assassin has since been caught and now sits on death row.

THE MEAT WAGON CREW

By 1984, years after I had lost my clerical job, I was working as an infirmary janitor. Stabbings, murders, and serious injuries had become so frequent that the medical staff created a special unit, to which I was assigned. Our job was to respond to the medical emergencies on the general population blocks.

They called us the "Meat Wagon Crew." When summoned, we would rush to the scene of a medical emergency, a staff nurse in the lead, one inmate pushing a gurney, another carrying an emergency medical kit, and a third bearing oxygen or medical equipment. Although our crew was originally intended to serve as an ambulance service, it in fact more closely resembled a coroner's wagon. Two or three times a week, we could be seen rushing through the many long concrete corridors in response to an emergency call. Often we arrived only in time to remove a dead body or the unconscious victim of an assault.

In one case, an inmate had died of a drug overdose. He sat frozen on his bed, his lifeless eyes staring out a window. Inattentive (or poorly trained) guards simply added him to their usual count, while passing inmates wondered what could be so interesting outside. Finally, someone asked the stiff body that question, only to discover that dead men don't talk. When the Meat Wagon arrived, we had to struggle to get the rigid corpse out of the cell's narrow opening to the waiting gurney.

In most cases, if the medical emergency didn't involve a drug overdose, it was usually some aftermath of violence. One inmate, who had been attacked over nonpayment of a two-cigarette-pack debt, was found with his intestines spilling out from a razor slash across his stomach. We had to keep pushing his entrails back into place as we raced the gurney down the corridor. Another man's face had been so badly beaten that I didn't recognize him as one of my friends until a guard identified him from his ID card.

By 1985, the body count was so high that we stopped running to answer our calls. The helpless victimization of our fellow inmates and our own frustration eventually rendered us indifferent to violence.

Violence or degradation, self-defense or lost self-esteem, kill or be killed—these are not real choices. In the same way, Graterford offered no real choices to the multitude of men overcrowded within its walls. The violence of inmates was no worse than the brutality and insensitivity of an indifferent, omnipotent bureaucracy. In the long run Graterford's great walls would never be high enough to contain the hatred, violence, and rage swelling out of proportion inside.

5

The Underground Economy

EDITORS' NOTE

The underground economy in prisons balances the supply and demand of goods and services. It flourishes when the official prison economy falters. In extreme cases, as seen in this chapter, the official economy may undermine the black market. Prisoners live with many deprivations and are highly motivated to secure goods and services. In the process, they create a culture of their own. In this situation, a virtual "Kingdom of Inmates" is created. Officials cannot fully control the underground economy nor easily banish inmates from their subterranean kingdom, but this arrangement only lasts as long as a degree of order is achieved.

Sooner or later, however, some key event will mobilize the staff to constrain the excesses of the inmate culture. It might be a full-scale riot or a public scandal, after which the prison will be retaken and a new order under officials will be put in place. Soon thereafter, the pressure to expand the underground economy will grow, and the cycle will likely unfold once again.

Drug dealers in prison often use homosexuals to smuggle contraband. For this reason, some homosexuals in prison enlarge their anal cavities so they can hide drugs in greater quantities. Since many prison "mules" work on a percentage basis, larger cavities translate into more money. Mules are sometimes even paid to carry contraband in their cavities all day long. They become walking safe-deposit boxes.

By the mid-1980s, Graterford was in the advanced stages of a complete system breakdown. Not only had the prison become an extremely violent place, but the administration was showing signs of an inability to meet the inmate population's basic need for food and shelter. This breakdown, however, opened the door for a thriving underground economy provided virtually every kind of goods and services that the legitimate prison system now lacked.

For example, if I wanted my laundry done, I could pay an inmate laundry worker with cigarettes to have my laundry picked up, cleaned, and delivered back to me. If, on the other hand, I had tried to send my laundry through the institution's authorized laundry system, I probably would never have gotten it back. Thieves and hustlers who profited from the underground laundry made sure that the prison laundry was unable to meet the population's needs. So for two or three fifty-cent packs a week, an inmate could get his laundry cleaned and returned, which was a real bargain. Those who had no cigarettes wore dirty clothes or washed their own laundry.

Other black-market services abounded at Graterford, especially in the main corridor where most business was conducted. For a few packs a week, a swag man could deliver specialized cooked foods and pastries to your cell on a daily basis. The food was smuggled out of the kitchen by inmate workers who would then openly hawk them on any housing block. These swag men were the most prolific of the underground service providers and, since the food cost them nothing, also the best paid. The quality of bootlegged sandwiches was comparable to or better than that of the food served in the dining hall. But this said more about the breakdown of Graterford's food service than about the culinary skills of the swag men.

Eventually, I worked my way into a situation where my own basic needs were being met. I had at my disposal the eager services of swag men, laundry men, ice men (for summer ice cubes), barbers (to cut my hair in my cell), and phone men (to make sure I was signed up for phone calls). I could even have a cell cleaner, though I felt there were certain things a man should do for himself.

All in all, Graterford had become a predatory institution where nothing worked right and everything was for sale.

A KINGDOM OF TRIBAL GANGS

Through this gradual process of deterioration, Graterford the prison became Graterford the ghetto: A place where men forgot about courts of law or the differences between right and wrong because they were too busy thinking about living, dying, or worse.

Reform, rehabilitation, and redemption do not exist in a ghetto. There is only survival of the fittest. Crime, punishment, and accountability are of little significance when men are living in a lawless society where their actions are restrained only by the presence of concrete and steel. Where a prison in any real or abstract sense might promote the greater good, once it becomes a ghetto it can do nothing but promise violent upheaval.

As weapons in Graterford proliferated, violence escalated, and gang leadership emerged; the administration gradually ceded control of the institution to independent gang tribes. During this period of gang expansion, there was no method to the madness. Violence was as unpredictable as the weather. By 1986, it was still epidemic, but it had more direction. Most of the violence was now directed at people who failed to pay their debts. The underground economy was so healthy at this point that it needed to take further steps to defend and preserve its fiscal survival.

DOUBLE D AND ROCKY

It is hard to find friends in prison because most inmates are anti-social by disposition or through prison conditioning. One of the cruelest aspects of a penitentiary is the way it leaves one isolated and lonely despite the overcrowded surroundings. Yet, because of all the fear and hardship we experienced together, the friends I made at Graterford turned out to be my closest. The harsher the conditions, the closer the bonds between us. Dan, my chess companion and one of my earliest friends at Graterford, was a quiet, soft-spoken man who stood a tall six feet and weighed about 180 pounds. His prison handle was Double D, an abbreviation for Dangerous Dan.

I had met Double D when I was in the county jail awaiting trial. For some reason he took a liking to me. I would prefer to think it was because of my dynamic personality, charm, and wit, but in prison such qualities don't count for much. Chances are, he liked me because he felt I was of some use to him. I've never really been certain why but, whatever the reason, I valued his friendship highly in those early years.

Dan never talked much, didn't lie, didn't steal, and didn't mince words. Though he belonged to no prison gang, he was respected by everyone. Those who didn't respect him feared him to the very marrow of their bones.

We both loved chess and, while he was a much better opponent, I played well enough for him to enjoy beating me. We played a lot on the block, because I didn't like being too far away from my cell. The good thing about chess is that it's not a spectator sport and is so boring to watch that it kept people away. Dan and I were able to have long, leisurely games and conversations without distraction.

"Why do they call you 'Dangerous'?" I once asked.

"Because they know I won't take any shit from any of these fleas."

"A lot of guys are afraid of you."

Dan rubbed his forehead and pushed up the brim of his ever-present prison work cap. Its tightly creased brim stood at a crisp forty-five degrees to the ceiling, moving around like the dorsal fin of a shark. After a long silence, he replied, "I like it like that."

I must confess that being a friend of Double D's had certain advantages.

One was the freedom to play chess without ever having to worry about an ambush or an attack, fairly common events in those days.

Once while we were playing, a mountain of a brute walked by. Dan never looked up, but I could sense he was watching the man's every move. I could also sense there was no love lost between them.

Rocky was the biggest and toughest convict in Graterford, and inmates and staff alike paid deference to him. He led a gang of black and white thugs called the "Terminators," which he liked to refer to as a paramilitary organization of anti-government terrorists. I had been told that Rocky's Terminators were the largest gang of extortionists, drug dealers, and smugglers in the prison. But to Double D, "Rocky's just another flea."

"You don't like him?" I asked one day after I made a rather stupid chess move.

"No. Pay attention to the board," Dan said in that soft voice.

"Why do you think they let him do the shit he does?"

Dan gritted his teeth with annoyance and rubbed his forehead, the shark fin of his cap circling the air. "Because he works for the prison. He's doing exactly what they want him to."

I had played enough chess with Double D to know his words were as complicated as his chess strategy.

"What do you mean?"

The fin came toward me. "This place only lets happen what it wants to happen. Rocky's no bigger than the three hundred guards they got working here. That silly Terminator stuff is just bullshit. They use Rocky to keep everybody in line. He does their dirty work." Then he proceeded to beat me mercilessly on the chessboard, as if to emphasize his point.

According to Double D, Graterford had gone through some violent changes in the 1970s. Despite its rigidity and strict military discipline, three staff members had been murdered. One was a captain of the guard who in 1979 had had his head split open by a baseball bat in the main corridor. By the early 1980s, prison gangs had become firmly entrenched and the administration did not have the manpower or the know-how to deal with them. Furthermore, the rigidity and discipline did nothing to make their jobs any easier.

So, as Dan saw it, the administration decided to play a gambit: They relaxed the rules and, instead of trying to end the gangs, they manipulated them by playing one against the other. In this way gangs would be too busy fighting each other to work together against the system. To destabilize these gangs, the administration threw its support behind one gang to maintain a balance of power. So Rocky's Terminators became the administration's flavor of the month.

To me, this seemed too far-fetched to be the product of any rational administrative policy. Besides, it sounded illegal; you can't support corruption if you're paid to combat it. But in those days I knew very little about the prison system. So I discounted Double D's story, reasoning that the Terminators' success was more likely due to administrative ineptitude. The staff was simply as frightened of Rocky as were most of the inmates.

"Rocky's going to get himself killed," volunteered Double D one day, as he murdered me on the chess board.

"Why do you say that?" I asked, knocking my king over.

"Because people are getting tired of his bullshit. The administration can't protect him forever."

The conversation ended there. I couldn't imagine a thug like Rocky needing protection from anyone.

About a year later, gang wars broke out and numerous inmates were getting stabbed. Double D and I still played chess together regularly, but we were a lot more wary.

One day a friend of Dan's, Shorty, got beat up by Rocky over a phone call. Rocky wanted to use a phone Shorty was on, so he just picked up the little guy and threw him to the ground like a rag. Shorty was no coward, but Rocky was twice his size. It was a no-win situation.

Later that same day, Double D took the time to warn me: "Don't come out in the main corridor when they open up tonight. Just stay on the block."

But I was too young and curious, unable to imagine that the main corridor could be any more dangerous than it already was. When the evening bell rang, I locked my cell and ventured out, staying close to the guard's station just to play it safe. All seemed normal, except the traffic was extremely light. Too light for a prison of over 2,000 men. The main corridor exhibited a dreary glow, like the light of a fading fluorescent lamp.

Suddenly, the corridor became completely empty. A deadly silence gripped the scene. Some feet away, a guard ordered me back to my block as he scanned the corridor in puzzlement. Usually there would be last-minute stragglers loitering about, but now there was not a soul in sight.

As I started for B-Block, I felt a slight breeze. I looked up the corridor to see the auditorium door angled open—inmates were spilling out into the corridor. I was too far away to make out details, but I could tell that a huge mob was quietly filling the back end of the corridor and heading in my direction. It was an eerie, unsettling sight to see hundreds of men rush down a long corridor in utter silence.

Rocky happened to be coming out of the door directly to my right. When he saw the approaching mob, he ran as fast as a man his size could toward A-Block. He banged on the gate, yelling, "Key up! Key up!"

When the mob saw this, they all bolted in unison down the corridor toward him, shouting angrily.

The guard on A-Block, instead of retreating to the safety of the guards' station, courageously rushed to Rocky's aid, keyed the convict into his block, and locked the door behind him. Then in some fit of insanity he stood in the center of the corridor, raised his hand, and hollered, "Everybody back to your blocks! That's an order!" But the unstoppable mob ran over him on their way to confront Rocky and his Terminators.

Some men banged on the door to A-Block and screamed, "Key! Key!" Amazingly enough, another guard opened it and let through a stream of men before he realized his folly and slammed the door shut. The rest of the crowd streamed through the door from which Rocky had emerged moments earlier.

Leading the pack were Double D and Shorty. When he saw me watching in amazement from the corridor, Dan waved me away. His mob then disappeared into the dark doorway until all of them had emptied out of the main corridor. All that was left were me and the trampled guard still lying on the floor. Quickly guards hurried out of their station to drag their coworker to safety. I myself rushed to the B-Block door and was lucky enough to be let in.

Soon the mob returned to occupy the corridor, hollering in triumph. This wasn't the Battle of Lexington or the Boston Tea Party, but the consequences were just as profound for Graterford.

No one was killed in this bloodless coup, but things changed rapidly. Rocky, the Terminator's leader, was transferred out of the prison that night. The next day, a number of his gang members were stabbed in separate incidents. Many of the others took self-lockup.

From that day forward, no one gang dominated at Graterford. If Double D's story was true, then the administration had lost its balance of power. Soon whole gangs of cell thieves were being stabbed and beaten. Just as these gangs had once made the administration superfluous, the collective will of the inmate population had now made the gangs superfluous.

Hence, the "Kingdom of Inmates" was born. Its new offensive curtailed much of the stealing that the administration had been unable to control. A collective conscience had risen among the inmates, as Graterford evolved from a ragtag nation of independent tribal gangs into a unified conglomerate of collective and competing interests. It was only a matter of time before the new kingdom would begin to test its boundaries by challenging the power of the prison administration.

THE INMATE CODE OF CONDUCT

In retrospect, it was primarily the inability of Graterford's guards to ensure inmates' safety that brought about the demise of their control over their own prison. When things got so bad that inmates couldn't even commit themselves to protective custody, the population knew it had to fend for itself. The only thing guards could do for inmates now was to keep them locked in their cells.

Because of this, the population developed its own unwritten "Inmate Code of Conduct," which stood apart from the prison administration's rules and regulations. The code went something like this: "Don't gamble, don't mess with drugs, don't mess with homosexuals, don't steal, don't borrow or lend, and you might survive."

By itself, this simple rule would never have worked unless something tangible and powerful prevented the inmates from killing each other and forced them to abide by it. That something was the flourishing underground economy. The black market of goods and services had grown so much as a result of overcrowding and failed security that a stable class of merchants and consumers had established itself within the prison population.

The swag man who sold me and others his sandwiches became my friend. But if it hadn't been so easy and profitable to steal from the kitchen, he probably would have ended up stealing from me. The more he provided his clandestine services, the more he created a demand, which in turn ensured him a steady income that was far less risky than breaking into another man's cell.

Every inmate in general population was either a buyer or a seller. It was now to everyone's benefit to abide by the Inmate Code of Conduct, so that the economic heart of the Inmate Kingdom could continue to beat.

The only threat to this economic stability, then, became the guards. Since they were no longer the mainstays of stability or providers of protection, their petty rules, shake-downs, and confiscations served only as an irritating nuisance that hindered the inmate population's new economic order. The Kingdom of Inmates had no choice but to challenge the authority of the guards in order to discourage their interference with the socioeconomic balance.

CHICKEN SUNDAY

It is difficult to determine exactly when Graterford's guards yielded their authority to their charges, but one significant turning point took place on Super Bowl Sunday of 1983. An inmate left the C-Block dining room and headed for his cell, openly carrying a paper plate piled high with the usual Sunday chicken dinner and all its trimmings. It was his intention not to let his favorite meal interfere with his watching the Super Bowl on the TV in his cell. Posted everywhere around him were signs dictating, "NO FOOD IS TO LEAVE THE DINING ROOM."

While violations of this rule were commonplace, the usual practice was to hide one's food before leaving the dining hall. To accommodate this minimal demand for obedience, most inmates smuggled out food in anything from trash-bag liners to empty potato-chip bags, often stashed in the split lining of one's institutional prison coat. Guards never searched for food, and no harm was done.

But on this particular day, this inmate had decided to blatantly ignore convention. As was expected, a guard saw him with the food plate, followed him to his cell, and ordered him either to eat his food in the dining hall or throw it out. Considering the circumstances, this was a reasonable request.

The inmate told the guard in no uncertain terms that he planned to eat his Super Bowl meal in the comfort of his cell and there was nothing he could do about it. The guard, frustrated by this display of disrespect, grabbed the plate of food out of the man's hands.

What ensued became known as the Super Bowl Sunday Chicken Riot. Since C-Block housed many winemakers and this was a big sports day, a good number of the block's four hundred occupants were drunk on "pruno," or prison hootch. When they saw this inmate's fight with the guard, everybody decided it was time to show the staff who was boss. Every inmate related to the incident as if the guard had tried to take away something of *his*. The chicken was more than just food—it represented each man's hustle, and its confiscation challenged everyone's livelihood.

Dozens of men swarmed to the aid of the inmate and beat the guard. Dozens more mobbed the dining room to defiantly take chicken dinners back to their cells. In quick order, every guard on the block was assaulted and some were even locked in cells.

Notably, the inmates attacked only guards and not each other. Not a single inmate was hurt in the uprising, which made this event uniquely different from other prison riots. If anything, the inmates actually joined together with a coherent plan. Some seized a guard's radio transmitter and called for reinforcements, while others armed with sticks and clubs waited in ambush by the block's main entrance. When a dozen or so guards rushed into the block, inmates fell upon them like swashbuckling pirates and quickly subdued them. Then they locked their new victims into cells.

What happened next was the most convincing proof that a kingdom had arisen. The inmates abused and humiliated the guards—but they didn't seriously injure any of them. Once they were satisfied, they simply opened the main door to C-Block and allowed other guards to tend to their fallen comrades, just so they could see what might one day await them. Some inmates even assisted the nursing staff in tending to the wounds of guards they had attacked only moments before. There were no demands for better conditions, amnesty, media, the superintendent, or anything else.

And that was the end of the Super Bowl Sunday Chicken Riot. Most of the inmates simply returned to their cells to watch the Super Bowl Game, drink jailhouse wine, and eat chicken. Nothing else happened for the rest of the day. At the 5:00 PM count, everyone locked up in their cells as usual. It wasn't until then that guards quietly gathered the rebellious inmates from their cells and escorted them to the Hole.

By then it was too late. The point had been made. Inmates had joined together to defeat the guards fair and square. The interests of the inmate population had been advanced and defended, thus ensuring the livelihood of each and every man in the triumphant Kingdom of Inmates.

To this day, Graterford is still the most violent prison in the state system. It now houses over four thousand men and is home to the most politically active inmate population in Pennsylvania.

6

Prison Politics

EDITORS' NOTE

All political systems are premised on the provision of security. The safety of the citizenry is the first obligation of all rulers. This obligation is even more salient in prison than in the free world. Prisoners are captives under the control of officials, who are fully responsible for their welfare. A prison that cannot protect its own is a scandalous failure.

We in the corrections field have become acclimated to such profound failure, as have many inmates, but this dereliction throws in doubt the legitimacy of the entire system. As a practical matter, the prison population has a moral right to self-preservation and is forced to protect itself if officials fail to do so. Inmates will arm themselves, join informal groups, establish gangs, and come to see themselves as a constituency in opposition to an impotent staff. This is the formula for a riot—us (the aggrieved inmates) against them (the powerless staff). A change in political power is the end result.

Prisoners have a vibrant political system because the failure of officials has necessitated their participation in the daily stability of the prison environment. The staff must cooperate, sometimes even collude, with influential inmates if things are to get done. In this chapter, Victor Hassine describes how a prison's political system operates on a daily basis. He argues that inmates and staff who participate in the prison's political process tend to benefit from the status quo. By resisting change, the political system perpetuates the existing arrangement and hence ensures that those few who are on top today stay on top tomorrow. The main differences between inmates and guards are the methods that each uses to maintain the existing order. As described by the author, a prison's political system does not seem much different from political systems everywhere. This is a paradox of modern punishment, since prisoners are by definition disenfranchised and should have no political power at all.

> "Put your trust in the Lord; your ass belongs to me!"——Warden Norton, addressing new inmates, *The Shawshank Redemption*, Castle Rock Entertainment, 1994.

The balance of power has changed much in prisons since the 1950s, when real superintendents like the fictional Warden Norton often made this infamous boast. The process of change within the prison system can be as treacherous as the most notorious of its inhabitants.

The danger associated with navigating the murky waters of jailhouse politics makes that change sometimes very difficult to control.

Change in society is inevitable, but in prison there are powerful competing groups of differing interests with much time on their hands and a strong motivation to prevent change. A prison's very existence often depends on the struggles to control change. Its soul is not reflected by the preciseness of its construction nor the orderly appearance of its uniformed staff. Nor does the calculated chaos and deliberately random violence of its inmates necessarily expose the real belly of the beast. Only on the battlefield of resistance to change will one be likely to find the naked prison as it exists.

Much like soldiers in combat, inmates and prison staff have little overview of the arena where their conflicts play out. They can only glean narrow glimpses of it from the small plots of turf they happen to occupy at any given moment. Consequently, inmates and guards alike can never afford themselves a complete view of the prison in which they live, work, and struggle.

In any prison system, the parties of competing interests are represented by the inmate population, the rank-and-file uniformed staff, and the managerial administration. The interaction among these three groups defines a prison at any given time. Those few times when all three parties are in agreement over some particular change, the result is a quick and effective implementation of that change. Likewise, when all three parties are completely united in their opposition to an impending change, the result is unanimous rejection, even though other unrelated and unexpected changes might occur because of competitive tactics employed by one or more of them to resist the original change.

By far the most common and most volatile type of change in a modern prison comes as the result of two groups attempting to impose change over the objections and resistance of the third group. Even though the decision of the majority will be upheld, the resisting minority will nevertheless be relentless in its attempt to undermine that change. The end result is most often some dysfunctional change where conditions are worsened by the minority's resistance. Thus, the intended change is never fully realized. Reluctant change is always more destructive because jailhouse politics tends to maintain and perpetuate any ongoing struggle.

THE SERGEANT, THE MAJOR, AND ME

One illustration of the complexity of prison politics was revealed to me soon after my ill-fated hamburger caper in 1981. There was an unexpected consequence to that infraction of which I was not initially aware.

After my misconduct hearing, I returned to my cell to begin serving my sixty days of cell restriction. At the time, I genuinely felt I was being mistreated. Compared to the rampant thievery and abundance of violence I had witnessed in Graterford, my measly infraction was hardly worth the bother. Losing my job and paying for the burgers made sense, but two months locked in my cell for twenty-two hours a day seemed unfair to me.

Little did I realize that there were higher forces who felt I had been treated too leniently and who wanted to thrust me into the lions'den of jailhouse politics. In actual fact, stealing food from a penitentiary kitchen was a serious offense because it involved two vital concerns of the administration: spending and control. Graterford spent an average of $2.75 per day to feed a single inmate, in contrast to the statewide average of about $2.10 per day. To the powers that be, the ease with which I was able to buy smuggled food from the kitchen meant that the prison could not control its inmates. If other inmates similarly challenged its control, the per diem cost of feeding the population could rise drastically.

Ten pounds of bootlegged ground beef should have landed me directly in the Hole. The fact that I used the major of the guards' bathroom in my plot normally should also have cost me double time in cold storage for my arrogant defiance of authority. If anything, cell restriction was a lucky break for me. But what did I know? I hadn't been in prison long enough to appreciate the seriousness of the situation.

When I finally arrived at my cell, I was unexpectedly greeted by the B-Block sergeant. A man of military bearing, he stood a rigid six feet tall in a starched and precisely creased uniform. His prison dress cap added height to his authority.

"Didn't think I'd be seeing you back so soon," the sergeant said, chewing on a lump of tobacco in his cheek that gave his southern drawl a lazier tone. He spat to accentuate his words.

I assumed he was referring to my returning so soon from the misconduct hearing. Usually men given cell restriction took their time coming back in an effort to extend their liberties.

"I got sixty days cell restriction, Sarge," I complained naively. "Can you believe that?"

The sergeant spat again. "Boy, the way I see it, you must be a real important inmate to have talked your way out of the Hole. I don't like important inmates on my block, so you just watch yourself because you can be right sure I'll be watching you."

With that, he double-locked me in and walked away like a general who had just reviewed his troops. Amazed by his hostility, I foolishly thought he was singling me out for some personal reason, perhaps because I was Jewish.

However, the truth was that the sergeant's attitude had nothing to do with me but with my former work supervisor, the major of the guard, who had intervened on my behalf to keep me out of the Hole. This recently appointed officer happened to be the only African American in Pennsylvania history to hold such a position. As such, he was the first member of a minority to personally direct the actions of an historically all-white guard force at Graterford. In addition he had been promoted from the rank of lieutenant, which was not only unprecedented but caused a stir among the several captains he was promoted over.

To further complicate the situation, the major was also a reformer, a compassionate and decent man who did not feel that physical force was the way to solve Graterford's problems. In his view, such a traditional style of prison management often led to the unfair treatment that had thrust Graterford into a crisis in the first place.

While the prison administration and the overwhelmingly African American inmate population were hopeful about the major, the almost all-white, rank-and-file staff were disgruntled over his appointment. Not only had a longstanding race barrier been broken, but there was genuine concern that the major's management style would give the prison away to the inmates. Militarism and white leadership had been the way at Graterford for generations.

When the major had decided that my actions were not serious enough to warrant sending me to the Hole, battle lines were drawn. Derogatory slurs were already being made about him by the uniformed staff, often in the presence of inmates, which only served to undermine the major's authority.

There I was in the middle of all this, and I didn't even know it. I simply wasn't yet tuned in to the political undercurrents sweeping through Graterford.

While on cell restriction, I was let out of my cell for two hours each day for recreation. During this time, I found myself and my cell constantly being searched by the block guards. Though they were not as intrusive as they could have been, even one search of a man's cell or body is an assault on his sense of dignity and freedom.

Naturally, my resentment and paranoia grew with each search, as if every guard was out to get me. Helpless to stop them, I began to hate these men in uniform. To make matters worse, some of them would ridicule and taunt me by calling me the "major's boy." At times they would even imply that I had avoided the Hole by being a snitch. The mere suggestion of such a label in a prison like Graterford was life threatening.

On the fifty-ninth day of my sixty days of cell restriction, I was issued another misconduct—for taking more than two hours for recreation. Reporting to another misconduct hearing, I was given an additional thirty days of cell restriction. As I returned to my cell, the sergeant was again waiting for me.

He spat a wad. "Boy, I don't know why you came back to this block. You got no job and you just keep breaking the rules." He spat again. "You must know some real important people. But let me tell you this. Let any of my officers catch you wrong again and nobody's going to be able to save you then."

This time I said nothing, though I'm certain the hatred beating in my heart could be heard by the sergeant as he locked me in and paraded out of sight. For all my frustration and anger, I was too young and inexperienced to realize that his malice was focused elsewhere. The old soldier was just trying to stop the process of change. His real enemy was the black major with his liberal notions. I was just someone who was unlucky enough to be chosen as the vehicle for his resentment.

Resistance to change in a prison can foment enough resentment and malice to result in changes so riddled with compromise that more problems are created than solved. The only beneficiaries of this kind of change are those who will profit from the system's breakdown. As a twenty-two-year veteran of jailhouse politics, I can now only speculate what could have transpired had the sergeant approved of the major. Could Graterford have become a better place? No one will ever know.

THE POLITICS OF ANGER

I have always considered myself a proud American and, despite my incarceration, I still subscribe to the traditional American system of values. Before coming to prison, I expected it to be a very unpleasant place, staffed by the otherwise unemployable and inhabited by the generally unredeemable. While I was not surprised by the amount of violence and corruption at Graterford, I was genuinely shocked by the level of persecution.

The sergeant did much to shape my current reality. He accomplished this by continuing to have the block guards pat me down and search my cell, even after I had completed all my cell-restriction time. Generally, this type of treatment was reserved for troublemakers and drug dealers. I was neither. Though the searches never turned up anything of consequence, my cell was always left in total disarray. My creature comforts, such as an extra pillow, bed sheet, and towel, were taken away from me.

Beyond the unfair treatment, the sergeant had succeeded in making me feel even more isolated from the world that existed outside the prison walls. I was no longer so proud to be an American. I was just a convict without rights. Again, I had simply misconstrued the motives behind his actions.

When prison guards feel they are losing control, their first response is to crack down hardest on the segment of the population over whom they still have control. This is done as a show of force to let the general population know that they mean business. Furthermore, if cooperative inmates are being treated this harshly, then the troublesome ones can expect much more serious treatment.

The problem with this control tactic is that it doesn't always work. Often the uncooperative elements of the population don't necessarily get the message or don't care about the consequences of their actions. When this happens, conditions usually worsen. There is still a control problem, only now it exists with the added hostility and resentment of the more stable inmates.

I was now made to feel the full weight of forced confinement in an imposed egalitarian police state. All my life I had been taught to work for my livelihood; the harder I worked and the more resourceful I was, the greater would be my reward. Now everything was turned around. No matter how hard I worked, or even if I worked at all, I received the same portion as everyone else. There was no incentive to achieve anything or improve myself. In fact, the more well-behaved I was, the more likely it was that I would be mistreated by inmates and staff.

Prison anger affects every aspect of prison life and management. At Graterford it made victims of the major, the sergeant, and me. We were all left wondering what kind of world we had fashioned and, each in our own way, resented having to live in it. While anger usually demands satisfaction, it often settles just for company. I had now resolved that the inmate population would be my new nation. And the first thing I would do was join the Graterford Lifers Organization.

OMAR AND THE LIFERS GROUP

"I need a pass for the Lifers meeting," I told the guard seated at a small, shabby desk in the middle of the B-Block "Bridge." The Bridge was a ten-foot walkway that spanned the two upper tier walkways of the block like the center crossline of a big "H." Behind me stood twenty other men waiting for their passes off the block. I spent a good deal of my time at Graterford waiting in one line or another.

"I didn't know you were a lifer," replied the weary, disaffected bridge officer, a phone receiver cradled between his shoulder and ear. Routine had just about made him a part of the furniture he was stuck in. His hands quickly fingered my inmate ID card, but he never looked up. He knew me only from the identity photo.

Without answering, I silently waited for my pass. He slid back to me a standardized slip of paper and my ID card. I took both immediately and headed down to the ground floor of B-Block.

Once I reached the block's main entrance, I waited my turn in yet another line, this time for the front-door officer to allow me off the block.

"I didn't know you were a lifer," the door guard said, echoing the bridge officer.

Again I waited silently until he decided to verify my pass. I then entered the main corridor and merged with a moving mass of inmates. During general movement, hundreds of men walked quickly up and down the corridor. Most of them wore prison uniforms for work or exercise clothes for the yard, but there were always some in pajamas and bathrobes whose only apparent purpose was to be part of the confusion.

As I headed for the auditorium, I could hear the familiar voices of hustlers hawking sandwiches, drugs, and anything else worth selling. Hundreds of voices bounced off the concrete walls, the usual disconcerting din that always heightened my concern that I might accidentally collide with the wrong guy. Sometimes the carnival atmosphere here made me forget the dangers of this place. But invariably, I would witness the all too common corridor knifing and be reminded once again how risky it was to commute on this prison's main boulevard.

Halfway to E-Block, I arrived at the main entrance of the auditorium, one of its four doors wedged open with a guard blocking the way inside. I gave him my pass, which he glanced at and quickly returned without a word. All his attention was focused on the many shadows speeding past him in both directions. There were no other guards in sight, so his safety was more of a priority than my status as a lifer. Besides, who would attend a Lifers meeting if he wasn't a lifer?

Crumpling the pass and tossing it, I stepped inside into a dusky twilight. The auditorium, used on weekends as a movie theater, had its lights dimmed down to ambush dark. This would explain why the door guard chose to take his chances in the more brightly lit corridor.

A few feet inside, I was greeted by the first row of steel-framed theater chairs. The auditorium could seat about a thousand men in three descending columns of these battered folding seats. Deep within was a flat area of space flanked by two basketball hoops mounted on the wall. Directly adjacent to this was an elevated stage that stood a few feet off the floor. It had a large, dirty white projection screen pulled down in front of it.

As I looked down at the farthest row of seats, I could see about a hundred indistinguishable figures either standing, sitting, or slouching. Three men stood alone together, facing the audience.

I couldn't make out anybody I knew well enough to sit next to, so I just walked down to the third row and took an aisle seat. Soon after, I heard the sound of a heavy steel door slam and lock. Shut in from the noisy corridor, I was unaccustomed to such eerie quiet.

"I call this meeting to order," said the tallest of the three standing men.

I had never been to a Lifers meeting and I wasn't sure I wanted to be there now to listen to some of Pennsylvania's most vicious killers. But since I'd become one of the boys, I decided it was time to meet my fellow lifers. Besides, I longed to be a part of a self-governing body.

There were three inmate social organizations in Graterford at the time: the Lifers Organization, the Knights of Henry Christof, and the Jaycees (Junior Chamber of Commerce). Each of them was allowed to raise funds in the prison through the sale of food or by providing services, such as showing movies and taking photos in the visiting room. Prison gangs would inevitably dominate these groups and try to control or manipulate any money-making ventures that they undertook.

As the tall man spoke, everyone appeared attentive. The meeting followed a reasonable order of business, with questions asked and politely answered. I soon felt so completely at ease that I wanted to join the discussion in some way.

The tall man gave the floor to the shortest man, apparently the financial officer, who started giving a business report. I knew the Lifers sold soda and potato chips to the population on weekends during the auditorium movies. What I didn't know was that they were allowed to make profits and maintain a bank account. I was thrilled to hear that a private enterprise zone actually existed in Graterford. Maybe a little too thrilled.

When the speaker concluded his report, I enthusiastically stood up and asked a question. "Excuse me, I heard you say we have money in a bank account. I just wondered, how much do we have on deposit and how much revenue do we generate?"

I don't know why I stood up but, from the sudden focus of attention on me and the mumbling around me, I realized that standing up in a Lifers meeting meant a lot more than I had intended. Things got ugly real quick.

"Why do you want to know?" asked the speaker.

"Well, I just wondered how much money we were making," I replied a little defensively.

"What are you, a troublemaker?"

"What are you talking about? I asked a simple question and I'd like an answer." Instinct had trained me not to let anyone talk down to me.

It was obvious I had hit a nerve. The prudent thing would have been to sit down quietly and forget the whole matter. But prudence in Graterford was seldom a viable option since it was often mistaken for weakness.

"Why don't you sit down and dig yourself," said the tall speaker.

At this point I felt a tugging at my shirt sleeve. An older man in his mid-forties materialized in the seat beside mine, smiling up at me. As my focus was on the escalating trouble in front of me, I just pulled my arm away and answered the speaker.

"I'll sit down when I get an answer."

The tall man took a step toward me, and I turned toward the aisle to confront him. Once again I felt that tugging at my sleeve and glanced over at the widening smile of my neighbor.

The short speaker reclaimed my attention. "Look, why don't you just sit down."

Someone behind me called out, "Sit the fuck down, motherfucker!"

Then someone else shouted, "Answer the man's question!"

Things were obviously getting out of control, as my fellow lifers now tried to egg on a confrontation. Painfully, I knew I would have to remain standing until I got an answer, no matter what happened.

The third man, who had said nothing so far, finally broke his silence. "Look, all of this noise is going to get the guards into our business." Then he addressed me, "Now look, I ain't never seen you at a meeting before. I don't even know if you're really a lifer. Besides, we ain't got this month's statement yet."

The three then began to speak among themselves. The tallest one had to be pulled back from advancing toward me.

Before I got a chance to decide what to do, I was pulled down into my seat by the smiling man. He never gave me a chance to speak.

"You are either the bravest man I have ever met or the dumbest. It's too early to tell which." This wasn't said offensively, and the man's demeanor was so kindly that I had to appreciate his sense of humor. But I still kept one eye on the three speakers.

"Now just sit where you're at and try not to say anything," he continued. "You made your point. What you need to do now is take a look behind you and see what you got started. Those three guys up there are really not your major problem."

Cautiously I glanced back. I was surprised to see how many men were standing up and looking in our direction. There was a lot of cursing, mumbling, and even a few snarls. I turned back around.

"What are they all so mad about?"

"Mad?" The smiling man belly laughed. "They're not mad. They're just warming up."

Almost on cue, one of the men directly behind us stood up and hollered, "You know I'm a lifer, motherfucker, now you tell me about that money. And don't give me no shit about you don't know. You ain't pulling that on me. This ain't my first time here."

Someone else shouted out, "Man, don't be feeding into that negative shit. Sit the fuck down!"

Yet another voice called out, "Man, fuck that! What's wrong with knowing how much money we got?"

The guy directly behind me answered, "They stealing, that's what's wrong."

"So who ain't?" shouted a faraway voice.

A dozen men were now arguing among themselves, some holding others back. It looked like a fight was about to break out at any minute. Nevertheless, my companion just continued to smile as he shook his head.

"It sure doesn't take much to get these men started," he said.

Still a little confused about what was going on, I just looked at him in silent amazement.

"Let me ask you a question," he said. "Did you happen to notice that the guard locked us all in here with no supervision? Do you know why he did that?"

I shook my head.

"Because he knows that everybody in this room has at least one confirmed homicide to his credit. And obviously being smarter than us both, he decided he didn't want to be caught in a dark room alone with a bunch of murderers who might start fighting. Now tell me, what do you suggest we do if things turn ugly?"

His words left me speechless.

"I thought so. You haven't got a plan. You're just playing out of pocket. Well then, you might as well tell me your name so, if I get my old behind in a tussle, I'll know who to thank."

It took me a moment to answer. "My name's Victor, but I really didn't mean..."

"It's too late to sweat it now. I just hope you can fight as good as you can talk, because you managed to embarrass some of the men in here."

"But all I did was ask a question."

"That's all it takes in this place. People don't like to answer a whole lot of questions, especially about money, especially if They're stealing. I'd be surprised if they weren't. By the way, my name is Harold, but I prefer to be called Omar. I don't like being called by my slave name." With that he extended his hand to me.

I gladly shook Omar's hand. It looked like I might be needing a friend. Besides, there was something about him that I really liked and admired. Nothing seemed to rattle him.

To our relief, things were settling down. Almost everybody was sitting down now, though with a cautious edge.

"Why does everyone seem so angry all the time?" I asked my new friend.

"Good question. It's probably because most of the men in here take everything personally. Nothing's really personal unless you want it to be. Or it could be that anger is really all the authorities leave you that's your own. They take everything else away from you at Receiving. Now, why don't we start easing toward the door so that, when the guard decides to open up, we can slip out of here without getting our feelings hurt."

With that sage advice, Omar and I got up and walked up the aisle. He was smiling and chuckling, which took some of the tension out of the air, occasionally calling out or waving to one of his friends.

Once we made it to the auditorium door, Omar turned to me and said, "Victor, you live a charmed life. You may even manage to come out of this with a little rep [reputation]. In the future, try not to upset anybody and always make sure you have a way out before you start asking questions. Frankly, you like things a little too exciting for me."

In time, Omar and I became as close as brothers. The population would come to know us collectively as the Muslim and the Jew. And it was through Omar's wisdom that I learned that nothing in prison is personal.

Race Relations in Prison

7

EDITORS' NOTE

Race is a central feature of life in most American prisons. An inmate's race may determine where he can stand, sit, or work, and what he can say and to whom he may speak. In many prisons, unwritten race-based rules of behavior are common, and violation of these rules can have serious consequences. Knowing these rules is part of being a convict. As one might suspect, race-based rules lie in the purview of the prison's political system and are part of the status quo. But as Victor Hassine's experience illustrates, race can be transcended by other factors. A prisoner's best friend and confidante might well be a man from another race.

The racial makeup of a prison's staff is influenced by the racial makeup of the locale. Prisons located in rural areas tend to have predominately white staffs, while urban prisons tend to have racially mixed or predominately black staffs. This generalization excludes the effects of affirmative action programs, unions, and organizational philosophies, which can further complicate the demographic configuration of staff groups.

Little is known about relations between officers and inmates of the same race. One is left with the impression that staff may allow racial prejudices to operate in some circumstances. This may happen in unexpected ways, as when officers are harder on inmates of their own race because they are more comfortable exercising their authority on them. Studies of correctional officers at work suggest that their first allegiance is generally to other officers and that racial sentiments are secondary.

"...A gang leader in Philadelphia has led Graterford's Muslim movement, officials said, controlling part of the prison's drug trade. A prison guard, Lieutenant Cynthia Link, said that when the lights in the prison's mosque suddenly went out one night two years ago, the 100 inmates ignored her order to leave. Finally, one of them said, 'Ms. Link, these people aren't going to move until [the gang leader] tells them to.' Link said, 'Well, go get him, tell him I need him.' He came, told the prisoners to leave, and they did...." *The New York Times*, October 30, 1995 (Complete article reprinted in Appendix A.)

Every Pennsylvania prison that I have been to, regardless of the ratio between black and white inmates, was operated by an almost entirely white staff. In Graterford between 1981 and 1982, over 80 percent of the staff were white, while over 80 percent of the inmates were black. By July 1987, according to two Pennsylvania Department of Corrections surveys on a racial breakdown of inmates and a corrections-workforce comparison, the disparity remained relatively the same with 76 percent white staff and 76 percent black inmates. To its credit, however, Graterford employed the highest percentage of minority employees out of all of Pennsylvania's state prisons.

Though the prison had been desegregated since the late 1960s, the inmates of Graterford continued to impose their own form of segregation. For example, it was an unspoken rule that the dining hall be divided into a black section and a white section. The administration did its part as well, for example, by refusing to double-cell white inmates with black inmates. De facto segregation was very much alive in those days, as it is today.

At Graterford I observed that many of the new white guards had little experience interacting with people of different races. Presumably due to feelings of intimidation or discomfort with inmates of other races, they tended to be much stricter with those of their own race.

During my initial classification period at Graterford, I was required to identify myself as either black or white. There were no other options. Hispanics and Native Americans were classified as black or white, depending on their choice. It wasn't until the mid-1980s that the racial classification process at Graterford allowed inmates to designate themselves as anything other than black or white.

Among the African American population at Graterford was a large and well-established black Muslim community, the vast majority of which came from Philadelphia. On the other hand, most of the white prison staff were Christians, many of whom were raised in the rural communities around the prison. This extreme imbalance between the racial, regional, and religious composition of staff and inmates vividly reflected the general dysfunction of the prison that prevailed throughout my years there.

Though nonwhite inmates were usually embraced by the prison population, they were often viewed with suspicion by the white staff, who seemed to believe that only white inmates could be reformed into law-abiding citizens. This racial bias at Graterford did not result in favoritism by staff but rather provoked a divisive and relentless competition between the inmates themselves for the staff's favor. Everyone in the prison system was forced to play the bias game because the only group identity available to inmates was based on skin color.

As a rule, a prison administration is reluctant to promote any group activity or identity that might evolve into cliques or gangs. Graterford's sole purpose was custody, so its entire security force was geared toward discouraging and punishing any group affiliations. All inmates were issued identical uniforms, and there were strictly enforced rules against any congregation of more than five inmates. While some social and religious organizations were permitted to operate, the administration made the rules of participation so cumbersome that these groups constituted organizations in names only. Though the prison could not punish an inmate for belonging to a legitimate group, it could try to weaken his desire to belong. One of the ways in which this was accomplished was to influence every inmate, including myself, in the direction of racial polarization.

BLACK AND WHITE PRISON GANGS

Generally, black gangs in Graterford were extensions of Philadelphia's neighborhood street gangs. They bore names based on their urban location; for example, the 21st and Norris Gang, the 60th and Market Gang, the 10th Street Gang, and so forth. Many of their members had belonged to the original street gang before they were incarcerated. Once sent to Graterford, they joined their prison counterpart to carry on the gang's traditions. As more and more street-gang members arrived, their growing strength in numbers enabled them to conduct a wider array of prison-gang activities.

The moment any African American Philadelphian entered the prison, scouts immediately approached him to determine which part of the city he came from and whether he had been a member of a street gang. This sorting of incoming blacks based on geography dictated the character of black prison gangs, giving rise to the often used term "homey" for those who hailed from the same neighborhood or hometown. Homeys were the most common recruits for black-gang membership.

Black gangs competed vigorously with each other for turf and the control of contraband sales. While this competition often resulted in violent battles, gangs on many occasions merged their enterprises and worked together. For example, rival gangs had been known to fight each other over the business of selling drugs, yet they frequently cooperated in bringing the drugs into the prison.

Those black gangs formed by inmates from areas other than Philadelphia differed considerably from the black Philly gangs in that, for the most part, they had no counterparts on the streets. Such non-Philly gangs usually originated in the prison and their members were often strangers who happened to be from the same county or city. The competition between regional gangs and Philly gangs tended to be very hostile and violent. There was seldom any trust or cooperation between them. Numerically, Philly gangs greatly outnumbered other gangs, which allowed them to dominate the population and completely exclude outsiders from joint ventures.

Regardless of their numerical superiority, it is highly probable that Philly gangs still would have had more control, because their carry-over from street gangs gave them the distinct advantage of functioning under well-established rules, organizational structures, leadership systems, and ideologies. In contrast, regional or prison-based gangs tended to be weakened internally by frequent power struggles, uncertain leadership, and untested organizational processes.

Because Graterford's black gangs were determined almost exclusively by geography, gang membership was widely diverse. In any one gang you could expect to find drug addicts, thieves, murderers, and hustlers of every stripe, including Muslims, Christians, and atheists. This amalgam of homeys provided black-gang members with such strength and vitality that the administration was hard pressed to break them apart.

Black gangs at Graterford primarily operated as money-making enterprises. While geography helped to bring prison gang members together, it was money and drugs that kept them together. The goal of every gang was to earn money, which meant selling anything that anyone was willing to buy. As in a corporation, gang profits were then reinvested to buy more contraband for further distribution. Gang members gauged their individual value by the amount of money they were able to make. What they did with their earnings was of no consequence, since the hustle itself seemed to be all that mattered. Money earned was merely an indicator of how good a hustler an inmate could be.

White gangs at Graterford were a completely different story. These gangs almost always originated in prison and, like the non-Philly gangs, were not as well-structured or established. They too were comprised of members who were often strangers to each other, most of them brought together by the simple chance of their skin color.

Statistically, white gangs in Graterford were strictly a minority, usually formed for their own protection from other gangs. While they might be involved in some hustling, they were limited by their inability to protect their turf or business interests against the larger black gangs. They were more likely to be the buyers of drugs and contraband than the sellers.

Furthermore, most white gang members were not brought together by geography but rather out of a need to protect their mutual interests. White drug addicts tended to join together to pool their funds to buy drugs at a volume discount. Some white gangs were formed because of ethnic bonds, such as Catholics, Italians, and Protestants, or because of special interests, such as gamblers and body builders.

White gangs at Graterford were more likely to be small, improvised groups rather than organized teams with specific agendas, and were generally much less diverse than their black counterparts. Whereas black gangs required large memberships to generate income and protect their turf, white gangs preferred to have as few members as possible in an effort to stretch their resources. Any white gang that grew too large would promptly be challenged by the dominant black gangs.

The exceptions in Graterford were the outlaw motorcycle gangs that successfully managed to entrench themselves within the prison system. Like the Hell's Angels who had already established themselves on the street, they were far more business oriented and could compete directly with black gangs in the sale of contraband, drugs in particular. Despite their relatively small numbers in the prison, their connections to the much larger street gangs made them resourceful money makers and a power to be reckoned with.

THE MUSLIM AND THE JEW

Not long after my first Lifers meeting, Omar became my closest friend and my window into the workings of prison life. He knew many of the inmates at Graterford and understood better than I the language, games, players, and dangers of the prison system. Most important he was willing to share his wisdom with me. His profound insight into the system helped me to grope my way through a foreign country of which I had had no inkling before I arrived at Graterford. Thus, Omar became my Old Head and I became his eager disciple.

A few months after I had lost my job in the major's office, Omar was hired to take my place. Since he now lived on the same block as I did, I often visited him in his cell. We ate meals together, walked the yard together, and exchanged a lot of jailhouse philosophy to kill time. We became inseparable and were one of the more unusual sights in Graterford: the veteran black Muslim from Philadelphia and the young Jewish rookie from New Jersey. We were constantly arguing about one issue or another.

I would often find my Old Head sitting on the cold, hard concrete floor of his cell, deeply absorbed in writing a letter to his family but never turning his back to the doorway, always keeping one cautious eye on the inmate traffic a few feet away. His cell was drab and spartan, containing little more than state-issued clothing, bedding, and some old newspapers. I once asked Omar why he chose to have so few possessions.

"I don't like people taking things away from me," he replied. "If I don't have anything in here that's mine, then the authorities can't take away any more than they already have. Besides, I don't think it's healthy for a man to get too comfortable in the slammer."

On one occasion I had just returned from a prison basketball game that had ended in a vicious melee between a black and a white gang. Often one prison gang would field a team to play against a team backed by another gang, and the rivalry on the court usually led to violence. Watching who won the game was only half as exciting as watching who won the fight *after* the game.

But today I was particularly disturbed by the rampant hatred and racism between black and white inmates, so I posed a naive question to Omar: "Why do they hate and hurt each other so much? Why don't they just get together and channel their hatred toward the guards?"

Omar's ubiquitous grin vanished. After a long stare that was pregnant with pause, he finally said: "It's all a game."

"What, that's it?" I protested. "All the beatings, stabbings, and killings are just a game? It's no game. Men dying is no game."

Omar regarded me with some amazement. I must have been a bit more excited than I had intended. With a gentle but serious tone he cautioned, "Are you going to argue with me or are you going to listen?"

I sat quietly, waiting for him to share his view of the restless shadow world we lived in. Just outside his cell, silent, unfriendly faces glided past, glancing inside, never smiling. It was this kind of backdrop that kept a man alert in his cell at all times. Occasionally a prison guard would look in on us and then move on. Though I was not allowed to enter another man's cell, the rule was never enforced.

"Most of the hate and anger in here is all a game," Omar emphasized again. "It's a hustle, just another way for people to make money. Anger and hatred are a prison's cash crop.

"When whites hate blacks, they're stealing the sympathy and favor of a mostly white Christian administration. When blacks hate whites, they're strong-arming appeasements and concessions. The administration, they get the most out of it all. Violence and hatred in prison means more money, more guards, more overtime, and more prisons. What incentive is there to keep prisons safe and humane? All staff has to do is sit back and let the men here tear each other apart. Then they can cry to the legislatures and tell them how much more money they need to control their prison. Just like with the prison swag men, dope boys, and laundry men, there's something being sold and money being made. Only it's a lot more money than most of the guys in here can ever imagine. It's a lot easier for everyone to profit from hatred than it is to help the poor and ignorant do something positive with their lives."

I couldn't believe what I was hearing. "Come on, Omar, you can't believe that stuff. You're sounding real paranoid, like there's a conspiracy everywhere." His views were similar to those of Double D, who believed the administration was actually encouraging gang activity. But I wasn't ready to believe either one of them. The prison system was too chaotic to be that deliberate.

Omar replied, "Well, then you tell me why, with all the guards, guns, locks, gates, walls, and money, they still can't stop what's going on in here?"

I had no answer to that. "Okay, if this is all a game and everybody knows it, then why do the men in here play it? Why do they play when it can get them hurt and even killed?"

Omar smiled assuredly. "It's like a Dodge City crap game in here, Victor. Everyone who plays it knows it's crooked, but they play it anyway—because it's the only game in town."

8

Saying Goodbye

I t was a hot summer day, a Saturday, a time for recreation. Most of the inmates were wearing sweat suits, sweat shirts, or ragtag gym clothes homemade from scraps of stolen cloth. Many of them chose to spend all their recreation time on the block, most of them serious gamblers or avoiding the sun or avoiding a fight.

The gamblers were the easiest to spot because they always played cards on the most private picnic tables in the deepest interior. To a man, they slumped low in their seats, ready at a moment's notice to reach for their weapons. These weapons were usually hidden somewhere below the table, waiting for someone to be caught cheating or prematurely grabbing another man's money. Most other block loungers just milled around, talking, smoking, or drinking coffee as if they were somewhere other than in a maximum security prison.

I had just returned to my cell to change into state whites for my infirmary job. To me, the only difference between hard labor and imposed idleness is the change in a man's appearance. In the end, both will break a man's spirit as surely as his sentence will make him older.

As I left my cell, I heard a distant commotion from the upper range. Hearing it too, the table gamblers slumped a little deeper in their seats, easing closer to their weapons, their eyes never leaving their cards.

Soon I could make out an inmate called Hammerhead Fred, running toward me down the narrow walkway of the tier above, with guards in hot pursuit. He was carrying a five-gallon plastic bag, the kind used to dispense milk from a cafeteria cooler with a rubber nipple on one end. But this one was filled with homemade jailhouse liquor called hootch.

As he ran the length of a football field, Hammerhead lifted the bag over his head and forced the booze to flow into his open mouth. Much of it poured onto his face and chest, glazing his protruding forehead and staining his dirty clothes. The heavy bootlegged load was slowing him down, and the pursuing guards were gaining on him.

The whole cellblock was in an uproar, every man cheering him on. "Go Hammerhead! Fuck those hacks! Drink that wine! Don't give it up! Hammerhead! Hammerhead! Hammerhead!"

Just as the lead guard caught up to Hammerhead, an inmate suddenly stepped out of his cell and "accidentally" collided with the guard. The two fell down, and the other guards toppled over them in Keystone Kops fashion.

This gave Hammerhead enough time to take an extra long swallow of hootch. Then he jumped off the second-story walkway and landed upright on a tabletop below. Amazingly, he managed to hold onto his five-gallon bag. His legs spread boldly across the table, Hammerhead guzzled more wine until he had had his fill. Then he hurled the container at the frenzied crowd around him, beat his chest, and gave a savage victory cry.

The crowd screamed, hollered, and beat their chests as they drank from the contraband container, passing it from man to man in a victory-sharing ritual. Finally, the guards got themselves together enough to force Hammerhead down from the table. The inmates booed and hissed as they escorted Hammerhead away, no doubt to a waiting cell in the Hole.

But Hammerhead couldn't have cared less because he was too drunk to feel any pain and more important because today was his last day in captivity. He had served all ten years of his sentence, and he owed no parole time or probation. He was out tomorrow, free and clear.

This was how Hammerhead wanted to be remembered and how he would always be remembered. This is also how I have always remembered Graterford and its Kingdom of Inmates, since the day I myself said goodbye and good riddance to its wretched concrete walls.

PART II
INTERVIEWS

EDITORS' NOTE

Victor Hassine presents a series of interviews with fellow inmates, each with a specific theme. These personal views serve to broaden our perspective on prison life. Readers should be aware that in some cases the interviews have been edited to protect the true identities of the interviewees but are otherwise verbatim.

9

Anatomy of a False Confession

EDITORS' NOTE

Claims of innocence are said to be common in prison and just as commonly dismissed as feeble attempts by convicts to con the unwary. Even prisoners themselves are skeptical about such claims. After all, they live in a world in which "playing the opposites" is a way of life (see chapter 3). Victor Hassine recounts the story of Frank Stoppage, an innocent man who was released before DNA testing began to reveal the substantial fault lines that run through our justice system. This story is important for several reasons.

First, erroneous eyewitness testimony (as in Stoppage's case) is the root of many false convictions. A witness who has seen a suspect some time earlier in life—in a mall, at the police station, in a photo line-up, wherever—will find his or her face to be "familiar." With a minimal suggestion by the police, intended or unintended, that witness may then "locate" the suspect at the scene of the crime. One of the most remarkable things about human memory is the difficulty that we have keeping memories in their place, given the marked tendency to misplace them in time, especially under pressure or stress.

Second, bogus confessions (also as in Stoppage's case) are more common than one would suppose. Some are the product of limited intelligence, while others reflect the vagaries of memory. As just noted, people often forget where they came to learn something (true of eyewitnesses and suspects alike). If persistently questioned in a leading way, suspects may come to "know" the details of the crime as if they were there. They may even come to believe that they were there. Such is the force of isolation and suggestion, during which authorities are relentlessly shaping the situation in which the suspect is or feels trapped (see Schacter's The Seven Sins of Memory*).*

At the time of this writing, over 150 people have been released from Death Row due to errors of the legal system. They are legally and, in many instances, factually innocent. These cases often came to light, however, only because others looked at them closely. The prospect of executing an innocent person seems to focus more the mind of the reformer. How many prisoners with sentences of five or ten years or life, even life without parole, would be set free if their cases were examined with care? Hassine's account reminds us that we simply do not know and may never take the time to find out.

As Americans hurry through their high-tech lives, they seldom allow themselves enough time to sit back and reflect upon the things they have done, should have done, or dreaded having done. Their rush to stay busy seems calculated to relieve them of the painful responsibility of personal reflection. Yet, despite their efforts to occupy every single waking moment with one crisis after another, every now and then an event occurs that forces them to stop dead in their tracks and consider what they have done and what kind of people they have become. In the answering of such questions, their lives become changed, forever altered in the way they live or at least view their lives.

About a decade ago, long before the current wave of publicity about people wrongly convicted of crimes, a friend and I were talking about the unfairness of the criminal justice system. Being fair people ourselves, we decided to find out whether our views were correct. We reasoned that the best, most convincing way to demonstrate the unfairness of the system was to find the proverbial innocent man in prison. After all, if the system was as unfair as we claimed, our jailhouse home of two-thousand-plus inmates should certainly hold at least one innocent man.

Thus began our search for an innocent convict or even someone who just might be innocent. In honesty, neither of us thought we would ever find such a person. We thought it would be impossible to determine anyone's actual innocence; after all, it is an old line that everyone in prison claims to be innocent.

One day, my friend excitedly announced that he had found someone who claimed to be innocent and who in fact might be truly innocent. His name was Frank Stoppage, a young man whom my friend and I sometimes played handball with in the prison yard. About two years earlier, in a bar one night, a man who introduced himself as "Keith" had picked up a woman named Wilma Smith. The woman's friend, Nadine, later identified Frank Stoppage as the man who had introduced himself as Keith. Wilma disappeared, and her body was found in a landfill about three weeks later. Subsequently, Frank was questioned by police about the murder. Within four hours, he had confessed and provided a considerable amount of information about the crime. The next day, police questioned him again to clear up some of the details. Frank again confessed, and this time the confession was tape-recorded and later transcribed. As part of a plea bargain, Frank was sentenced to ten to twenty years in prison for the murder.

Despite his tape-recorded confession, Frank insisted that he was innocent. He gave me the transcript of his confession, which I read with initial skepticism. The following are some excerpts:

Q: Frank, we are investigating the disappearance of one Wilma Smith. Do you know who we are talking about?
A: Yes.

Q: Did you know Wilma Smith?
A: Not until the 8th of January when I met her.

Q: Where did you meet her?
A: It was at Ranger's bar.

Q: What time did you get to Rangers?
A: I got to Rangers at 4 in the afternoon.

Q: What time did Wilma get to Rangers?
A: It was 8:30 going on 9:00 PM

Q: What time did you leave the bar?
A: Between midnight and 12:30.

Q: Did you leave alone?
A: Left with two girls, Wilma and Nadine.

Q: Where did you go with them?
A: Dropped Nadine off at home and drove around with Wilma.

Q: Where did you go after?
A: Went up into that landfill area.

Q: How far in did you go?
A: It was back in the area where they did some dumping at.

Q: What did you do once you and Wilma got back there?
A: Got out of the car, went, and laid down in the flat area and started having sex.

Q: When did you decide to have sex?
A: When we were driving around in the car.

Q: How did the conversation start?
A: I was talking to her about what she liked to do. That's when it led to talking about making out. She kind of popped the question to me and I asked her the same thing back.

Q: What did she ask you?
A: If I wanted to have sex.

Q: What did you say to that?
A: I told her it was all right.

Q: Was there ever any mention of money for sex?
A: Not, not until it was over with.

Q: What was the weather like that night?
A: A bunch of snow laying on the ground.

Q: Was there ice on the road?
A: In certain areas we were driving.

Q: Was it icy back in the landfill?
A: There was some snow and ice when you first went in. Then going back the road there was patches of ice laying around.

Q: Once you were inside the landfill, where did you have sex?
A: It was up on a hill part, a flat area.

Q: Were you outside the car?
A: Yes

Q: Did you do any necking inside the car?
A: No. We were walking up the hill, we were holding hands and petting and stuff. When we got to this one part of the hill, she put her coat out on this area.

Q: Did you have sex on the coat?
A: We were laying on top of the coat.

Q: Did you remove all your clothing?
A: She had her underwear off and her dress up. I had my pants unzipped and halfway down.

Q: What happened afterwards?
A: She got up and started running and I started chasing after her.

Q: Did you catch up to her?
A: After she had lost her one shoe.

Q: What did you do when you caught her?
A: I hit her with a stick.

Q: How much money did she have?
A: $65.00

Q: Did you give her the money?
A: Yes.

Q: What did she do with it?
A: She put it in her purse.

Q: What kind of purse was that?
A: Black one with a shoulder strap.

Q: You said that you hit her with a stick, where did you get that stick?
A: Picked up from a pile that was laying off to the right when I was running.

Q: How many times did you hit her?
A: Four times in the front and four times in the back of the head.

Q: Where did you hit her first?
A: In the front part.

Q: Was that in her head also?
A: Front part of her face.

Q: What did she do when you hit her?
A: After the fourth time I hit her in the front, I caught her above her right eyebrow, and she fell flat on her face.

Q: When did you hit her in the back of her head?
A: When she was falling forward.

Q: How many times did you hit her in the back of the head?
A: Four.

Q: After you hit her in the back of the head, what did she do?
A: She was laying unconscious.

Q: What did you do then?
A: That's when I started dragging her.

Q: Where did you drag her to?
A: To like a level ground down in the wooded area.

Q: What did you do once you got her there?
A: Covered her up with some leaves and branches.

Q: Did she bleed at all?
A: Front part of her face was.

Q: Did you do anything with her coat and underwear?
A: Nope.

Q: Did you want to talk with us here today?
A: Yes.

Q: Why?
A: To get more of it cleared up.

Despite his taped confession, Frank insisted he was innocent. He said that he was with his girlfriend on the night of Wilma's disappearance, that he never met Wilma or Nadine. When asked why he pleaded guilty, he replied that his lawyer, whom his parents and his girlfriend had hired and paid more than thirteen thousand dollars, told him that if he did not plead guilty, he would probably be found guilty and given a life sentence without parole. He was scared. At the time, it seemed like the right thing to do.

I did not believe him. Instead, I felt the confession seemed too detailed to be fabricated. My reasoning was simple: since the confession was taped, the police could not have inserted false statements. All the facts came from Frank's own mouth, and it was unlikely that the police could prep anybody well enough to remember all those details. Besides, anybody who knew Frank knew that he was a bit slow and could not possibly remember anything with such detail, unless he was speaking from experience.

It seemed pretty clear to me that Frank was guilty and suffering from a bad case of denial, probably aggravated by the medication he was taking (daily doses of Lithium, a mind-altering drug). My friend and I both agreed that Frank was lucky that he wasn't on Death Row.

Not long after we reached this conclusion, however, police raided the home of James F. Carnivore. Carnivore had picked up a woman in a bar and promised her money for sex. The woman accompanied him to a remote wooded area on railroad property. He then bound the woman with duct tape, raped her, beat her, and told her that he was going to kill her "like the others." A railroad security officer happened to be patrolling the area, and Carnivore was forced to run away before he had a chance to commit murder. When the police showed up at his house later that evening, he knew he was in deep trouble.

For six hours, he held the police at bay on the roof of his house, threatening to jump off. When he finally surrendered, he confessed to raping, beating, and killing four different women in the previous four years—including Wilma Smith. The police tested Carnivore and discovered that the semen found in Wilma Smith's body (which did not match with Frank Stoppage) did in fact match with Carnivore. In the meantime, Wilma's friend Nadine changed her previous testimony and now identified Carnivore as the man who had introduced himself as "Keith" in the bar that night.

As a consequence of Carnivore's arrest, the police (1) had a confession from Carnivore that he raped and killed Wilma Smith, (2) knew that Carnivore had killed several other women the same way that Wilma had been killed, (3) knew that Carnivore's semen was found in Wilma's body, and (4) knew Wilma's friend Nadine now identified Carnivore as the man who had picked up Wilma the night she was killed.

Nothing happened, however, for four and a half months. No one in our prison, including Frank, knew that anything was happening with his case. Then without warning, a newspaper ran a picture of Frank on its front page with large captions: WRONG MAN IS IN JAIL, D. A. SAYS. CARNIVORE ADMITS SLAYING.

When I saw the news headline, I leapt out of my cell and ran up the cellblock tiers toward Frank's cell, hollering his name. When Frank stuck his head out of his cell, I showed him his picture on the front page. He was as astounded as I was. I could not believe that I had found an actual innocent man who had been framed and wrongly imprisoned.

For the next several days, Frank and I talked about his childhood, the days before and after his arrest, and why he confessed to a crime he had not committed. All that time, I kept asking myself: Why was I talking to an innocent man still incarcerated in a prison meant to hold only the guilty? Oddly enough, a criminal justice system designed to instantly remove suspects from the community has no speedy process by which to release the innocent. This can only be accomplished through a long, slow judicial process controlled by the officials who, in most cases, made the error in the first place and may be reluctant to admit their mistake. Innocent people can remain in prison for months after their innocence has been established because public perception of the system's infallibility is more important than any single person's innocence.

Two weeks after the news headline—five months after the real offender was apprehended—Frank was transferred to another state prison. Days later, I read another newspaper report that a judge had released him and dismissed all charges against him. The attorney who had convinced Frank to plead guilty was quoted as saying he was seeking "retribution" for his client. I wondered if he meant that he would return the money he took from Frank's parents and girlfriend for convincing him to plead guilty.

Frank's IQ tested at 69, the article reported, and a court-appointed psychiatrist concluded that he pleaded guilty to the slaying because he wanted to please the detectives interrogating him. Nowhere in the article did the press, the judge, or even Frank's lawyer ask the obvious questions. Who gave Frank, a man with a low IQ, all the details to a crime he never committed? Once Carnivore had confessed, why did it take five months to release Frank? Why were the two detectives who questioned Frank not charged with fabricating a false confession? After all, every detail of the taped confession was a fabricated lie. Frank had never even met Wilma or Nadine.

Finally, why did Frank confess? He explained to me that when the detectives brought him in for questioning, they convinced him that they had reliable eyewitnesses who swore he had been with the victim on the fateful night. Frank never considered the possibility that they were deceiving him. To him, police officers always told the truth. The detectives told him that if he did not confess to the crime, he would receive the death penalty and die in the electric chair; but if he confessed, they would make sure that he only got ten to twenty years because they thought he was a nice guy.

Frank knew that he was innocent, but because of his limited ability to reason, he confessed to the crime so the detectives would not be mad at him and would let him out of the interrogation room. He also believed that once the detectives were pleased with him, he would be allowed to call his girlfriend who would tell them that he could not have committed the crime. Unfortunately, once he had confessed, his alibi witness became meaningless. Frank could not have known this, given his limited mental abilities. Instead, he childishly believed that the truth would always prevail over a lie.

I find Frank's case deeply disturbing. These cases happen too frequently to be ignored. Like the rest of the country, I am too often willing to accept as true anything that people in authority claim to be true. This case and others like it makes me wonder if our criminal justice system sometimes ignores actual guilt or innocence, or if the police have become experts in procuring false confessions. What hope is there when lawyers who are paid thousands of dollars to defend their clients are willing to let them plead guilty to crimes they did not commit, simply because it is easier to get a good deal from the D.A. than it is to prove their innocence?

The Frank Stoppage story tells us three things: (1) Never take rides from strangers; (2) never believe detailed confessions recorded by the police; and (3) never believe there are no innocent people in prison.

10

David
A Sexual Victim

EDITORS' NOTE

David's story is troubling. We see a young man transformed from a naïve innocent to a merciless predator. Viciously abused in prison, David comes to abuse other innocent prisoners—to vent his anger and find some semblance of love. Were David's victimizers angry men on a misguided search for affection or simply violent predators? Does it matter? The catalyst here is what Victor Hassine calls senseless violence, of which David is a sad product.

I first met David, my current next-door cell neighbor, in Graterford. He was starting a two-to-five-year sentence, and I was two years into my life sentence. David was nineteen then and "cute as a button"—a curse for any young man in prison.

At the time, I was working as a clerk in the Chapel, which was how I met David. It was there that he was assaulted and raped repeatedly by at least three prisoners. I was present to see the aftermath of young David's introduction into Graterford's criminal justice system, one of many lessons on the facts of life in prison.

It is now about ten years later. This is David's second time back in prison and my fourth transfer to a different institution. We both have landed in SCI-Rockview, which is a medium/minimum security prison in the mountainous central region of Pennsylvania. Rockview is considered to be one of the less restrictive "soft stops" in the Pennsylvania state prison system.

It was here not too long ago that another attractive young man like David was gang-raped by four of his weight-lifting buddies. The head "booty bandit" (jailhouse rapist) was named Pac Man, also a cute-looking youth when he first rolled into Graterford to do his time. Ironically, the same "beef rustlers" who raped David in the Chapel had also "long-dicked" Pac Man a year or two earlier. This is but one of many examples of prison's vicious cycle of victims-turned-attackers.

David was gang-raped not once, but twice. Now in his late twenties, he has served close to half his life in institutions and has made most of the important decisions of his life based on the experience interacting with inmates.

David's story, a grim portrait of today's incarcerated youth, presents a too-common slice of prison life that is sadder than that of many of the broken men who are my neighbors, and sadder still than the prison pallor that greets me in the mirror every morning. The following is excerpted from a 1991 interview.

"[In the county jail I had] sexual pressure, fighting over my manhood. I was playing chess for money and lost several times, and it became like a twenty- or thirty- dollar debt. I couldn't immediately cover it. I was given a choice, either borrow it or have sex with him. We got into a fight. [After that] he left me alone....

"There were a couple of guys who tried to take me under their wings, but I didn't really trust them. I had heard stories about this. The ones who wanted to take me under their wing I didn't even know until I went to jail. It was strictly a con; [these guys] were like predators....

"When I got to Graterford, I took protective custody lockup twenty-four hours a day. A guard came down one day who had a pass for me to go get legal mail. He unlocked my door and left. I got up out of bed in my underwear and was rushed by approximately six or more inmates. I was raped numerous times. They rushed me, then threw me to the floor and hit me a few times. Before I had a chance to react, a knife was placed at my neck. I was already on my side or stomach. I don't remember what was said. I somewhat knew what they wanted and it wasn't my commissary. All they did was fuck me with no emotion. I was hoping while this was happening that they would ask me to have oral sex and I would then bite them. Had it been under other circumstances, I would have fought back. At that time I was in good shape. I would guess logically that it was a 'set up.' They left as soon as it was over. I was angry, bleeding, and in quite a bit of pain. Because I was in protective custody and it happened there, telling or reporting it was pointless and also very dangerous....

"I lost all hope for about six months. I was totally stripped of emotion. I just didn't give a fuck anymore. When I was much younger, I was a vengeful person. But I didn't want to get even because where there is an action, there is always a reaction....

"I don't think it was fair that I was raped, because I did nothing to deserve the vicious assault that has haunted my mind for almost ten years. They had no right to victimize me, and now I have become a product of that assault. It has caused me to become attracted to other young men sexually, so as to continue the nightmare by further subjecting myself to punishment for my past crimes, and to also inflict my nightmare on others so they too can carry the terrible burden I've carried....

"The administration could have done more to protect me, or others that are in protective custody, by totally segregating them, which ultimately wouldn't be fair, because you would be deprived of all activities enjoyed by the regular inmates. But, on the other hand, isn't this the same reason most of us are here, for depriving those of society of their normal routines and enjoyments of life? Basically these types of occurrences can be avoided by tighter security for these young individuals, because most of the booty bandits are already known by the administration. Again, these occurrences are so commonplace that the administration often looks the other way, unless the person who is victimized is willing to put his life on the line and prosecute the perpetrators. The reason I say the perpetrators, instead of the guilty ones or rapers, is because most of these individuals are the victims of violence themselves....

"After the first time I was raped while in protective custody, I convinced the officials to let me out in population without telling them that I was assaulted. They let me out into population and I ran into a friend who I met on the street. I hung around with him for a while, figuring he could teach me the ropes of survival in the 'Big House'. He introduced me to a fellow who was too nice, who one day invited me to the Chapel to get high. I met him, and he had a few friends with him. We smoked a couple of joints, and the next thing I knew I was getting physically beaten and again was viciously raped by at least three guys....

"After I was raped, the only medical attention that I received was a physical examination of my rectum to confirm that I had been assaulted. I was placed back in protective custody by myself without anyone, to talk to, alone and deserted like a dirty rag. I received no therapy from either a psychologist or a psychiatrist. I was left to deal with it on my own. I didn't cry out then because no one seemed to care, and so I stripped myself of all and any emotions. If there were people who cared, they really didn't come forward, which is natural, because it is a very difficult thing to respond to. I can sympathize with women victims. It is a devastating experience to not only cope with, but even more to live with....

"Once I was released from prison, I was very demanding of people because I felt they owed me something. And more than often, if my wishes were not complied with, I took what I desired from them. Don't get me wrong, I never raped anyone, but I did lash out on all the supposed predators and even those, both family and friends, who I felt deserved to be tormented. I didn't discriminate. I did it to anyone I felt had it coming to them. Anyway, that was how sick I was then, or rather that was how obsessed I was, until recently. Now, mostly I feel guilty about what I've done in an act of retaliation. But I also realize I was really crying for help in the only way I could, by acting out.

"I am a very confused person now, sexually that is, because I am insecure about what is natural combined with what I've been through and seen with my own eyes through the many years that I've been in institutions, thirteen years altogether. I am attracted to younger guys because of their innocent look and naive personalities, more so because it's that very innocence that I was robbed of. Sometimes I feel really guilty after I have sex with a guy, because I know or feel that I have violated their minds subconsciously, and eventually they'll have to face the music about who they are or cop out and remain a victim. But I am realizing that all that is happening is that I am doing it because that's the only way I can get any kind of love, affection, and attention that I so desperately need.

"[As for the system], I still don't trust them because they are the true predators and rapers of the people."

David is getting out soon. I wonder whether he will find that desperately needed love, affection, and attention in the outside world. And if he doesn't, I wonder what he will do.

11

Chaser
A Medication Addict

EDITORS' NOTE

Prescription medications are ubiquitous in most prisons. Psychotropic drugs, essentially heavy-duty tranquilizers, are common in virtually all penal institutions. These medications are prescribed to inmates under the supervision of a physician, but they are often distributed to inmates by corrections officers and fellow prisoners. Because prescriptions are readily available, these drugs can be readily bartered for other goods. Any prisoner with a prescription can hoard pills then sell or trade them with others.

Victor Hassine's observations indicate that theses drugs are used almost exclusively to achieve social control—to render prisoners numb, submissive to authority, and virtual automatons. Any therapeutic benefits are, in Hassine's opinion, secondary. Whether one agrees or not, medications have become part of the fabric of prison life, contributing directly or indirectly to maintaining order. Given the increasing use of penal institutions for housing the mentally ill, it is unlikely that we will see a drop in prescription medications. With these vulnerable and unstable offenders, medication may be a better means to maintain control than a reliance on punishment.

I met Chaser in 1984, my fourth year at Graterford, when he first arrived to serve time on a robbery conviction. I can still remember the frightened look on his face that first day. As I was adapting to the rapidly changing rules and conditions of a prison in total meltdown, Chaser became the beneficiary of my hard-learned lessons on inmate survival. We managed to forge a mutual friendship.

Many outsiders who have met Chaser would comment, "He doesn't look like he belongs in here." I've heard this often when people encounter an inmate who doesn't have some grotesque feature that neatly fits their preconceived notion of the "criminal look." Experience has taught me that the less an inmate appears like a criminal, the more likely he is to be particularly vicious and unrepentant. Criminals who look like criminals keep people on guard; the honest-looking ones put them at ease, which allows them the greater advantage of misjudgment. But in Chaser's case they were right. He didn't belong in prison, let alone deserve to become a victim of the system.

I did my best to look after my friend until, about nine months later, he was transferred to the Rockview facility. This was a relief for me, since protecting a naive and scared young man from the predators at Graterford was no easy task.

Once he was transferred, I quickly forgot about Chaser. Frankly, it is nearly impossible for me to remember all the people that have come in and out of my life, especially nowadays with the influx of so many frightened young kids. Almost all my relationships with fellow inmates today are superficial, as prison life becomes more and more a case of every man for himself.

What Chaser and I didn't know at the time was that prison administrators were feverishly trying to figure out how to stop the imminent collapse of Graterford and other overcrowded prisons. With thousands of new, young Chasers coming in, it was becoming more impossible to feed, house, and clothe them all, let alone rehabilitate them. More important to officials, an increasing number of guards and staff were becoming victims of inmate attacks. As employee safety was their first priority, the administrators realized that something had to be done to shore up the cracks in Graterford's foundation—and it had to be quick, cheap, and effective. But Chaser and I never concerned ourselves with the administration's problems. After all, we had swag men to deal with and predators to avoid.

In 1990, as I made my way to chow at Rockview, I ran into Chaser again. He was walking out of the dining hall's special section reserved for the "nuts," whom the administration refer to euphemistically as "special-needs inmates." Chaser walked sluggishly with a disheveled, glassy-eyed appearance. In short, he *looked* like one of the nuts.

"Chaser, is that you?" I asked.

"Hey, Vic," he replied, "I've got to talk to you. It's real important. Meet me in the yard."

That evening in the yard, my old friend explained to me how he had returned to the streets two years earlier, only to lose his wife and son, develop a voracious drug habit, and end up committing burglaries to support his habit.

I was unmoved by Chaser's story, since almost every returning con I've ever met recounts a similar tale of woe. All I wanted to know was why he was on the nut block and why he was taking "brake fluid" [prescribed psychotropic medication]. It was obvious because of his very slow, disjointed movement, and his shakes. Another alarming clue was the noticeable scars on his wrists from razor cuts.

Chaser described how his return to prison had exposed him to the "medicate-and-forget-them" system of modern prison management. This new system of mind-altering and mood-altering psychotropic drugs was rapidly becoming the prison administration's "quick, cheap (psychotropic drugs are expensive, so instead of cheap, I would say effortless), and effective" solution to warehousing masses of inmates into smaller spaces, while using fewer and fewer support services.

The reasoning seemed to be that every dose of medication taken by an inmate equaled one less fraction of a guard needed to watch that inmate, and one less inmate who may pose a threat to anyone other than himself. Hence, overcrowding had brought about a merging of the psychiatric and corrections communities. The resulting effect on inmates can be best described by Chaser during this 1994 interview.

"The first time [I came to prison] I was terrified because I didn't know what to expect and I knew no one. I was awkward and didn't know my way around. I had not acquired a prison or inmate mentality. The second time I was much more at ease because I knew a lot of people still in prison and I knew what to expect. I had also learned quite fast how to become as comfortable as possible. I had to take a lot of psychotropic drugs to achieve this comfortable state of mind. . . .

"In November of 1989, after telling the shrink in the county prison that I wished I was dead, I was unknowingly given Sinequan which knocked me out for three days. But since I was in a special quiet section of the jail, I continued the medication, because to me it was better than being in population. . . .

"I think the biggest difference between street drugs and psychotropic drugs is that street drugs give me some kind of feeling of well-being, high, confidence, euphoria, and contentment. But psychotropic drugs cause all feeling to cease. It stops self-awareness and sucks the soul out of a man. It slows or stops a man from striving to better himself and he stops caring about everything. It also creates total laziness. That laziness becomes his entire attitude and also is 100 percent habit-forming. . . .

"After almost three months at the county prison in Philly, I was sent to Graterford to start my four-to-ten-year sentence. I had abruptly stopped taking the Sinequan and felt totally disoriented. I lasted three weeks in population. Looking for drugs, I ended up taking another inmate's Thorazine at times. I was out of control and all I could think of or look forward to was getting stoned.

"One day I got very drunk and went into a blackout and refused to lock up. Four guards carried me to a room and I was put into restraints. I was given nine months in the Hole. I did five at Graterford and was sent to Rockview to complete it....

"[Getting medication in Rockview] was quite easy. I said I wished I was dead, which was the same thing I said in the county. Every week the shrink would ask, 'How do you feel now?' All I had to do was say, 'Bad,' and ask for more or different meds. I always got what I asked for, as long as I told them I thought of killing myself.... I took Sinequan, Mellaril, Elavil, Klonopin, first separately, while always asking for Valium. Then in desperation, I mixed the medications and the dosages. The ultimate effect was total numbness. My body was numb. My feelings were numb, and then my mind was numb. I did not care what happened to me and just stopped thinking about anything....

"While taking the meds, I was put on a special block and given a single cell. I got only a reprimand at misconduct hearings and did not have to go to work. I felt I was being placated and given special attention and I liked that. But when I stopped taking the meds, I was shook down [cell-searched] a lot and went to the Hole if I was ever given a misconduct. Once in the Hole, I would say I wish I was dead, and again they'd give me medication....

"I admitted to staff many times that I had a severe drug addiction and that I had an abusive personality. I tried numerous times to get in the drug-therapy groups and on the D- and A-[Drug and Alcohol] Blocks. I was refused and ignored every time....

"I lost all sense of dignity and self-worth. I had no pride. I lost all interest in the outside world and eventually did not care if I ever returned to it. All I knew or cared about was what times I went to get my fix.... [I] hurried to be first in line. I constantly had the shakes and inner tremors. My speech was slurred and slowed, and so was my thinking. I could not think ahead. I was like a small child only looking for instant gratification. My entire metabolism changed, and I gained a lot of weight fast. It damaged my memory, even to this day....

"Since I was under constant supervision and being evaluated once or twice a month, prerelease and parole became much harder to obtain. So for the luxury of being comfortable and in a fantasy world, I had to abandon the idea of early release or furloughs. Since my number-one priority was no longer a goal, it became easy for me to forget or stop striving for what was once important to me. The side effects of the medication, such as tremors and shakes, made it impossible for me to get and keep a job. Education, reading, learning, and working to strengthen my mind became things of the past. Giving up became repetitious and habit-forming (not unlike street drugs) and eventually I lost and gave up my self-respect, dignity, and morals until my only interest in life was getting in line three times a day to receive my medication.

"I had given up on all these things, and I woke up one day and realized I was a very sad man. But I was willing to give up on life, because the medications I was taking made me think I was comfortable.... I had given up on Chaser....

"I was seeing a shrink two times a week because I was depressed. I was not diagnosed as having any kind of mental illness or chemical imbalance, but despite that I was taking large dosages of Thorazine, Sinequan, Lithium, Elavil, and Melloril. I took them at 7 AM, 11 AM, 4 PM, 8 PM....

"One night just before lockup, I got another misconduct. I didn't care if I went to the Hole or got cell restriction. What concerned me was that the administration might possibly take away my medication. So after weighing my options, it seemed only logical to kill myself, or at the least, give that appearance. I opened my window, pressed my wrists against the frozen bars, then took an old razor and opened my wrists. I figured that, if I died, that would be fine. But, if I lived, I would definitely get more medication, and that thought satisfied me. I lived this madness and insanity for well over a year, until I ran into you. You offered me your time and energy to explain to me what I was doing to myself and what I was becoming. Within six months, I was totally off the special-needs block and off 99 percent of the medication and my will to live and succeed returned . . . with a vengeance. I never needed the medications for my depressed condition. I just needed someone to say they cared. I needed a friend. I got both from you. I owe you my life, not the prison, and not the medication....

"I have been medication-free for two years now and, although I'm usually uncomfortable with prison conditions, I can look in the mirror and see Chaser looking back with a smile. So to me, giving up the medication was a small price to pay to be myself again.

"[Psychotropic medication] is one of the easiest things to get in prison. It is easier to go to the shrink and ask for 500 mg of Thorazine than it is to get on the phone or get a pass to the Chapel. If a guy goes to the doc saying he feels depressed, violent, or suicidal, the doc will give him one of numerous medications. He is usually given a choice. All the medications are geared to slow a man down or fog his thinking so bad he can't think of why he's depressed, violent, or suicidal. This will continue for years, as long as he says he needs the medications to a staff person once a month....

"I'd say 40 percent of the population here is taking some form of psychotropic medication. They are treated less harshly than those unmedicated. They are seen and talked to by staff much more often than those not on medications. They are given special consideration at misconduct hearings. They are permitted to come in from night yard earlier than the other inmates and, in a lot of cases, are given a single cell. When it comes to working, someone on psychotropic medication can usually pick whatever job he says he can handle. On the other hand, most of us were not required to work at all. . . .

"I believe that, when a guard or any staff member puts on a uniform, they know it stands for authority. So they demand respect and control. When someone rebels or stands up to them, they feel their authority and control is threatened and they take steps to eliminate the rebellion. They put on the appearance of power, so they act cold, mean, negative, and harsh to display this power.

"Now when a guy is on medication, the threat is almost nonexistent. They [the staff] feel safe and secure with the men that are medicated. So the use of force and display of power is not necessary, and they act more leniently to the medicated inmate. They treat these men like children. To staff, a medicated inmate is a controlled inmate. . . .

"[If all inmates were required to take psychotropic drugs], I would be shocked and scared. It would be like they were turning the prison into a brainwashing institution. I would think they had lost all control and were attempting to gain it back by stopping our wills and brains from functioning properly. I believe they are headed in that direction because of how easy the medications are to get and how many people are taking them. . . .

"I think that, as the prison populations continue to grow and grow, and a younger and more violent crowd comes in, it will become harder and harder for the administration to control all the blocks. I think they are now learning that the best way to control inmates or pacify them is to totally medicate them. It may even become a reward system."

Psychotropic drugs are nothing new to the psychiatric community, which has been using them on the mentally ill for years. However, its use in corrections as a population-management tool and behavior modifier is relatively new. The effects of prolonged use of such medication on an ever growing number of inmates are unknown.

Just from the increasing size of medication lines and the growing number of inmates doing the brake-fluid shuffle, I have observed that psychotropic medications (also known as "chemical shackles") are defining the behavior of an increasing percentage of inmates in the general population.

As politicians and bureaucrats continue to debate the loftier issues facing the criminal justice system, the mother of invention has required front-line prison administrators to quickly implement any practice that might help them to keep their prisons intact and functioning. The practice of medicating inmates is becoming popular because it has proven to be a relatively inexpensive and efficient prison-control tool. The two governing estates of custody and treatment are being pushed aside by the rising third estate of psychiatric medication.

A bureaucratic system that subdues whole populations with drugs must certainly give us pause. The wisdom of turning means into ultimate ends in this way needs to be questioned. Today in prison, I find myself longing for any glimpse of an attempt to rehabilitate, not because I believe that treatment works, but because I worry about a society that no longer cares enough to try to help.

In my opinion, today's prison managers are only interested in their ability to confine an ever-increasing number of people for an ever-longer period of time. Because there is only so much that can be done in terms of cell and prison design, the search for solutions has focused not on changing the nature of prisons but on changing the nature of prisoners.

As of this interview, Chaser has been off medication for about two years. He has successfully gone through drug-rehabilitation therapy and is soon due for release. Once released, he will join a growing number of mind-altered men who are leaving prison and entering the mainstream of society. Only time will tell whether chemically treated inmates do in fact make law-abiding citizens. But, if you ask me, we should go back to trying to build a better mouse trap and, for God's sake, leave the mice alone.

12

Toney
An AIDS Tragedy

EDITORS' NOTE

A pattern of benign discrimination against homosexuals can be found in many prisons. Openly homosexual inmates, for example, may be denied access to programs and employment opportunities "for their own protection." This pattern has expanded steadily since the onset of the AIDS epidemic. Yet, these prisoners are not protected from the real dangers that surround them, given their sexual preferences and the easy availability of sex in prison today. Condoms are largely unavailable, and education about risk is limited or absent altogether. When a gay prisoner becomes infected, he is told to say "no" to sex. Too often, little or nothing is done to help him deal with the trauma of this death sentence or to change his lifestyle in the prison community.

Toney's interview vividly illustrates these points. Readers may note Toney's despair and perhaps be shocked by his candor. More shocking, however, is the power of loneliness in prison to drive some inmates to engage in life-threatening sexual behavior for the sake of fleeting pleasures and impermanent relationships.

Toney is a young homosexual inmate dying of AIDS in a Pennsylvania prison. In his own words, he takes us through the gauntlet of prison life that has beaten down his spirit with all its ordeals of love and hate, crime and punishment, and compassion and indifference.

Unlike the multitude of other incurable diseases afflicting mankind, AIDS not only threatens our emotional and physical well-being but tears at the very fabric of our society. It is for this reason that AIDS can devastate the uninfected living as mercilessly as it already has its living dead. Equally ominous is how AIDS has served as a catalyst to the social changes brought about by the ills of promiscuity, drug addiction, crime, violence, and incarceration.

In this 1992 interview, Toney relates how the lack of education about AIDS affects homosexual activity in prison, and how AIDS is used among the inmate population as a tool for self-destructive love or as a weapon of hatred that can be deadlier than a concealed knife.

"My being gay in prison [has put] a lot of pressure on me from men constantly wanting to have sex with me because of the way I look, which is on the attractive side. They constantly beg me for either a blow job or anal sex and are most of the time willing to pay for it. A gay person can be treated like royalty in prison. Homosexuals have the choice of making it easy or tough....

"It is very easy to have sex in prison, at least for me it was and is. The only difference that varies from prison to prison is where you may have to do it and how careful you have to be about being caught; for example, at Graterford you could lay up all day with another man and have sex without being bothered by the COs [correction officers]. Whereas, [at Rockview] you're lucky to get a good nonstop fifteen minutes of sex. Yet it still happens. Some days in prison I have twenty men a day. "I can surmise when I may have contracted [AIDS], but I cannot say for sure. I've been an active IV drug user for twenty-one years, a homosexual all my life, and had a blood transfusion in 1985 before there was the start of screening blood. So you see, I cannot pinpoint it and I've had thousands of sexual partners and most of them were for one-time shots or one night only, and I used to prostitute. I do know when I first got sick in the fall of 1986. I had a tremendous loss of weight and night sweats. I had all the symptoms and that was while I was in the Philadelphia Detention Center....

"I had the test taken in 1987. I was a little stunned, but I was expecting my blood test to come back positive. Why? Because of the impact of the symptoms I had in 1986 at the Detention Center.... The reason I say I was only stunned was that, at the time I was told, I didn't realize the seriousness of what I had.... A normal person's T-cell count is 2,000 or more. Mine is down to 88, and I am considered to have full-blown AIDS....

"The prison administration didn't give me any support when I was first told. No physical or psychological help. I was only told to stop having sex and that, if I was caught having sex, they would put me in the Hole. They did nothing to help me in any way for the remainder of the 18 months I had left to do. I didn't get any help until I went home and went to a specialist who prescribed AZT and Bactium to try and prolong my life. That's when I realized the seriousness of my illness and that it was a matter of life or death....

"I sincerely believe [the prison administration] should have more accurately informed me—by the proper medical staff—of what I had and what could happen or couldn't happen. There should have been more facts given to me than the words 'don't have sex.' With this type of illness, a person, or I should say myself, should have been more educated on what was necessary to try to maintain life for as long as I could and the prevention of getting sicker. And as a result of just being told not to have sex—without strict reasons—I continued to have sex and more than likely infected others who infected others. At the time I was not aware that AIDS could so easily be passed from one person to another. I believed that you could not get it from oral sex or that sex with the same partner only a few times was safe. I was wrong because of the lack of education, or should I say no education, from the prison administration. If they can tell you you're slowly dying, they should also give you the facts as to what can harm others as well as harm yourself.... I remained sexually active [for two years] until I was educated by doctors on the street and read and educated myself about AIDS....

"I now realize the dangers that are involved in having unprotected sex. So, therefore, I have made it a practice to be honest and direct with anyone who asks me about my condition, whether it be a sexual partner or someone asking out of curiosity. I explain as well as inform others of the risk involved in dealing with someone like me, with the illness that I have. Even as I warn them, my partners usually don't care whether they get it or not. All they're concerned about is loving me or making love to me. I have allowed myself to be in relationships where no protection was used, and it is not because I did not tell them. It is because they wanted to be a part of me and make lifelong commitments to me. Or they wanted a lifelong commitment from me. So once they started having unprotected sex with me, it was my spouse's way of saying, 'You belong to me forever.'

"This happened with my last spouse whom I love very much, and we didn't use anything. So he now has [AIDS] and he knew all the risks. Yet he wanted it that way, so I allowed it to happen. He has a life sentence and he wanted to die and lay side by side with me in a coffin when I die. He did it out of love, and I thought I let it happen out of love. I realize that what we did was the insanity of being human beings. We were both wrong, or more so me, for allowing it to happen. But there's a saying, 'love can sometimes be blinding,' and in this case it was true. Because I loved him, and yet I hurt him. I learned not to let my emotions overcome my reality....

"I know some associates of mine who are out to get revenge on people and are passing [AIDS] on. A homosexual I know says he is going to kill as many people as possible. I'll never understand it, but that is the way human nature is and the way some of us accept or cannot accept life's situations. It happened and there is very little chance of a person knowing whom to hurt anyway. So they want everyone to hurt as they hurt. I myself may have gotten AIDS because of someone not caring and out to kill everyone else. I'll never know....

"I am doing this [interview] of my own free will, because I care for human life. Also so I may make people more aware [that] ... a person [who] is HIV positive can feel, cope, and deal with it. Also to enlighten the minds of others with or without AIDS. And to let people know that prison is not a way of life and AIDS is not either and is no joke....

"[If I were standing in front of the governor of Pennsylvania], I would first tell him that it should be mandatory to ask inmates if they want to be tested for the HIV virus. Not mandatory testing, but mandatory to ask inmates if they want to be tested for the HIV virus. That way it can stop the spreading of a lot of illness and death in prison, because a lot of inmates have it and don't know it because they're not tested. Even though the administration doesn't condone homosexual acts, it is a fact of life that goes on, and I believe I would tell him to supply condoms to inmates. Just by issuing condoms doesn't say that everyone should go out and have sex, because there are a lot of people that don't mess around. But it would save lives in prison and in the streets. Sex is being practiced at an alarming rate throughout the prison system. And if it is going to happen anyway, why not make it safe?

"And I would also tell him inmates are transmitting the disease rapidly among themselves and then allowed back into society to spread it even more. Think of the men who have it and make HIV babies. The reason that is happening is because inmates don't know they have it because they were not tested. And also there should be medical specialists that deal in infectious diseases and not just a medical doctor who gets all his information from pamphlets and books and seminars. A doctor treating HIV patients should work and have firsthand knowledge of dealing with the disease. That's what I would tell the governor."

This interview frightened me, not because it threatened my moral beliefs or my conservative way of life, but because it threatened my very *life*. AIDS has bound us all to Toney, because the virus that is eating away at his immune system is also eating away at our ability to trust each other. We are becoming as unforgiving as the deadly disease itself.

We no longer welcome the stranger, pardon infidelities, or excuse even our own indiscretions. Our nightmare of the hopelessly desperate AIDS carrier has forced us to live in a purgatory of doubt and distrust, limiting our lives to the certainty of condoms, blood tests, and our own fidelities.

Toney died of AIDS in 1994.

13

Albert Brown
A Permanent Resident

EDITORS' NOTE

The author's interview with Albert Brown skillfully contrasts the old with the new. In the old days, prisoners lined up in an orderly rank and file for every daily routine. A silent system was routinely enforced with sanctions that verged on corporal punishment. All races were segregated.

By contrast, some of today's prisons, particularly those that are poorly managed, are places of remarkable freedom and privilege but also lax security that breeds disorder and even anarchy. The safe if sterile Big House has given way to a prison urban ghetto, a world where noise reigns and silence is a rare, prized commodity. Old prison or new, Victor Hassine makes it clear that those who chose a life of prison, like Brown, are so institutionalized that they have become mere husks of human beings.

Today's prison, which is supposed to be the bastion of the status quo and the hallmark of uniformity, is changing faster than one can possibly imagine. There are more inmates and more prisons than ever before. There are women guards, doctors, lawyers, gym coaches, and teachers working in prisons today. There are even children in prisons. What would an Old Head who has spent a lifetime of incarceration think of these rapid changes?

Every day when I rushed out of my cell on some busy agenda, I always passed an elderly black neighbor quietly and contentedly sweeping the range floor. The only reason I even noticed him was the steady routine of his life was in stark contrast to the fast-paced upheaval around him. He seemed so impervious to it all.

Then one day I observed him explaining to a much younger man how he would be willing to relieve him of his burden of doing time. I sensed there was more to this very Old Head than met the eye, so I decided to interview him.

Albert Brown is a seventy-four-year-old lifer who looks more like he's in his late fifties. He stands a tall six foot one and has a deep, strong voice that hints at a hearing problem. One of the most impressive things about Mr. Brown is his air of honesty, something you don't hear very much of in prison.

Listening to his observations about prison life, past and present, I learned why Mr. Brown cares little about change and even less about the rest of the world. As I watched this man, it was hard to resist the feeling that I was looking at the face of my future. I shuddered at the possibility that he represented the natural consequences of a lifetime in prison.

When Mr. Brown first came to prison in 1945 at age twenty-five, separate but equal was the law of the land in the relations between blacks and whites. It was a very different world when he started serving his life sentence in the now abandoned Eastern Penitentiary in Philadelphia, which was built in 1829. In 1958, he was transferred to Western Penitentiary, which opened in 1826. (Eastern and Western Penitentiaries were among the first prisons built in the world.) In 1962, he was transferred back to Eastern, where he got into a fight with a white man. To avoid trouble, he asked for a transfer to Graterford Penitentiary and arrived there in 1964. Here is Mr. Brown's experience, in his own words.

PRISON THEN

"At nine o'clock a guy would blow a trumpet and all the lights would go off and it was time to sleep. At six o'clock they would blow that trumpet again and it was time to eat breakfast. You would have to hurry and line up to eat. You better not butt in line or go out of place like they do today. No sir, you couldn't do none of that back then....

"Whites and blacks were segregated. We were completely apart. There were about eleven blocks and they were almost even blacks and whites.... I never went to other blocks so I don't know what happened in the white blocks.... I have to say everybody was treated the same, [except that] white guys always got the best jobs.... Everybody ate the same thing. Even the guards would eat what we ate....

"No dayroom, no TV, no radio, or nothing. They gave you headphones that plugged into the wall. There was no newspapers and you were lucky if you got over an hour of yard when you got yard. There was no gym equipment. Nothing like that. The only magazine they would let you have was the *Christian Science Monitor*. People could write, but it was censored going and coming...."

"They had a library you could go to sometimes in the afternoon, but they only had some old books. Plus I couldn't read too well then. Blacks worked on the blocks as janitors or in the kitchen. All labor jobs....

"They had novelty shops then. Inmates made things and they were allowed to sell them. Some had a big business with people coming and picking up their things regular. Some people would work for others. But only whites were allowed to do this. Sometimes if you had the right connection you could work for a white guy and make some money....

"I could barely read or write. I went to school, and it was inmates who taught me how to read and write. Inmates did almost everything back then. There were inmate nurses, clerks, and teachers. There was even an ex-inmate pharmacist. He had been pardoned. Only whites had these jobs. We did have one black that did machine work. But the rest of us did labor. I worked in the laundry....

"In 1956, there was a riot in Western Penitentiary. The inmates took control of the prison for a few days. After they took the prison back, the governor hired a new commissioner to clean up things in the prisons. He made a lot of changes for the better. They hired two black guards for the first time. One of them quit and soon returned to prison as an inmate. He said he quit because he couldn't lock people up. He's still at Graterford today, I think.... In 1960–61, the commissioner ordered an end to segregation. The Warden at Graterford refused to integrate. They fired him and forced desegregation. There was a few fights after they desegregated but no big problems. People didn't like it but they lived with it.... Afterwards, it was inmates that kept the dining room segregated. I remember there were people written up for not wanting to sit with blacks or whites in the dining hall.... I can't really say whether desegregation made things better or worse. They are pretty fair now. If there is racism, it is the inmates, not the prison....

"I remember in the '60s I watched them [try to] put double cells in Graterford for the first time. The commissioner was there and he looked at it and said it was too small for two people and made them move them all out. He changed a lot of things for the better....

"I never knew how important *Gideon* [the landmark case of *Gideon v. Wainwright* that established an accused criminal's right to counsel] would be. Before then, people couldn't come near any law things. They'd get in real trouble if they even tried...."

THE HOLE

"I was in the Hole at old Eastern. I got two slices of bread at nine o'clock and two slices at three o'clock. No lights. A half a blanket on a metal bed.... The Hole weren't no joke back then. No, sir, they didn't fuck around with you back then like they do now. If a guard writes you up, they'd lock you up right away in your cell and just tell you what you done wrong. Nothing complicated and official like you get now.

"After a few days in your cell, guards would come and get you out of your cell and take you to the deputy's [superintendent's] office. You know, back in them days the deputy ran the prison. He wasn't like a figurehead the way they are now. Anyway, if the deputy wasn't available, the major or captain took his place.

"The guards would take you to a waiting room off the deputy's office. Then they'd make you stand facing the wall with your nose on that wall. And you'd better not take that nose off that wall if you knew what was good for you. Those guards had them big sticks back then and they'd use 'em. Quick!

"They'd let you stand like that for a while and then they would take you into the deputy's office. He'd be sitting down at his big desk in front of you. You'd be standing in front of him with the guards around you. He'd ask you why you done whatever they say you did. You'd say your piece and then he'd tell you what he was going to do with you.

"At that time there was four places they could send you if they wanted to punish you. One place was the punishment block where they put all of the real bad troublemakers. Men that was always fighting or getting into some kind of trouble. They'd keep a man in the punishment block for a long time. They put him there years before they let him out. It was a whole separate block where everyone stayed locked in their cell. They never came out. No commissary or nothing. They might let them have a smoke every once in a while and they'd feed them three full meals a day, but they didn't get much more.

"Another place was the Gallery which was the top range of one of the blocks. It was just like the punishment block except they'd only keep a man up there for no more than a year. Usually a few months or so.

"Then there was what they called the Klondike. It was the back part of one of the blocks. I was there a few times when I was at Eastern. They put me in a small cell and gave me half a thin blanket and I had to sleep on a steel bed with no mattress. There were no lights inside, but it wasn't cold. I got two slices of bread twice a day. There was a cold-water spigot in the cell so I had all the water I needed. Every seventy-two hours I got one full meal. I was in there a few times, but the most time I did in there was fifteen days.

"Then there was what they called the Hole. I remember there was a guy they say cursed at the deputy. They put him in the Hole for four days. Then they took him to the deputy and they say he cursed at him again, so they put him back in the Hole for thirty days. When they took him to the deputy again, they say he acted up again. But they figured he was crazy and so they just let him alone after that. The Hole was a four-by-four-by-four-foot cell with a solid door they kept shut. You couldn't stand up or lay down all the way. You'd get bread and water in there with a full meal every three days. No sir, that Hole was no joke."

PRISON TODAY

"The food changed a lot. It got a lot better. When I first came to prison we ate everything out of one bowl. They didn't have no trays like they do now. We would go through the line with our bowl and utensils and they would put all the food into the bowl. Everything went into that bowl. It took me about eleven years before I got used to the food. But [in the 1960s] things got better, everything got better. You got chicken and beef. They didn't have none of that [before]....

"They treat you a lot better now. They have better medical care with real doctors and nurses. Inmates used to do all that. They have medication. I remember all they would give you was Epsom Salts for everything. They have college and schools now with teachers. They didn't have none of that.... It's a lot better now. It's more human....

"What makes me happy? Truthfully? If I could get a couple of Snickers Bars tonight and go to bed full and not hungry—I'm happy. Before they let you buy commissary in prison, I used to go to sleep hungry. Now with commissary and the eighteen cents an hour I make, I'm happy...."

Mr. Brown refuses to apply for parole, even though he has been eligible for many years. He has decided to remain a permanent resident of the Department of Corrections. Ironically, the cruelest thing the prison system could do to this man would be to release him into a society where he can no longer survive.

There are many more people like Mr. Brown in institutions throughout the country: spiritless, frightened souls who are quietly waiting to die in the only environment they feel comfortable in. These people represent a growing underclass of dependents in a world of change.

If this doesn't disturb you, maybe it should. Our system has become expert at making people forget about ever being free. If that doesn't bother you, then Mr. Brown wishes to thank you for being generous enough to pay the thirty thousand dollars a year it takes to keep him where he wants to be.

14

Jacko
Surviving the Hole

EDITORS' NOTE

In 1840, Alexander Maconochie, the superintendent of the Norfolk Island penal colony off the coast of Australia, invented a system of "grades" that is still in use in some American prisons. A typical system uses three grades. For any serious infraction, a prisoner is sentenced to the lowest grade: solitary confinement for thirty days, with the first days spent in what is colloquially known as "the Hole."

The solid door of the Hole closes out all light and sound. Meals consist of two slices of bread per day and water, with a full meal every third day. After six days of good behavior, the prisoner graduates to second-grade solitary, where the barred door provides light and sound. Three full meals are served daily, but no smoking or reading materials are allowed. After nine days of good behavior, the prisoner is then given first-grade solitary, where he has full access to smoking and reading materials. After fifteen days of good behavior, the prisoner may be released back into the general population.

Victor Hassine begins his interview of Jacko with a short description of the Pennsylvania system. What they refer to as "the Hole" is actually first-grade solitary confinement, the lower grades since abolished. Does this make the Pennsylvania system more humane than the graded systems? Hassine thinks not. He argues that these reforms were imposed from outside the prisons and deeply resented by prison officials. Resourceful prison staff members have devised ways to make even first-grade solitary confinement remarkably painful.

The following interview demonstrates this point and shows how the policy on the books may diverge widely from the policy one finds in the trenches of our prisons. As a general matter, reforms must be embraced by line officers if they are to have any chance of affecting daily life in the prison community.

While prison is punishment for those who have violated society's laws, the Hole is punishment for those who have violated a prison's rules. The Hole represents a penal institution's harshest form of legalized punishment short of the death penalty. On the one hand, a prison always feeds an inmate to keep him strong and healthy; on the other, it develops and imposes new and more creative forms of punishment that seem to defy all standards of human decency.

When Mr. Brown recalled the Hole between the years of 1945 and 1955, he was describing the beginning of a twisted path that found its way to me some thirty-five years later. While the nature of punishment in prison seems to have changed, its intensity certainly has not.

In the 1950s, the governor of Pennsylvania assigned the new commissioner of corrections the task of reforming the prison system. One of the things the new commissioner changed was the way inmates were punished. The four-by-four-by-four-foot punishment cell described by Mr. Brown could no longer be used. Furthermore, it was required that inmates in solitary confinement be given three full meals per day and allowed exercise periods out of their cell. Corporal punishment was prohibited.

These profound changes generated a lot of resentment from prison employees, who felt unruly inmates were not being adequately punished. In response, what solitary confinement lost in severity it gained in total confinement time. Inmates who broke the rules were now sent to the Hole for much longer periods of time—in many cases, years at a time.

Other changes required that lights be provided for the men confined in solitary. In response to that, guards left bright, glaring lights shining in these isolated cells for twenty-four hours a day. One Pennsylvania prison went so far as to build a special disciplinary cell out of translucent glass-block, known as the "glass cage," which allowed bright security lights to unyieldingly glare down on the fully exposed inmate.

Bright lights and more time were not the end to the backlash of postreform punishments. Whenever possible, the cells in solitary were kept either shivering cold in the winter or stifling hot in the summer. Those three full meals a day were often served cold and in the most cruel manner. Trays would be thrown in the cell so most of the food would spill on the floor; the food was sometimes mixed together in the tray, making it look more like garbage than a meal; fingers would sometimes be openly inserted into the food when it was being served; hair, dirt, bugs, even body fluids seemed to find their way clandestinely onto these sorry food trays. And, although corporal punishment was prohibited, "goon squads" were formed by the guards to administer unofficial physical punishment. These goon squads were often comprised of guards who were not assigned to the general population, so inmates could not recognize them. They never wore name tags and their activities were never reported, at least not by the staff.

Thus, despite all the reforms, deprivation and physical force remained the peacemaker at Graterford and other Pennsylvania prisons. While it was true that inmates in solitary were now fed three meals per day, given exercise time, and allowed lights in their cell, the degree of cruelty remained the same or was more severe than it had been in the past.

In fact, conditions in the punishment units of Pennsylvania's prisons became such an outrage that in 1973 the Bureau of Corrections was faced with a court-ordered Consent Decree resulting from a class-action suit, *Incarcerated Citizens Union (ICU) v. Shapp,* filed in Federal District Court to challenge conditions in the state's solitary-confinement cells. The Court had decided to try to institute and enforce the reforms that the first commissioner had attempted in the 1950s. The ICU Consent Decree once again significantly changed the way Pennsylvania punished its inmates.

In this interview with a fellow inmate, Jacko describes the Hole at Graterford from 1976 to 1978. He recalls a much different place than Mr. Brown's Klondike at old Eastern Penitentiary.

"I stayed in the Hole back then and, to tell you the truth, it wasn't really too bad. They would call you over to the day captain's office and give you a misconduct report. Then you would go about your business. Unless it was a real serious misconduct, like hitting a guard or something, they never locked a man up until after the misconduct hearing.

"A few days later you would get a pass to the old phone room which was off of the main corridor right across from the laundry. There was always a lot of people sitting on the benches in the waiting room of the Hearing Room who were waiting for their hearing. The room was small and stayed hot because there were no windows and a whole lot of people. You'd sit there for hours sometimes until a guard from the Hearing Room would come out and call your number.

"Once you finally got inside the Hearing Room, a guard would pat you down and tell you to sit down in a chair that was right in front of a big table. Sitting on the other side of the table was the major, a counselor, and a work supervisor. If the major wasn't there, it would be a captain or another white shirt [officer]. One of them would read the misconduct to you and ask you how you wanted to plead.

"At this time, you got a chance to say whatever you wanted to and then the guard would ask you to step outside. You always got found guilty, so basically all you were doing was waiting to see what punishment they were going to give you. You'd sit in the waiting room for a little while more until the guard would call you back in the Hearing Room. He would pat you down again and make you sit down in the same chair. Then the major or one of the other guys would tell you what you got.

"They didn't really have cell restriction, loss of privileges, or any of that stuff back then. If they didn't send you to the Hole, they put you on probation or put you on the Gallery. Probation was when they would warn you that, if you got another misconduct any time soon, you would go to the Hole. That was it.

"The Gallery was the back half [fifty cells] of the top range of B-Block on the A-Block side. If they sent you there, you went right from the hearing. But once you got to your cell in the Gallery, you could give the guard a list of things that he would bring to you from your cell. You could even have a TV and radio in the Gallery, and you also got commissary once a week.

"The section of B-Block where the Gallery was at had a steel mesh screen running along the outside of the top-tier walkway, which separated it from the rest of the block. But you could still see and holler down to your friends in general population on B-Block. It got pretty noisy at times, but the guards didn't really mess with you about that. For recreation, you went to a small yard area between A- and B-Block two hours a day and they brought food to you off the main line three times a day.

"If you went to the Hole, you went right to Siberia. That was a whole separate building out by the wall on the opposite side of the cellblocks. The official name was the Behavioral Adjustment Unit [BAU]. We'd call it Bad Actors University.

"When you went to Siberia, you didn't take anything with you. You got the same meals and yard time as in the Gallery, but that was about it. Plus the guards kept it real cold in there. And if you made a lot of noise, they'd tell you to be quiet. If you didn't stop, the goon squad rushed you and beat your ass. That kept things pretty quiet.

"But to tell you the truth, I didn't mind the Hole, because they would give me all the medication I asked for. I mean I got Valium and Darvons—all I wanted. I stayed high. And as long as you didn't mess with the guards, they pretty much left you alone. But it was cold."

In addition to the improved conditions in what was now called "Punitive Segregation," Jacko was afforded the right to appeal his misconduct to a program review committee and then to the superintendent. If the superintendent would not give him the relief he asked for, he could take his appeal up to the commissioner. When Mr. Brown went to the Hole decades before, however, all he could do was his time.

The ICU Consent Decree also brought about a limit to the amount of time a hearing committee could confine a man in Punitive Segregation: a maximum of 180 days in the BAU or Gallery for every misconduct report. In response to this, guards who had previously listed all of an inmate's infractions on one misconduct report now issued separate misconduct reports for every infraction. In this way, the hearing committee could continue its practice of sending troublemakers to the Hole for years at a time.

This rush to fill the Hole with long-term residents resulted in a long-term shortage of cells in the Gallery and BAU (now renamed the "Restrictive Housing Unit," or RHU). By the time I faced my first misconduct hearing in 1982 for the hamburger caper, the Gallery had been expanded to double its former capacity. Furthermore, part of the RHU was double-celled, so that solitary confinement at Graterford was not so solitary anymore.

Aggravating the problem was the violence at Graterford, which had caused a dramatic increase in the number of inmates seeking protective custody, or self-lockup. For a multitude of reasons, these men could not be protected in general population, so they chose to live in the safety of solitary confinement. By housing them on the Gallery, the prison administration imposed on them the same restrictions used for many of the men who were serving punitive-segregation time. Unfortunately, as the violence escalated, these restrictions were not enough to stem the tide of inmates seeking protective custody.

Consequently, the hearing committee was no longer free to punish misbehaving inmates by sending them to the RHU or the Gallery. There just weren't enough cells. So new sanctions were developed, one of which was the cell restriction I received for my burger infraction. Another was "double lock feed-in," which allowed an inmate to serve RHU time in his cell until such time as a cell in the RHU or the Gallery became available.

The nature and the effect of punishment at Graterford and other prisons are still in flux. In my view, guards' resistance to reform, combined with overcrowding, have to this day prevented a reasonable system of punishment from being realized or evaluated. In fact, crisis management, along with a heavy dose of resentment and spite, seem to be resulting in an increase in the level of punishments.

One final thought about the Hole and other harsh punishments is that people adapt. If you throw a prisoner into a dark cave, he'll learn how to see. If you feed him rats, he'll still eat. In fact, if you give him enough rats, he'll get fat. You can try feeding him cockroaches to punish him more, but he'll eventually get fat on those, too. As inmates sometimes boast, "What doesn't kill me only makes me stronger." Once you start down the road toward ruthless punishments, there's no turning back.

15

Coach
A Changeling

EDITORS' NOTE

A famous social-psychology experiment conducted at Stanford University in the early 1970s tried to simulate the conditions of imprisonment for two weeks by randomly dividing male college volunteers into two groups of prisoners and guards. The study was abandoned after only six days because the behavior of the subjects quickly deteriorated. Almost overnight, average young men changed into either depressed and withdrawn prisoners or tyrannical and brutal guards. The researchers concluded that a "pathology of imprisonment" led to these rapid personality changes.

Scholars still dispute whether corruption and brutality among guards is the product of prison conditions or outside influences that predate correctional work. The Stanford experiment suggests the former, though the study allowed stereotypical roles to flourish. For example, the young males assigned the role of "officers" dressed like redneck Southern police with all the trappings of power, while the "inmates" wore sack-like dresses and ankle shackles to display a look of passivity. However, few inmates in the real Graterford prison would ever be considered passive.

Victor Hassine's interview with Coach suggests that simply working in a violent, morally corrupt prison will have harmful effects for some officers. As a general rule, however, officers, like inmates, adapt in ways that reflect their personal history as well as the prison environment in which they find themselves.

It has been my experience that violence—inside *and* outside of prison—is learned behavior. Even the gentlest person in the world will discover that he has to become violent after spending five years in a prison like Graterford. He will learn violence not because of shame, not because of some personal slight, but because that's the way business is done in this part of town.

What goes for prisoners also goes for prison staff. Logic dictates that if overcrowded, violent, and understaffed prisons teach rage, violence, and criminality to prisoners, then these conditions inevitably will affect staff members, who spend a significant amount of their waking hours in the same environment.

Recently I read a newspaper report about three inmates who were savagely beaten by a group of corrections officers in a particularly overcrowded county prison in Pennsylvania. The three inmates had each struck a corrections officer in separate, unrelated incidents. These incidents resulted in retaliation by a mob of angry corrections officers, beating and kicking the three inmates with batons, fists, and boots *after* the inmates had been subdued, placed in handcuffs, and secured in isolation cells.

Eventually a nurse and a corrections officer were persuaded to come forward and give eyewitness accounts of the incident. The nurse described how one inmate had been beaten so badly that when prison guards brought him to her for medical treatment, his body resembled a "Frankenstein" monster. The nurse also recalled how she had heard the pleadings of the inmate during the beating. Despite having witnessed this horrifying incident, the nurse stated that she had not immediately reported the event because she feared the loss of her job and the retaliation of the same officers, whose job it was to protect her whenever she worked in the prison.

During the course of a subsequent federal investigation into the beatings, several corrections officers decided to plead guilty for their parts in the crime and also agreed to testify against other officers who participated in the beatings. In April 1997, four corrections officers were tried in a Federal District Court for the beatings of the three inmates.

"I became almost blind with rage when these incidents happened," testified one of the cooperating corrections officers. "I just got out of hand." When he was asked why he reacted the way he did, the prison guard answered, "I think I would need a psychiatrist to figure that out." And when he was asked if he later received mental health treatment, he responded, "The best treatment I got was getting out of there."

The remorseful prison guard went on to describe how during one of the beatings a lieutenant had scolded him for not using two hands to strike a helpless inmate with a baton. The Lieutenant, who "...seemed like he was showing off...," just began "...flailing away..." at the inmate with a series of two-handed baton blows.

When an attorney for one of the accused corrections officers defended his client by suggesting that beating inmates who struck prison guards was the only way to maintain order in prison, a cooperating officer firmly disagreed. "I thought at the time it was necessary. That's the thinking I had. My thinking now is [that] you have to have people in there who are suitable.... The inmates aren't perfect. But then, neither are the guards."

Another cooperating officer testified at the trial that he participated in the beatings because he was just "...trying to fit in with fellow officers." A third cooperating guard explained that he kept quiet about the incident because he didn't want to be labeled a "snitch."

The brutality of the corrections officers—their inmate-like behavior, conspiratorial silence, fear, and rage—suggests that they became morally depraved by working in prison. Something altered their understanding of right and wrong. Something made them as perverse as the men they guarded and despised—perhaps even more so. As a result of their working environment, they had become mentally unfit.

One example of this mysterious personality change is a man who answers to the prison handle "Coach." Coach is currently serving prison time for robbery and rape. Before becoming an inmate, he was a big-city police officer and a corrections officer. Coach's journey helps us to understand the process that changes the jailer into the jailed.

"I grew up [in Philadelphia in the 1940s and 1950s]. I had a good childhood considering the racism and discrimination that existed at the time. That was the heyday of the gang era, and I was a gang leader and had a well-known reputation in our neighborhood of being from a family where everyone knew how to fight. In some respects, my childhood upbringing had a lot to do with my adult behavior before getting into trouble. I learned to share and care for others early in life because I came from a large family. I learned to be accountable for my actions and [I learned] a sense of responsibility from taking care of and protecting my younger sisters.

"My father died while I was very young. My mother raised me and my ... brothers and sisters by doing housework as well as [from] my father's Social Security survivors' benefits. I can remember every holiday we would get together with my aunts, uncles, and other family for dinners at our house....

"My father had been a boxer and, as a result, all of my brothers would try out boxing.... We were a close-knit family. To this day I have a very close relationship with my siblings....

"Actually, although I didn't get a high school diploma until I got out of the Army, I had been an A student in elementary school and middle school. I dropped out of school for no reason other than to have more time to hang out in the streets. Eventually I met the woman (then a girl) who I would later marry. She became pregnant, and I knew that I would have to do something with my life. That's when I went into the Army.

"After getting out of the Army, I took the civil service test for the post office. I was hired within ninety days. I worked for the post office for five years and it was during this time I went back to school. I got my GED and went on to take college courses.... I left the post office and became ... a police officer. This was during the late '60s and early '70s, a time of great strife when civil rights workers were becoming active.

"I left the police force but I retained my police commission and became a bail enforcement officer—a bounty hunter—for a bail bonding agency. It was then that I decided to become a corrections officer. I worked for both the Philadelphia prison system and the Pennsylvania Department of Corrections. My goal was to become a criminal psychoanalyst or a counselor. I was working toward that goal by taking college courses in those fields.

"In 1974, I became a state corrections officer at Graterford. I preferred corrections over police work because, as a cop, my only contact with offenders was to arrest them. That was it. My college courses were in the behavioral sciences, psychology and sociology, which gave me a desire to get to know and possibly be of some assistance to the offenders. As a police officer, I knew that I couldn't do that, but also as a corrections officer I found that it was hard to do. I was always chided by other officers for being too much of a social worker. I left Graterford in 1981 and went into the Philadelphia county prison system until 1985.

"There has always been a lot of racism in law enforcement [and] corrections work,... which often got me into trouble at Graterford. In Holmesburg [a Philadelphia County prison], it wasn't a problem since most of the guards and supervisors were black. My relationship with inmates has always been good no matter where I worked. Many of the COs wanted to see inmates treated like trash; they expected all COs [corrections officers] to act the same. But all of us didn't feel that way.

"When I worked at Graterford, it was a very dangerous and violent jail. Corruption was everywhere. During my tenure, I had a take in the gambling games that were run on A-Block. I knew guards were pimping the homos and selling weed and drugs. Graterford was still better than Holmesburg. There was a lot of money to be made. White Hats [high-ranking corrections officials] were in on it as well.

"I saw so many instances of abuse and cruel treatment of inmates that, for the most part, I would disassociate myself from it. There were a few times when I subjected an unruly inmate to my own private brand of cruel treatment, like an ass-whooping, up close and personal.

But I never rushed an inmate with a gang of guards. I saw many incidents of guards putting shanks [prison knives] in inmates' mattresses and then come back to shake them down, beat 'em up and write 'em up [issue a misconduct citation].

"Over the years I have cut down inmates who hung up [tried to commit suicide]. Sometimes I saved their lives. Sometimes they were dead when I found them. I saw one inmate get his throat cut wide open over his commissary at Graterford. He was dead by the time he got to the hospital.

"[I once saw an inmate] ... punch a guard in the face in the dining hall at Graterford.... The guard fell and hit his head on ... [a] table and was killed. There was a minor riot in the D-Block kitchen. Once we quelled it, [the inmate] was placed in the Hole. He was charged with murder.

"While he waited for trial, he was kept at Graterford instead of being moved to another institution. He was kept naked in his cell [in Siberia] without blankets or sheets. He was hosed down with cold water every time he tried to sleep. Eventually he came down with a very bad viral infection and died in the infirmary.

"Another incident that sticks out in my mind was when [another officer] was killed ... in the main corridor of Graterford. I was working the door on D-Block corridor. The men from the yard were coming in and [the officer was standing there].... [An inmate] came in with a [baseball] bat and the officer stopped him, verbally chastised him, and told him to return the bat to the yard.... [As the officer] turned to walk away, [the inmate] ... hit him in the back of the head with the bat.

"A crowd of inmates was blocking the view, so me and some other guards went to see what was going on.... [The officer's] head was smashed in. There was a big puddle of brains and blood....

"[Several years later] ... I was the officer in charge of ... [protective custody] in another Philadelphia County prison.... While in my charge, [one] inmate got into a fight with another inmate and was beaten in the head with a mop wringer. [The inmate] ... was injured very badly and later died. I was charged with negligence for allowing that to happen, and I was suspended and fired. I was unemployed with a new home, new car, plus a wife and kids; economically I was strapped. Eventually, I took my retirement funds, bought a large amount of cocaine, and became a drug dealer. Soon I became the leader of a large organized drug ring, which led me to be charged with a variety of crimes. I took a deal for a guilty plea and ... [was sent to prison].

"I have run into a lot of inmates who knew me when I was a guard. No one has shown me any resentment. If they did, it was behind my back. I've never had a problem since I've been down. It was very humiliating after being a CO for so long and then being a convicted felon. The guards have always treated me well. My block card is marked so the guards know who I am.

"Prison hasn't helped me. I think I am a better person for coming to prison, but not for being in prison, if you know what I mean. ..."

When you consider the atrocities that Coach witnessed while he was trying to "be of some assistance to the offenders," his later crimes seem predictable. Certainly the corruption, hostility, violence, and criminality in his workplace must bear some blame for Coach's fall from grace.

Because I have lived for so long in prison, I understand the perversity that transforms inmates and staff. A crucial ingredient in this metamorphosis is the daily hatred and disregard that staff express toward inmates, *and* that inmates express toward staff. Like carnival mirrors, captives and captors reflect, distort, and amplify each other's basest personality defects and worst behavioral deficiencies.

Some years ago, while Coach was working at Holmesburg, I was privileged to hear a survivor of the Nazi concentration camp at Auschwitz speak to the Jewish inmates at Graterford. Itka was her name, and she was a woman I will never forget. I knew that she had been deeply wounded by an experience much worse than mine, yet I never detected the unmistakable bitterness, hostility, and cynicism in her that binds the ignominious fraternity of prison inmates together like a secret handshake.

One of the inmates asked Itka how she felt about the Germans today. I could tell that he and most of the other men wanted to share in the bitter feast of her hatred. She responded by crossing the index and middle fingers of her right hand, like a child making a wish, and raised them over her head for all the men to see.

"When two people hate each other they become like my two fingers. No matter who is the stronger or the more powerful, each one is enslaved by his hatred of the other. The same way you cannot determine which of my crossed fingers subdues the other, two people joined by their hatred of each other cannot be free from the restraints they place on the other through their hatred, because the effort needed to hate is as oppressive as any act of malice."

Itka then displayed her fingers in the sign of a "V." "Even after I was liberated from Auschwitz, I was not truly free. Only when I stopped hating the Germans was I able to uncross my fingers and free myself from the bondage of those feelings that had kept us both captive. Today

I come to you a free woman to tell you the secret to freedom: you have to stop hating."

It takes a courageous person like Itka to bury the hatred that seems to be the inevitable byproduct of the human warehouses called prisons. As a result, the construction of each new warehouse poses an immense harm to our moral landscape. Collectively, as politicians and citizens, victims and offenders, correctional officials and prisoners, we all now must be brave enough to uncross our fingers.

16

The Dancing Man

EDITORS' NOTE

In the form of a self-interview, Victor Hassine offers a vivid first-hand account of a prison riot. During this riot, he witnessed an incident that would become his saddest prison memory: The repeated beating and gang rape of a young inmate taken from protective custody.

The author criticizes prison staff for videotaping the episode and not acting to stop the torture. He is also critical of his own inaction, having lived for years with the memory of this tragic event. We learn that some situations in life are arguably worse than death. When savage violence is allowed to flourish, everyone—victim and bystander alike—is sullied in the process.

When I interview people for the pieces that I write, I begin by asking questions that spark memories of the major events that shaped their impressions of prison. I ask my interviewees what their happiest memory was during their incarceration, then what their saddest memory was, then what their angriest memory was, and so on. You can tell a lot by what a person chooses to remember as well as by what he chooses to forget.

My saddest memory of prison is the dancing man. The experience taught me that death isn't the worst thing that can happen to you in prison. Living can be far worse: living in fear in protective custody; living as somebody's sex slave; living under somebody's thumb, helpless to do anything about it. This is existing, not living, and it is a condition worse, far worse, than death.

During the fall of 1986, I was transferred from Graterford to SCI-Pittsburgh (Western Penitentiary). An inmate at Graterford had attacked me for no apparent reason. To me, it was just another act of random violence at Dodge City, but to the prison administration, it offered a good excuse to get rid of me.

A prison transfer is much more than just a move from one place to another. It is more like moving from one country to another, because all prisons are unique. The rules are different, the guards are different, the inmates are different, even the food is different. This particular transfer took me far away from my loved ones. At Graterford, my family in Trenton, New Jersey, was only two and a half hours away. Now here I was in Pittsburgh, seven hours away by car. Visits became sporadic.

The move devastated and embittered me. I felt isolated, victimized, and alone. To make matters worse, I was now in a badly overcrowded prison. Graterford was single-celled when I left, but inmates in SCI-Pittsburgh were double-celled. Furthermore, Pittsburgh's inmate population (about 2,200 men) was only slightly smaller than Graterford's, but the prison was so small that you could almost fit its entire physical structure into Graterford's main yard.

In the early morning hours of a very cold October day, soon after I arrived at Western Penitentiary, I was awakened by the smell of smoke and cries of "Fire! Fire!" A guard, covering his mouth and nose with a wet cloth, opened my cell with one free hand and quickly moved down the range, opening other cells that were out of sight. The smoke was thick and the confusion grew as startled inmates ran from their cells. I stayed in my cell until I was dressed, putting on my heaviest boots and several layers of shirts and pants. Remembering a lesson I had learned at Graterford, I stuffed a thick stack of old newspapers against my chest and my back as protection from a possible knife attack. Finally, I took my gloves, a lighter, and a few packs of cigarettes.

When I finished dressing, I carefully pushed my belongings out of sight under my bed, turned out the light, and then locked my cell with a padlock. For a moment, I stood motionless on the range to watch what was happening. Suddenly, the guard who had unlocked my door came running past me, heading down a flight of stairs and off the cell-block, but not before he dropped a set of block keys on the floor a few feet away from me. I could hear men above me yelling, "Let me out, CO! Let me out!" As I eyed the keys, I wondered if I should risk danger to release the hundreds of men trapped on the upper tiers of the block. However, another inmate picked up the keys and began unlocking the cells. Just in case his bravery turned into larceny, I decided to check to make sure the padlock was secure on my cell.

The smoke thickened, but because I was on the second of five levels, I could still breathe and see. Looking up the tiers, I saw no flames, just a thick, black cloud of smoke floating downward.

The sound of inmates screaming and running down steel stairs probably would frighten most people, but I was a veteran of three riots at Graterford, so smoke, disorder, and noise didn't scare me. I cautiously headed toward the ground floor of the cellblock, trying to discern if I was witnessing a fire or a riot.

During times of confusion in prison, it is wise to travel with a pack, in case things get ugly. But I had only been in Pittsburgh for a month, so I didn't know many people. My only alternative was to walk slowly and deliberately to a place where my back was protected, where I had a clear, unobstructed view of the unfolding events. When I got to the "flats" (what inmates call the ground floor of a cellblock), I went to a brightly lit area next to the exit door, keeping my back to the wall. In the mounting chaos, I became a proverbial fly on the wall that nobody noticed.

I soon realized that I was looking at a fire, not a riot. A subsequent investigation revealed that an unknown guard on the graveyard shift had gone into the basement of the block, deliberately setting the fire next to several giant ventilation fans. The massive air ducts located on the ceiling of the five-story cellblock spewed out the thick, black smoke from the basement, choking inmates locked in their cells on the top tiers. No one ever discovered who that guard was or why he or she set the fire.

Because no one knew yet that there was smoke but no real fire, inmates were carrying armloads of belongings from their cells. Men with TVs, radios, and typewriters streamed out into the ranges. I could see inmates on the upper tiers covering their faces with wet rags, going from cell to cell to make sure that no one was locked inside. I stayed to watch the pandemonium, because I was in no mood to brave the wind and the cold outside.

After about thirty minutes of general chaos and confusion, things gradually turned ugly. By this time most inmates realized that the smoke was coming from the air ducts and there was no immediate danger from a real fire, so men began returning to the block to escape the cold and to keep an eye on their possessions. Right in front of me, a gang of about ten hooded men who had been roaming through the ranges tried to throw someone over the third tier to his certain death. For the first time, I could see flames in the back of the block from inmates setting cell fires. I knew that this chaos was quickly turning into a riot.

A small inmate who walked by was suddenly attacked from behind by two men, who beat him to the ground and kicked him. A third man soon appeared, who grabbed the small inmate by the hair and dragged him to a cell off the flats. I knew what fate awaited the small man. About this time, ten inmates carrying metal rods began to hammer at the steel mesh fence that surrounded fifty cells in the adjacent protective custody unit. I could see two guards nervously pacing up and down the unit, calling for help on their handheld, two-way radios.

The steel mesh gates finally collapsed, and a mob of twenty or more inmates rushed inside the unit. The two guards were beaten, kicked, and clubbed. Once the guards stopped struggling, the inmates spat on them and urinated on them, only to begin beating them again. Eventually, the guards were stripped and dragged into empty, unlit cells. Several inmates took the guards' keys and began to unlock the protective custody cells.

The two guards had been out of my view for several minutes when one captain and two city police officers (I think one was a woman) came into the block. Amazingly, the riotous frenzy stopped in its tracks. Maybe it was the fear of uniformed authority, or possibly no one was certain whether the officers were armed, but the three rescued the two injured guards without any resistance. Only the fear of brute force prompted the inmates' humanitarianism.

After the five officers left the block, the mob became far more enraged and violent, probably because they realized they hadn't mustered the courage needed to attack the rescuers. Inmates now fell on the men who had been confined to protective custody with unbridled savagery and ferocity. I finally walked out of the building from sheer disgust. As I exited, I saw several inmates carrying a blonde-haired, blue-eyed youngster over their heads, away from isolation.

The sudden sting of frigid air on my face restored my senses. The thick stack of newspapers that I had stuffed into my shirt now protected me from the knife-like wind. I walked in relative warmth around the small prison yard, watching shivering men in bathrobes huddle in groups around the bonfires they had built. Graterford had taught me well.

For an hour or so, I stayed outside. My block was now engulfed in flames, so all the men (over six hundred) had left the building. The police and prison staff had managed to maintain control of the entire prison, except for the yard, the burning cellblock, and the auditorium (a rectangular building next to the cellblock). There was an elevated corridor about fifteen feet above the ground that connected the auditorium projection room with the administrative building.

Eventually, I decided to escape the bitter cold by taking my chances in the auditorium. Inside, there were a hundred or so men, which meant the building wasn't as crowded as it should have been. It was enclosed, dark, and out of the reach of the authorities, so it was very dangerous. But I was colder than I was frightened. Prison riots were becoming mostly a nuisance to me, so I cautiously entered this no man's land.

At first, I saw what I wanted to see: a cast-iron heating element against one wall. I inched toward the heater, carefully keeping my back to the wall. I leaned against that heater for several hours, trading immediate warmth for a lifetime of terrible memories, nightmares, and disillusionment.

It took a while for my eyes to adjust to the darkness, even though there were small fires of burning furniture scattered around the auditorium. Eventually, in the flickering light, I saw roving gangs of inmates attacking and beating each other. I saw a couple of men thrown into a bonfire. But what haunts me to this day was what was happening on the stage: a satanic performance at the gates of hell. A hole was torn open in the curtain of humanity that day.

The men who had carried the blonde youngster from protective custody had taken him to the auditorium. They had stripped him naked and were repeatedly beating him, forcing him to dance around the stage for his life. Between these dances, hooded inmates alone and in groups raped him, striking him time and again until he performed every imaginable sex act. Some of the inmates cut the young man, others urinated on him or shoved various objects in every opening in his body. When they weren't raping or beating him, they forced him to dance on and on, like a marionette on strings. For hours, he screamed and pleaded for mercy. He must have prayed for his own death.

What made this even worse was that the police were watching the scene from the safety of the projection room above the auditorium. They videotaped the atrocities that were performed on the stage, but they never tried to help the dancing man. They simply watched.

To me, the tragedy lies not only in the senseless fate of the young man but more so in the failure to stop his suffering. The police certainly could have done something; maybe I could have, too. At the time, the police recorded the incident on videotape; now I've recorded it years later on paper. Sometimes I see us all standing in that projection room, staff and inmates together, watching and condemning the brutality but without the moral indignation needed to stop the hideous music that compelled this man to dance. The sinner or the pitiless: who is worse?

These thoughts haunt me every day. I will never forget the dancing man looking up toward the projection room—and toward me—begging for someone's help. I should have stayed outdoors on that frigid October day because, as it turned out, it was far colder indoors.

17

Scenes from a Prison

EDITORS' NOTE

Victor Hassine introduces us to several interesting characters whose lives tell us something important about prison life. Cherokee is an aging lifer who has become a mascot of sorts for his keepers and an invisible man for his fellow inmates—a prop, not a person. Quietly crazy and superficially happy, he is a model inmate but at the cost of his soul. Has Cherokee been relegated to the margins of society, even prison society?

Kareem, described as a prison gangster, is a tough convict who is losing his mind. He is beginning to unravel psychologically, a process he thinks began in solitary confinement. One can sense a long downhill road for Kareem, who can do little but fight to hold on to his sanity—to tough it out on his own.

Tony, a bank robber turned jailhouse lawyer, presents an upbeat persona. He hangs a sign outside his cell each morning, advertising "Legal Aid," and arranges his cell like an office. He has modest skills and a thriving business. One day, he simply snaps. Shocking as is his fate, we learn that it is surprisingly common in prison.

We hear the words of an anonymous fourteen-year-old boy, sent to the Big House where he is raped and slowly emerges as a lonely, confused predator in his own right.

Finally, we meet the Old Man, who hunts down his breakfast like Hemingway's Santiago (The Old Man and the Sea) *hunts down his marlin, picked to pieces by petty officials, who (like Hemingway's sharks) nibble at the Old Man's dignity until there is almost nothing left. Yet our Old Man (like Santiago) asserts himself through his struggle. He lives in a degrading human warehouse, though we sense that he may yet transcend his surroundings and the humiliating abuses of indifferent prison officials.*

GOOD OLD CHEROKEE

When was the last time you thought about going crazy, living crazy, or dying crazy? Chances are, you never thought about it at all, assuming that insanity is something that happens to other people. I thought the same, even after I had been in prison for many years. I never considered that my mental health was in any peril because I focused all my attention on trying to keep myself physically intact. Only after I had overcome the physical dangers of prison did I discover the greater challenge of maintaining sanity. In truth, the American prison experience includes a slow, steady regression toward the threshold of madness.

Most convicts manage to survive this ordeal, but none remain unscarred by it. Those fortunate to outlive the physical prison find themselves thrust inexorably into the greater struggle to overcome the psychological prison. American society, which always values the mental health of its citizens, should be more concerned about a criminal justice system designed ultimately to drive millions of its incarcerated population insane.

My introduction to prison-induced madness came in the form of Cherokee, one of Graterford Prison's most esteemed inmates. When I first arrived there in 1981 to begin serving my life sentence, Cherokee had already been incarcerated for more than forty years. At some time during his long imprisonment, the Graterford staff ceased treating him like an inmate and elevated him to what amounted to the status of a mascot. To the inmate population, he was as ingrained into Graterford as its bricks and mortar. But whether anyone considered Cherokee a mascot or a fixture, neither description seemed a fitting way to view a gentle human being who for forty years did nothing more than exactly what the administration expected of him.

When I first met Cherokee, he was scavenging inside a fifty-five-gallon drum of prison trash. As I stood beside it, he took me off guard when he surfaced with a handful of pickings. Having lived in New York, I was unsurprised by the sight of a man mining refuse and paid little attention to him. Gripping a load of garbage, Cherokee produced a huge smile and quickly placed his catch into a large plastic bag.

"Hey there, you must be a new fellow," he addressed me politely. "My name's Cherokee." He stood over six feet tall, sporting a pot belly bulging from his worn, faded brown prison uniform. His hair was a dingy yellow like wind-blown straw, with streaks of white and gray, and his yellow teeth matched the color of his hair. His friendly, gentle tone obliged a response.

"My name's Victor," I replied.

His puffy cheeks swelled, as his smile broadened. "We don't get many Victors in here," he offered pleasantly. "You look like such a nice young fellow. You don't look like you belong in here." From that moment, Cherokee became my friend for life.

The big man gazed down at his bag of goodies and said, "You'd be surprised how much good stuff I find around here, like cups, and shoes, and socks. Once I found me a pretty good coat. Wasn't nothing wrong with it. I gave it to another young fellow who didn't have one to wear." Then he chuckled, "You young folks today sure like to throw things away."

I returned his smile and nodded, as he continued. "I give a lot of stuff away to anyone who needs it. You know how fellows can get down on their luck in here. So, if you got anything you want to throw out, you be sure to let old Cherokee know. And you don't have to worry about me, I'm okay. Everybody knows me. Just ask anyone about Cherokee."

He picked up his bag and lumbered off toward the next trash drum, also overflowing with garbage. After a few steps, he stopped and turned. "Oh, did I tell you I collect stamps? If you get any, I hope you'll give them to me. I'll stop around your cell." Cherokee and his bag moved on without looking back.

Throughout my stay at Graterford, I saw Cherokee frequently. Usually, he was digging his way into or out of a trash can or a dumpster. Sometimes, he would stop by my cell and ask if I had any stamps for him. I would give him all the canceled letter stamps I had received, and this seemed to make him very happy. Once in a while, I offered him some cigarettes, candy, or coffee, but he refused to accept anything, as it somehow interfered with the intention of his visit. Soon, I was storing commissary items in a brown bag for his next visit. He always took the offering, never saying a word. His smile was all the thanks I needed.

Cherokee's demeanor suggested that he no longer recognized his surroundings as those of a prison. His unique behavior was not what set him apart from all other inmates but rather the way the prison staff treated him. He was allowed to run free in the prison so he could forage anywhere he wanted. His only requirement was to return to his cell for count; his cell usually only locked at 9:00 PM. He needed no pass to go anywhere and could visit the kitchen at any time, eating anything he liked. Staff members often gave him candy bars and snacks purchased from an employees' vending machine. No inmate dared say an unkind word to Cherokee, because both guards and prisoners were fiercely protective of him. In a maximum-security prison, this kind of high status was rare and extraordinary.

I did not give any of this much thought at first and assumed that such long-toothed seniority entitled Cherokee to special consideration. After all, forty years of captivity had turned him into a harmless old man who was kind, likeable, and unlikely to escape even if the prison walls came tumbling down.

My suspicions of this apparent altruism toward Cherokee grew after I met other convicts who had served as much or more time. The institutional policy was to treat long-timers the same as other inmates, with no special consideration or privileges. I kept wondering why Cherokee had been singled out to receive the benefit of the staff's mercy and kindness. If prison managers wanted to do the decent thing for Cherokee, they would have sent him to a minimum-security prison or helped him to get a commutation of his sentence, so he could be committed to a nursing home. At the very least, they could have provided him with some mental health care. Allowing this harmless old man to live out his life rummaging in prison trash cans did not reveal any real decency—it was actually a form of degradation and humiliation.

I eventually came to understand that Cherokee's privileges were not meant to benefit him but to advance the prison's interest in displaying a "model inmate."

For forty years, Graterford had invested money and resources to hammer, bend, fold, and shape Cherokee into the mold of rehabilitation. The old convict was now obedient, functional, low maintenance, dependent, and virtually harmless. What more could prison management want? It made no difference that in the process of conditioning him into a model inmate, Cherokee had been driven to quiet madness. He had to be punished for his crime, and apparently forfeiting his sanity was a fair price to pay. This was Graterford's brand of mercy and redemption.

What the prison staff passed off as acts of kindness were actually inducements for others to conform their behavior to that of their model inmate. Certainly, staff members were genuinely fond of Cherokee; but in a prison, fondness must always stand a distant second to control. Cherokee, first and foremost, was a helpless, unwitting tool in a prison's long-term effort to achieve absolute control over the inmate population.

Anyone who has not felt the pinch of prison shackles will likely scoff at the notion that a modern governmental bureaucracy would knowingly induce insanity to maintain control. But consider this: if you were the warden of an overcrowded prison plagued with violence, corruption, drugs, disease, and lack of resources, Cherokee's smiling figure emerging from the trash to greet you might make you wish that all your inmate charges could be as respectful, obedient, and well-behaved as this old long-timer.

I THINK I'M GOING CRAZY

Finding the time and place to be alone in a prison is almost an impossibility. Overcrowding has seen to that. Whenever I discover an opportunity to be by myself, I try to exploit it. One hot summer day during my incarceration at Pittsburgh's Western Penitentiary, the heat was so oppressive that none of the other inmates dared to venture out into the small area of dirt and dust shamelessly designated as the "recreation yard."

In the early 1980s, some correctional bureaucrat had developed an ingenious plan to renovate Pennsylvania's oldest functioning penitentiary, beginning with the building of a new five-hundred-cell, one-thousand-bed housing unit within its walls. The plan called for three phases: new housing units replacing the main recreation yard of the prison; the shutting down of the old housing units and converting them into a massive work and counseling complex; and the demolition of the existing work and counseling buildings, to be replaced by a larger recreation yard and a field house.

The first phase of the plan was completed, and Western Penitentiary had gained five hundred new cells. Unfortunately, funding for the other two phases dried up. The state's oldest prison now held twice as many inmates—but it had no recreation yard. By now, it had become the most densely populated prison in the state.

That hot summer day, I was desperate for some privacy within the walkway area running between the new housing units that now replaced the old main yard. This area had no grass, no space, and no room to exercise. All that existed was a long, crooked concrete walk flanked by parallel strips of dirt with bleachers intermittently installed wherever they would fit.

Finding any unoccupied space under these circumstances was normally a ludicrous undertaking. But on this day, thanks to the stifling heat and burning sun, the yard was completely empty. I hurried to a remote spot to sit on one of the scorching bleachers, a small price to pay for privacy. I closed my eyes and ignored my discomfort as I drifted off into my own thoughts.

Before I had a chance to fully appreciate my solitude, I was startled by a tap on my shoulder, along with an urgent voice: "Victor, I need to talk to you."

Under normal circumstances, I would have ignored the intruder, but the voice belonged to Kareem, one of the more respected, honorable convicts in the institution. He was a prison gangster who took no nonsense from anyone, but he was also a fair and reasonable man who only challenged those who tried to interfere with his space. I had known Kareem at Graterford before I was transferred to Western and considered him a friend, though I always made a point of staying out of his way.

Hearing the urgency in his voice, my eyes immediately sprung open and my mind instantly focused on the possibility of danger nearby. "What's going on, Kareem?"

Kareem must have detected my concern, as he lowered his voice. "No, there ain't no trouble. I just need to talk with you about something personal." He moved next to me on the bleachers and sat down in the burning sun.

"What's going on?" I was a bit annoyed, but he had piqued my interest. Kareem was not the sort to waste anyone's time.

"I'm going crazy, Victor, I'm losing my shit," he blurted out, his eyes hawkishly searched our surroundings.

"What do you mean?"

Kareem's dark brown eyes fixed on me, wide and piercing. "I've been hearing voices. I know they're not real, but I hear them anyway."

What could I say? Prison life has taught me to be prepared for anything, so I collected my thoughts and asked calmly, "What do these voices say?"

"They tell me to do stupid stuff. You wouldn't believe it. I don't do any of them. I just hear the voices."

My curiosity rose, as I realized I was talking to a man on the verge of a mental breakdown. "Yeah, prison can make anyone hear voices. It's a shame what they do to a man in here."

"Ain't that the truth," he answered, sounding relieved that I understood his problem. "I've seen lots of Old Heads lose their shit, but I never thought it would happen to me."

"Well, maybe it's just a temporary thing and will go away," I suggested. "You're a strong man. You can beat this."

"No, man, I don't think so. I can feel myself slipping in and out. I tried to fight it a couple of times, but my mind just keeps snapping—I'm just going crazy." He added a chuckle to that.

"What do you think brought this on?"

"Nobody in my family's crazy—it has to be this prison. The time is getting to me. I've been doing this bit for a long time."

Kareem had served over twenty years of a life sentence, and his prison escapades had made commutation less than a remote possibility.

For a moment, I reasoned that perhaps he was a drug abuser whose mind had recently surrendered to his addiction. I worried about whether a similar fate might await me as my life sentence unfolded.

As if hearing my thoughts, Kareem added, "All my life I've avoided drinking and doing drugs because I'd seen what it did to other people. Now look at me anyway."

"I don't know what to tell you, Kareem. Sane or insane, these people want their time out of you. You're going to have to fight this thing."

"You know, I've done a lot of time in the hole. When I started my bit, I didn't care nothing about going to the hole. But these last few times, they were real rough."

"What happened in the hole?"

"Nothing this last time, but just being down there with these guards messing with you and all that time alone. I think I started slipping while I was in the hole."

"Did you hear these voices in the hole?"

"No. I just started hearing them. When I was in the hole, I didn't hear nothing. I'm not good with reading, so I just sat in my cell sleeping and thinking."

"You think the hole made you crazy?"

Kareem thought for a moment. "No. I don't think it was the hole alone. I think it's everything put together. You know, doing time ain't no joke."

"No, it isn't," I agreed.

"And you know what's the most amazing thing about all this?" He suddenly took on the animation of a child, eager to share a secret. "The way it just kind of crept up on me. One minute I was normal, the next minute I was bugging out in my cell, talking to myself. I didn't know going crazy could snatch me from behind like that."

A long silence lingered between us, both of us lost in our own separate thoughts.

"You're doing a life bit too, aren't you?" Kareem asked.

"Yeah, I got eight in and it's killing me. I can imagine how you feel."

"No, you can't, and you really don't want to." He reached out with his hand as if grabbing at something in the air. "Don't you worry about any of these motherfuckers messing with you. You just make sure you hold on to your mind. Don't let these people sneak up behind you and snatch your shit."

As he stood up and left me alone on the bleachers, Kareem's last words echoed back to me: "Nobody deserves to be treated like this. They might as well have killed me."

Suddenly, I did not feel much like being alone anymore.

IT HAPPENS ALL THE TIME

Tony was my neighbor at Graterford. I met him the first day I entered general population. He was a tall, rectangular man who cast an imposing shadow. His thick, black, well-trimmed beard with neatly groomed hair gave his block of a body a crown of sophistication.

"If you need to know anything about this joint, just ask me," he told me as I sorted through my belongings. "My name's Tony. I live a few cells down."

There was much that I needed to know about my new home, and Tony was more than willing to instruct me. He had read about my case in the newspaper and knew I had a background in law, which motivated him to be as helpful as possible. Nothing is free in prison, and the price for Tony's friendship was my assistance with some criminal cases he was appealing.

Tony was a jailhouse lawyer. Every morning, he hung a paper sign in front of his cell that announced *LEGAL AID*. His cell was arranged like a small office. The steel desk mounted on one side had all the necessary office supplies and adornments, including a manual typewriter. Alongside his desk was a makeshift chair assembled out of stacked boxes and old newspapers. The chair stood by the entrance to his cell, so a "client" did not have to enter too far to conduct business. On a shelf above his desk and peppered throughout his cell were thick law books to punctuate his "profession."

Tony was admittedly no legal wizard. When asked what he did for a living, he would proudly and without hesitation reply, "I rob banks." Helping people out with their legal work kept him busy and his cell filled with commissary items. He was doing fifteen to thirty years so he had plenty of time to occupy.

Tony was a well-disciplined man with streetwise intelligence, so he had managed to teach himself enough about the law to handle legal issues and fill out appeal forms. However, he lacked the ability to properly litigate an appeal to its end. With most cases, he would read an inmate's transcripts, fill out an appropriated appeal form, then have the court appoint a real attorney for his client. The charge for these services would amount to what he felt the client could afford, from a pack of commissary cigarettes to a couple of hundred dollars.

Tony functioned as effectively as any legal secretary I had ever known and provided a needed service. Many of the men at Graterford were illiterate, and the only way for them to begin the process of appealing their convictions was with the services of a jailhouse lawyer. In reality, most collateral appeals filed on behalf of inmates are the product of jailhouse lawyers—a poor man's last-ditch effort for justice.

As one can imagine, some jailhouse lawyers are honest and qualified, while others are con men hoping to hustle inmates out of money, often ruining their chances for a successful appeal. The caveat *Buyer Beware* holds true in prison as well.

To his credit, Tony was reliable and made up in enthusiasm what he lacked in legal expertise. As my own jailhouse legal practice began to thrive, I often referred minor cases like parole violations and guilty pleas to his able office. This spared me most of the nuisance cases and made Tony very happy. Once I became his neighbor, his clientele doubled and he gained a few pounds from all the commissary cakes and candies he was earning.

Every morning before I went about my business, I stopped at Tony's cell, sat on his client's chair, and enjoyed his offer of hot instant coffee and commissary pastry. Tony and I chatted for a half hour or more about legal issues, the prison, or anything else on our minds. It was always a good way to start off a morning.

In the afternoons, I performed my assigned prison job as a janitor in the infirmary. At times, I was asked by one of the nurses to escort her to the Special Needs Unit. This unit was a small caged-in section of the infirmary where the seriously mentally ill were housed. It was a dark, bleak place where men resembling zombies spent their days sitting or pacing, waiting for meals or medications. These inmates were not allowed outdoors for exercise, and some had spent years inside this forgotten purgatory.

Female nurses often preferred to be accompanied by an inmate janitor during their rounds in this ward for their own safety. In turn, janitors enjoyed the chance to serve as escorts, as it gave them an opportunity to flirt with a female. Men will be men, after all, and I was no exception.

As requested, I carried a tray of medication and walked behind the nurse toward the Special Needs Unit, referred to as "D-Rear." The guard assigned to D-Rear unlocked a wire-mesh gate and allowed us into the dark, dirty, foul-smelling cage.

Ghoulishly assembled around a large table were about twenty inmates eagerly awaiting their meds. Men of all colors, sizes, and shapes stared with wide-eyed expectation for the nurse to call out their name. Each inmate slowly shuffled over to the nurse, who handed him his medication. I gave him a paper cup of water with which to down his meds, then he moved away into the darkness to wait for the drug to spirit him away into his own netherworld.

It was such a sad sight. I could never wait to get out of there, nor did I wish to be reminded that places like this existed. When the nurse finished, she asked me to follow her to a new patient who was unable to walk. Reluctantly, I trailed deeper into the bowels of D-Rear.

Somewhere in a far corner sat a lone man obscured by shadows. Everyone else was walking a slow, tedious circle around the ward for daily recreation. It was too dark for me to be able to identify the man. I looked away, as the nurse gave him his medication. She asked me for water.

I approached and extended a water cup—only to be shocked by the sight of Tony, sitting motionless, drool oozing from his mouth.

"Tony, that can't be you!" I called out in astonishment. I had done my usual morning coffee and chat with this man less than eight hours ago. "This must be some kind of mistake," I told myself.

The nurse saw my alarm, as I tried to arouse Tony. "He can't hear you, Victor. He's on too much medication. Is he a friend of yours?"

I wanted to tell her about Tony, what a smart guy he was, the efficient, little office he had in the cell, and the way he never took advantage of people. But I couldn't. All I could do was stare at this shell of a man who slumped silently before me. "Yes, he is" was all I could say.

The nurse ushered me out of the unit. My body followed, but my eyes remained fixed on Tony.

"Look, there's nothing you can do for him," the nurse advised. "He's really out there right now."

"What happened?"

"No one really knows. I got a call to report to the block to pick up an inmate and take him to the infirmary. When I got to his cell, your friend was lying on his bed, mumbling gibberish and repeating that he couldn't do the time. He wasn't violent or anything. He was pretty much like you saw him. Do you know if he got some bad news about anything?"

"No," I answered, though I had no way of knowing. "What's going to happen to him?" I asked in a delayed panic. "What can I do?"

"Calm down, Victor. There's nothing you can do. The doctors will treat him. And soon he'll be back out in population. He'll probably have to stay on some kind of medication. There's lots of guys who go through this and they come around eventually. It happens all the time."

Years later, I filed a class action lawsuit against Graterford and the Department of Corrections, challenging among other things the conditions in D-Rear. A federal judge, after inspecting D-Rear, declared it an unfit place for human beings. Shortly thereafter, D-Rear was discontinued and a licensed mental health group arrived to operate an independent Special Needs Unit inside Graterford.

When the new mental health unit finally opened, I said a little prayer for my friend Tony and all the others who "couldn't do the time."

FAST WALK

"Why do you think so many people become insane after being in prison a while?" I asked my exercise partner, as he fast walked around the prison-yard track. Myth has it that inmates walk counter-clockwise around a prison to defy the measure of their time in captivity, as if walking in this way could "undo" or reverse time. In reality, the direction of inmate traffic is a prison yard is determined by staff, who are mindful of the angle and location of observation posts. The direction of inmate yard traffic does not represent some silent or symbolic resistance to the prison order.

"You writing some more stuff?"

"Yeah," I huffed, trying to keep up with his quickening pace. "I wanted to do something on insanity, like what it is about prison that drives people crazy."

"Why do you say prison drives people crazy? My experience is, a lot of people come into prison half crazy already."

"What do you mean?"

"Well, most guys coming into prison have some kind of drug or alcohol addiction. They've lived hard on the streets and by the time they come to prison, their madness just catches up with them."

"So, you think drugs cause all the insanity we see in here?"

"No. It's not only drugs and alcohol, but it's mostly that these guys are just weak individuals who crack under stress. It just so happened that they got the stress in prison, so these weak people lose their mind."

"So," I tried to clarify, "prison contributes to driving men crazy because of the stress?"

"No. I'm saying, these people are weak and while the stress from prison might have taken them over the edge, it really could have happened anywhere. If they were out on the streets, the job stress might have driven them crazy. If you're weak in prison, you'll go crazy in here."

"I don't know if I buy that. I mean, I've seen some pretty tough guys go crazy in here."

"How tough can a guy be if he goes crazy? When I first came to prison over twenty years ago, one of my Old Heads told me that prison will either build a man's character or break him down to a fool. Those were the truest words I've ever heard. If a man isn't strong enough to deal with prison, it will crush him."

"So what you're saying is, prison drives people crazy—but it's only weak people or people who are partially crazy already."

"Well, I'm not sure I'd put it like that, but sure. Prison doesn't make you crazy, your weakness does."

At this point, I was pretty confused, besides being out of breath from speed walking. I stopped and watched him zip on down the track, wondering if he was agreeing with me or not.

As I caught my breath, I mulled over his words. Some of his argument was true, but I thought that he placed too high a standard on human beings. Certainly, there were conditions that could drive the strongest man crazy—and to my mind, prison fostered those conditions. I began to wonder if prison had made my fast-walking friend a little crazy himself, and whether he thought the same about me.

OUT OF THE MOUTHS OF BABES

If asked to describe in minimalist fashion my first taste of prison life, I would have to answer the following way: busy, crammed, rigid, confusing, impersonal, unsafe, and lonely. I was twenty-five years old when I first entered "The Big House." (For a point of comparison, I am now fifty years old.) As an energetic young man thrust into confinement and trying to keep pace with my environment, I experienced profound change while in constant motion. My personality and habits changed quickly because the intense pressure, great needs, and dire consequences of the moment demanded such changes. It was as if I had suddenly fallen into an ice-cold ocean and my whole body instinctively transformed itself to protect me from dangerous, unknown elements. I became suspicious and aloof; I reacted quickly to insults, real or imagined. What little control I managed to exercise over these changes in my personality were certainly not enough to counteract their effect on my changing character. Prison made me a convict—a kind of outlaw to normal life—despite my best efforts to prevent it.

Once I had survived my forced metamorphosis, I was eventually able to critically examine these changes in myself. This was much more difficult to do than one might imagine, because I had forgotten what I was like when I first came to prison. Having lost my original identity, I had no way of gauging any of these changes.

Although I had been unable to identify and assess changes in myself, I could certainly recognize them in the many others passing through this prison assembly line. This had been especially true of younger men because their changes were always extreme and complete.

Case in point, a fourteen-year-old man-child was convicted ten years ago of murder and sentenced to life without parole. With great dispatch, this half-pint, "court-certified adult" was processed through the machinery of an adult prison, even though he had barely passed puberty.

To use the metaphorical analogy between a human being and a product, this young man was ultimately manufactured by the prison machine into a convict who now sits idle in a warehouse overcrowded with thousands of other finished products, most of whom are struggling to adapt to their new identities. Whether this is good, bad, helpful, or harmful only obscures his current identity and in the end obfuscates the true nature of contemporary prisons.

Allow this new creation to tell you in his own words what he has become as a product of the prison system.

"I don't know what exactly led me to have sex with another man in prison. I guess I could blame it on curiosity or from being molested as a child, but I believe what led me to have sex with another man was deprivation.

"As a child, I was exposed to sex all the time. My mother worked in a peep show and would take me to work with her, because I was too young to go to school. My father had sex with more women than I can count and often did it with me in the same room.

"As I grew older, I was completely transfixed with stacks of pornographic magazines which my father always left around the house. I even started masturbating at around the age of seven. My preoccupation with sex would often get me into trouble as I started school and when I entered juvenile institutions. I thought of sex constantly, no matter where I was. Always the first thought in my head was sex with any woman.

"I think something else that needs to be considered is the fact that I am a small guy. The runt of the litter. This caused me to be dominated by almost everybody I knew. So in my homosexual encounters, I was able to fulfill a deviant sexual need to dominate. These sexual acts are something I do not want to repeat. I found sexual gratification, but at the expense of degrading myself and sinking farther into my sexual dysfunction. What I really wanted wasn't sexual satisfaction, it was to dominate; to have someone submit themselves to me in the most debasing way possible. But there was also a part of me that only wanted to be with someone in an intimate way. I don't want to just fuck some woman, I would rather just hold her and be held by her. What I crave is not so much the physical pleasure, but the emotional bond that two people share.

"All I want is to be loved. I want the cuddling and holding, the caresses and tenderness that I didn't get growing up. That is not an excuse, just stating what I want most. But there is this part of me, psychologically, that wants to be in control. To dominate another human being the way I was always dominated in my life. To have that power to feel what they [those in control] felt.

"Being in prison, especially at age fourteen, certainly did not help at all. During the period of my life when I am just finding out about sex and experimenting, I am doubting my sexuality because of being raped and I am placed in a world surrounded by men; men that are perverts and child molesters, trying to take advantage of me. Placed in a world with no privacy. Thrust into this world with no preparation, no warning, no training. Sent there [to prison] for the rest of my life with no hope for release. Left with no way for physical satisfaction, but homosexual sex. Sent to a world of predators, victims and everything in between. Just a mixed up kid with no one to turn to. Just wanting to be held, to be loved."

THE OLD MAN, THE BREAKFAST, AND THE COFFEE

The old convict was pathetic, a dark portrait of indignity and suffering. He was oblivious to prison reality as he slowly, methodically swung his misshaped crutches forward to pull his broken body closer toward the dining hall. His distorted silhouette had shadowed the prison walkways for many years. He had come to a point in his life of captivity when the thought of freedom frightened him more than excited him.

With a hand-rolled "buckhorn" cigarette dangling from his lips, he mumbled, "Them eggs gonna be cold ... I hate cold eggs. They're always cold." He complained to himself the way men do when they are more bored than angry.

No one listened to his protests because he was completely alone. His fellow convicts had long shunned him because he no longer had anything worth taking. The prison staff avoided him because they feared his misery might be contagious. As he hobbled along, the other inmates whizzed by him on their way to breakfast.

The rain forced the cripple to swing his body forward in very small, cautious advances. In the past, his heavy wood crutches had slipped on the wet concrete, causing him to fall and suffer great pain. A prison study once found that wooden, rubber-tipped crutches were better suited for prison use; their solid core made them too cumbersome to use as a weapon, and the absence of hollows prevented the stashing of contraband. But he was a simple man who knew only that these crutches were bulky and unwieldy, leaving him with callused hands and chafed underarms.

"Damn, these crutches," he cursed. "They're gonna make me miss breakfast." A cigarette ash dropped and disappeared into his damp, gray coat collar, becoming an insignificant part of an even more insignificant man.

People did not die of starvation in American prisons, and the old man knew it. But many did die of obscurity and that worried him. The only person concerned with his living or dying was the staff member who counted him during meals, and that was just to make sure that he did not exceed his allotted three meals a day.

Suddenly, his crutches slipped out from under him. He fell face down on the wet concrete walk and spit out his wet cigarette. "Shit, I can't miss chow," he said as he mustered his strength to rise.

The suspicious eye of a tower guard focused on his activity, watching him like a vulture, as the old man struggled on his way to the chow hall. "Inmate on the walk," the guard shouted, "keep moving. No loitering on the walk."

The old man ignored him but hurried on to avoid missing breakfast. "He knew I fell down. Why do they do things like that?" he asked no one in particular. "Don't they know by now I'm gonna get mine? Three hots and a cot is what they owe me, and that's what I'm gonna get."

Breathless and hungry, he finally reached the indoor entrance of the dining hall just in time to have another guard slam the barred gate in his face. The scent of cafeteria food invaded the old man's senses.

"The kitchen is closed, return to your block," ordered the guard.

"It was raining, and I fell. Slipped with these damn crutches," replied the old man, so angry that he began to cry. "Please let me eat," he begged, fighting back tears. "Just some coffee or a piece of bread. I'm an old man and I'm soaking wet. Please!"

The guard did not answer right away, staring back at him. "I can't let you," he said finally. "Breakfast is over, you know the rules."

"The game," the old man muttered to himself. "They insist on playing the game. But I'll beat them. I'll get my three hots." Then he said to the guard in a sad voice, "Yeah, those are the rules. Thanks anyway."

He turned his crippled body and slowly shuffled away. After making two swings of his crutches, he heard the guard call out to him, which brought a smile to the old man's face. He swung himself around to face the guard, knowing that his sympathy ploy had worked again.

"Look, Pop," said the guard, "you never caused me any trouble, so I'll tell you what I'm going to do. You go ahead over to see the kitchen steward. He's the one who can help you out. I'll give him a call and put in a good word for you."

"Thank you," said the old man. *The game, they gotta play the game. He could have let me in,* he thought as he swung around in the direction of the kitchen steward's office.

"Watch the waxed floor, Pop," cautioned the guard. "We wouldn't want you to fall and hurt yourself."

The steward's office was located down a long, concrete corridor that had just been waxed, leaving a gray, treacherous film that even right-walking men slipped on. In the past, the old man never even knew it was there until he finally fell several times. In fact, it was the cumulative effects of all those occasional falls that had crippled his legs, bent his back, and broken his spirit.

"The damn game, the damn slippery floor, these damn crutches," he cursed in cadence with each swing of his crutches.

Surprisingly, he reached the steward's office without falling. A man sat at a desk, while inmate workers pushed large carts of cooked food back and forth through the kitchen.

"What do you need?" asked the desk man without looking up.

"The kitchen guard sent me. I missed breakfast."

"Yeah, he called a while ago. Sounds like you've been through a lot. You must be hungry."

"Yes, I am."

"You hurt? Need to go to the infirmary or something?"

"No, sir. I just need to eat, that's all."

"Yeah, I bet you do." There was a brief silence. "I'm going to have to get the steward. He's the man to see." The desk man rose and left the office.

"More games," mumbled the old man. "He should have told me he wasn't the steward."

Finally, a short, fat steward entered, still chewing his breakfast. "You missed breakfast?"

"Yes, sir, I did."

"The officer called and told me all about it."

"I've never been late before."

"No, you haven't. I would have recognized you. Look, I have no problem feeding you. God knows I have more than enough food. But first, you have to get permission from the major of the guards. He has the final say in these matters. I'll call and tell him you're coming. And," the steward added conspiratorially, "I'll tell him it's okay with me."

"Thank you, sir."

"No problem. You know where the major's office is?"

"Yes, sir, I do."

Another disappointment on this particularly trying day. Like a rat chasing a piece of cheese, the old cripple negotiated the long, slippery maze and ventured up two full flights of stairs. After a long ordeal, he eventually arrived at the major's office to find yet another desk man.

"Are you the major?"

"No," the desk clerk answered. "What is it you want?"

"I'm here to see the major."

"I kind of figured that. Now tell me why."

The old convict reluctantly recounted his tale, wondering if they all enjoyed hearing these bad-luck stories.

"You must be the one the steward called about," said the desk man. "The major's reading your file now. He's been expecting you." With that, he abruptly left the room.

The old man waited in silence, knowing that it was all part of the game to see how high he would jump or how low he would go. But he could not understand why he let himself be the main attraction in this dog-and-pony show.

The major finally arrived, a cup of coffee and an unfinished danish in his hands. He tossed both into a waste can close to the old man. The aroma of trashed coffee and pastry wafted its way up to the inmate's nose.

"I want you to know I'm a very busy man," said the major. "I don't really have the time to deal with matters like this. However, because the kitchen steward called me, I did read your file."

"Yes, sir, major, you can see I never did this before."

"Yes, I noticed that. It also tells me you never got caught before. You must be a very smooth operator."

The gambit had been played. The major was trying to provoke him.

"Sir, all I want is something to eat," countered the old man. "I really couldn't help falling."

"I'm sure you couldn't, and if it were up to me, I would certainly make sure you got your meal. It is bad policy to deny an inmate his food. Makes us appear cruel. But administrative directives require the warden to make such decisions."

The old man sighed. "I was only a few minutes late. That's all. These damn crutches, they're just no good in the rain."

"Don't blame your irresponsibility on your crutches. It always seems to be someone else's fault, never yours. Well, save your story for the warden. He'll want to know why you missed breakfast. Okay, you can go now."

The major disappeared from the room.

"All I want is a meal," mumbled the inmate, as he laboriously swung his crutches toward the warden's office. He endured yet another maze and two more upward flights of stairs, his mutterings echoing off the masonry walls.

"So it's come to this. They got me begging for a free meal. I've robbed, stolen, and done a lot of lousy things, but I never made a hungry man beg for food. And they wonder why I hate them. They're the real criminals."

At long last, he entered the warden's spacious, well-furnished office. A large basket of fruit caught his eye, within arm's reach, mocking his hunger.

"May I help you?" asked a secretary behind the fruit.

"The major sent me to talk to the warden."

"We've been expecting you. The warden will be with you in a moment."

Another long silence ensued, as the inmate tried not to think about his hunger or his misery. No matter what the Warden said, he knew that he would have to travel back down four flights of stairs, any victory ultimately his loss.

A deep voice startled him out of his reverie. "So, you're the man who missed his breakfast," said the warden, the convict's file in his hand.

"Yes, I am."

"I've reviewed your file. Despite your disability, there is no reason for you not to get to your meals on time. You've been issued crutches to accommodate your condition." He paused to study the old man's appearance. "The major of the guard tells me you claim to have fallen on your way to breakfast. Something about your crutches slipping on the wet concrete. Is that correct?"

"Yes, sir."

"Well, you know that is impossible. Those crutches are specially designed to resist slipping on wet surfaces. If you really did fall, it can only be because you were negligent in their use. Do you agree with that?"

During a moment that seemed a lifetime, the old man was forced to decide whether a meal was worth the humiliation of admitting to a wrong he had not committed. All he wanted was a meal. But if he did not agree with the warden, he knew he would not get his meal. If he did agree, he knew he would also be eating his own pride.

"Yes, sir," he said without hesitation.

"Good, good. I'm going to approve your request for a late break-fast. But rest assured, I will be closely monitoring your conduct in the future. I will not tolerate carelessness or lateness. You will eat with all the other inmates. Do you understand?"

"Yes, sir."

"Very good. You report to the steward's office. He'll give you a late pass to the dining hall."

The long, hazardous descent down four flights of stairs afforded the old man time to reflect on the events that had just transpired. He asked himself, "Why did I humiliate myself for that meal? They'll serve lunch in a few hours. I wouldn't have starved. Why did I do that?"

Suddenly, his crutches slipped and sent him tumbling down the final flight of stairs. He lay face down on the stairway, his crutches several feet below, knowing he would have to crawl down to get to his crutches and then to his pass. Then it struck him why he had agreed with the warden, who he was, and what he had become.

He decided not to move. Not to eat. Not to do anything. Then he remembered the bitter scent of coffee that had managed to lift itself up and out of the major's garbage.

TOMORROW'S MODEL INMATE

Until recent times, corporal punishment was the preferred method for correcting an intemperate will. Conformity, obedience, decency, and even morality were understood to be lessons learned best by physical means. The criminal justice community, having adopted this punitive model for the rehabilitation of convicts, operated its prisons as schools for felons and errants, whose good citizenship could be instilled through the creative and liberal administration of corporal punishment.

Gradually, a more enlightened science emerged that acknowledged the brain as the master of intentional behavior, thus making good citizenship a lesson learned best by mastering the mind rather than brutalizing the body. As a result, prison administrators began relying less on inflicting pain and more on conditioning minds. The criminal justice community eventually abandoned the crueler, less productive punitive model. This reform redefined the old system of enforcing obedience by physical means to develop new ways to break and bridle stubborn minds. Nightsticks, whips, straps, chains, and body blows were replaced by psychiatrists, psychologists, brain surgeons, medication, electric shock therapy, and solitary confinement. Following the precepts of B. F. Skinner's functional behaviorism, once used to teach Bible for the salvation, redemption, and rehabilitation of convicts, prisons were now turned into Skinner Boxes—complete with mazes, bells, whistles, carrots, and the occasional stick.* If Skinner could teach chickens how to play tic-tac-toe, after all, then prison administrators could certainly teach convicts how to be law-abiding citizens.

Seduced by science's reputation for infallibility, the criminal justice community applied the means of a functional behaviorism model toward the end of rehabilitating convicts, relying on the expected but as yet untested success of this new psychological model. The folly of applying this means to an end became apparent with the realization that the complexity of human behavior could not be manipulated in the same manner or degree as the behavior of chickens and laboratory rats. The criminal justice community, not known for taking risks, deserted the functional behaviorism model, which left prison administrators not only without the means of an effective model but also without the guidance of a unifying end. America's prisons were soon cast adrift into uncharted waters without the benefit of either compass or rudder.

This state of affairs, in my view, has led to the near universal use of prisons as little more than warehouses for convicts. Until a new prison management model is adopted, one that includes a unifying purpose, such tools as super-max prisons, solitary confinement, mind-altering drugs, psychologists, and psychiatrists will continue to be used for the limited purposes of inducing inmates to behave during confinement. The question of whether prisoners can be forced to behave through the use of medication and close supervision, thereby transformed into good citizens, is of little interest to prison managers who have adopted by default the more limiting end of facility and political expedience.

Because psychological manipulation and chemical inducement leave no visible evidence of injury, prison managers have been allowed to inflict more punishment on the mind than on flesh and bones. Mental and emotional suffering, yet to be recognized as legitimate grounds for inmate grievance, have left convicts without recourse to object to indiscriminate attacks on their psyche.

This is not to suggest the existence of some common conspiracy or plot to mentally torture inmates but to offer an explanation of why in the past three decades the criminal justice community has limited its prison management efforts to warehousing inmates and abandoned

---

* Skinner, B. F. 1976. *About Behaviorism.* New York: Vintage.

the development of such socially beneficial methods as rehabilitation. Men and women passing through prison systems today find themselves required to do little more than obey the many rules heaped on them. The goal of contemporary prisons has been severely limited to manufacturing convicts, training them over the years to live relatively orderly lives within the community of an overly policed warehouse.

Although convicts have always been subject to the detrimental impact of institutionalization—passivity—the purposelessness of prison management has accelerated and deepened this process by venturing into the unregulated business of applied psychology and psychiatric medication for the single-minded purpose of crowd control. Freed from the burden of any rehabilitative goals, prison managers have settled into the less complex, less expensive task of making "better inmates" out of hardened convicts.

The question of whether fashioning a better inmate proves to be a boon for society or a blueprint for insanity remains unanswered, left for the future to decide. Until then, I can only pray for the salvation of Cherokee, Kareem, Tony, the young kid, the old man, and many other victims of this crowded warehouse. I continue to hope that society will come to realize that most human beings are redeemable, so that all those who are incarcerated might be spared the unpleasant fate of being reformed into tomorrow's model inmate.

18

Interview with Judge Richard J. Nygaard

EDITORS' NOTE

Judges must sentence some offenders to prison. That is the law. This commentary by one judge is included here because he developed his ideas partly in reaction to this book. We learn here that officers of the court may have many reservations about current sentencing policies and correctional practices.

Judge Nygaard speaks with authority about our growing penal system and the ease with which we, as individuals and as a society, have come to live with prisons that operate as destructive human warehouses. His suggestion that prisons might be compared with toxic waste dumps is both startling and illuminating.

PRISONS AS I SEE THEM

An Interview with the Honorable Judge Richard J. Nygaard of the Third Circuit Court of Appeal

When I became a judge over two decades ago, my sense of frustration with the sentencing of offenders began almost immediately. I felt that I was "shoveling sand against the tide," that there was something terribly wrong with our entire system. And I felt powerless to facilitate real change in anyone who appeared before me for sentencing. What was needed, I thought, was a tough, no-nonsense approach. I was quite content to think that each person has a free will, and that each person was free to choose to commit or not commit crimes. This is what our system is based on, and I worried little that it also may be the reason for our system's failures. In short, I was content with the maxim "If you do the crime, you do the time."

That impression did not last, however. It began to change, as I learned about the real world from which offenders came; as I saw the real milieu into which I sent them and the communities to which they would someday return. At some point, I would have to reevaluate it all. Most particularly, I found my inner self in conflict with my professional action and the law itself, forcing me to rethink my most basic beliefs with respect to the criminal law. With that, a fascinating journey began for me.

First, I began to look at what prison does and is doing to the people I send there. Raw statistics indicated that something was seriously wrong. If our schools had more than 50 percent failure rates, then we would surely turn elsewhere for our education. If our physicians used nineteenth-century practices, losing more patients than they saved, then we would look elsewhere for our care. As I talked with offenders whom I had incarcerated, and others with whom I had become acquainted through my prison visits, I was appalled. Although many professionals within the penal system struggle mightily to make something productive out of it, all too many have simply given up. Prisons, which began as penitentiaries (places to do penance), have become human warehouses. Beneath it all, these warehouses are evil places, populated in substantial percentages by people whose evil is not sufficiently controlled; and being staffed by "watchers" who are insufficiently "watched" to prevent them from harassing or emotionally, even physically, tormenting their charges. The result is predictable: Prisons are rife with uncertainty, fear, and their concomitants—anger and violence. They are like hospitals infested with diseases, bacteria, and viruses. And, they are turning out damaged goods.

Second, I began to wonder what exactly prison does to us, to society. The way we treat our fellow citizens is a reflection of our self-worth, serving to create our self-image. I suggest that with respect to both sentencing and prison, we must ask ourselves, "Is our action a negation or an affirmation of our own humanity?" Are we proud of what we are doing? If it is not an affirmation, if we are not proud, we should seek to change it. Positive change is well within the range of possibilities, but only we can make change probable.

Our nation has become incredibly skilled at tracking, capturing, processing, and confining criminal elements within our communities. It is staggering how effectively and efficiently—almost seamlessly—our supercharged incarceration machine has swelled over these past two decades. There are now over two million citizens housed in prisons and jails across the nation. This is up from about three hundred thousand when I became a judge. Moreover, there are tens of millions more "graduates" who have been excreted from the belly of the beast to live tentatively among us, hopefully trying not to become part of the grim statistics of recidivism.

A most astonishing and unsettling aspect of this contemporary movement to uproot and relocate a large percentage of citizens into prisons is its explosive growth amidst little to no resistance from the displaced or their families and friends. Apparently, along with becoming experts at incarcerating citizens, as a society we have become adept at suppressing that cherished noble American spirit that would resist captivity at any and all costs. This success at incarceration has uncovered an unsettling reality: Most offenders will silently resign themselves in submission to the largest, most sustained government displacement of people for the purpose of incarceration that this nation and the world has ever experienced.

I must confess my own initial apathy to the fact that such an enormous undertaking was being so effectively, efficiently, and bloodlessly carried out. Not for long, however. Some outlaw spirit within me, some rebellious fire in my belly that covets personal freedom and liberty, was anguished, unsettled, and concerned that the incarceration supermachine has encountered so little resistance to its insatiable appetite for imprisoning human beings. The reality that most people will accept incarceration without protest leaves me praying for, wondering about, and concerned for the continued vitality and viability of the freedom and liberty that I have grown to idealize and worship. Today, it may just be one of "them." Tomorrow, it may just be one of "us."

To date, the debaters of crime and punishment have generally been bifurcated into those who believe that convicts can be healed of their criminality and those who believe that convicts must be punished into absolute and unconditional obedience. Since most everyone is either a victim of crime or of the criminal justice system's war on crime, it has become difficult and at times impossible to objectively debate differing strategies for the treatment of the convict class. As a result, the question of whether prisons go about curing or punishing has mostly depended on whether the majority relates to convicts as "victims of crime" or "victims of the criminal justice system." Which one are you? What about victims of society that never got a chance?

Recently, in this postmodern age of advanced technology, a third possibility intruded itself into the long-standing feud between those who would cure and those who would punish convicts. Locking away offenders indefinitely suddenly became an achievable possibility, and the warehousing model soon became the most widely used and accepted penological purpose in the nation. The broad-based acceptance of this warehousing model can be attributed to its seductive logic, winning over even the most devoted proponents from both the cure and punish camps.

The "honey-trap" logic of the warehousing model goes something like this: Since we have yet to develop an effective treatment against criminal behavior, the most logical thing to do is to quarantine criminals until an effective cure or punishment for crime can be developed. In addition, by safeguarding our law-abiding citizens from the malice of disruptive elements, we will be more willing and able to seek and develop a more effective treatment or cure for crime. This is the "leper colony" approach. Once banished, these social lepers are easily forgotten, and society finds it easier to embrace apathy, even antipathy, toward these social pariahs.

Everyone wants to be safe and secure in their homes and communities. Hence, this warehousing model seems to promise the next best thing: keeping known criminals far away from society. I myself accepted this seemingly foolproof logic. As I watched the ominous silhouettes of prisons rapidly defining our nation's landscape, I did not object. As laws were changed and enacted to make it easier to put more people in prisons for longer periods of time, I did not object. As more and more of my tax dollars were diverted for the use of building and maintaining prisons, I did not object. Stubbornly, I continued to hope that warehousing criminals meant increased safety for my family and myself. Behind it all, though, I suspected that I was ignoring a greater truth.

That truth is now becoming known to me: The warehousing model does not make anyone safer. If anything, it exposes us all to certain harm as a result of the false sense of security it provides, benignly inhibiting our resolve to discover real and lasting solutions to the problems of crime. By following this warehousing model, we are simply covering the cancerous lesion with a bandage, while the sore underneath insidiously continues its deadly progress. To better understand this fact, consider the following comparison:

Think of criminals as fifty-gallon drums of toxic waste, inexplicably and unavoidably produced as a by-product of some manufacturing process that your company is engaged in. Consequently, as your company prospers, more drums of toxic waste are produced. Because no agent has yet been developed to reuse or neutralize this toxic by-product, your waste management specialist has limited operations to collecting and storing each filled drum in a secure containment facility located in the most remote outpost of your community. Yet, you continue to face the problem of the continued management of future toxic waste drums.

As a result of the continued prosperity and expansion of your company, there has been a dramatic increase in the amount of toxic waste drums being filled. Over the years, as more toxic-waste containment facilities have to be built, any new one will have to be built closer to populous areas of your community. The number of waste-containment workers needed to operate and maintain these facilities has grown so dramatically that the cost of operating and maintaining them has required an increase in product cost.

Most important, you are now informed that because there has been no research and development in synthesizing an anti-toxin to these by-products, no matter how well you store the toxic waste, there will come the inevitable, unavoidable catastrophes that result from toxic spills and contamination, affecting our waste-management employees and endangering the community surrounding the containment facility. Aggravating this situation is the fact that because there is no antidote for the toxic waste, this threat will most likely spread unabated throughout your community.

Given this scenario, you commission a study to recommend new waste-management strategies. You receive the following recommendations:

1. Continue to warehouse the toxic waste in the current manner and double the amount of toxic waste you store at every facility, thus reducing costs by 50 percent and reducing the short-term need for the construction of new facilities.

2. Invest money in the development of more efficient, secure, super-warehousing facilities that will hold more waste, use fewer employees, and keep toxic spills locally contained.

3. Invest money in the development of a neutralization process that can eventually end your reliance on waste warehouses and make the growth of your enterprise less hazardous to your community.

The first two suggestions clearly do not eliminate the danger inherent in either the manufacturing process or in the warehousing of toxic waste. They only make waste storage less expensive, while delaying the likelihood of a catastrophic and contaminating spill. The third solution is the only one that holds out any promise for real, sustained, and long-term safety from the toxic substances.

As you consider this example, think about what is happening every time a bigger and better prison is built that promises nothing more than warehousing inmates indefinitely and inflicting upon them more severe punishment. Would you consider it reasonable for a waste manager to pay good money to have people shake up a drum of toxic waste, making it even more dangerous before releasing it to the community?

No? Neither would I. Yet, that is what is happening to prisoners in our mushrooming, understaffed institutions.

If I wish to be truly safe, I must apparently invest in developing an antidote to the toxic by-product being produced by our growing, prospering community. More important, I must invest in developing a way to break down toxic waste into its elementary components, so that I may make productive use of them again. This means that we must conduct research and require prison managers to direct their efforts and resources toward correcting convicts rather than tormenting them. Consequently, we must staff our facilities with persons who care about the by-product (convicts) they store and want to neutralize their dangerous propensities.

If no antidote, treatment, or cure exists, then we will be no better or worse for trying to discover them. However, if cures do exist, if treatments are effective, if antidotes can be used, and we do not try to discover and use them, or if we do not seek to apply them, then we condemn ourselves to the inevitable human equivalent of toxic waste spills—the release of more dangerous individuals into our communities.

PART III

OP-ED

EDITORS' NOTE

Victor Hassine presents several opinion essays that express his critical view of the prison system. Unlike the material presented in the first two sections, each of these op-ed chapters is intended to argue a point. Whether readers agree or disagree, the author offers his authentic perspective on some of the most pressing problems facing American prisons today.

19

Prison Overcrowding

EDITORS' NOTE

Prisons have always been crowded, as Victor Hassine notes. Under the best of conditions, prisons offer tight spaces to their reluctant inhabitants. Today, most prisons are filled well beyond their original capacity, thus becoming overcrowded.

The declining quality of life in our prison systems is the subject of this chapter. Hassine describes vividly how daily details of domestic life are radically affected by overcrowding, setting in motion destructive forces that will spread out from every cell to affect the very character of life in contemporary prisons.

WHAT IS OVERCROWDING?

Prison overcrowding is a much overused term to describe an aggregate of related conditions that plague prisons all over the country. Despite its overuse, it is seldom explained in graphic terms that students and lay people can fully grasp. Instead, it is depicted as a vague, generalized "social problem"—a euphemism for the extreme, hopeless, horrifying, and tragic conditions that truly exist. The blood and guts of what prison overcrowding is *inside* and what it really does to the insiders remains an enigma to most outsiders.

The thin but durable veneer of this euphemism was poignantly revealed to me by a fellow inmate as we sat on the crowded bleachers of a crowded yard in a very overcrowded prison. After reading a newspaper article on the topic, he spat a plug of tobacco on the ground, turned to me, and said: "These people keep blaming everything in here on overcrowding. It's overcrowding this and overcrowding that. Well, who the hell *is* this guy that's overcrowding us, anyway? And, if they know he's causing all these problems, why the hell don't they lock his ass up?"

His comment was more than just an angry sarcasm. It suggested some fundamental questions: What *is* prison overcrowding? What impact does overcrowding have on the experience of imprisonment?

FIRST CAME CROWDED

As the term implies, prisons must have been crowded before they became overcrowded. Crowding in prisons was planned; overcrowding was not. Since the early 1800s when penitentiaries were first built, the one aspect of prison design that has survived is the practice of housing as many inmates as possible in the smallest cells possible, while meeting their minimal needs using a minimum of staff.

When I first came to Graterford, I entered a very crowded place supported by a very controlled, structured system designed to confine a mass of inmates, yet provide for them in the most economical way. Years of prison riots, reform, trial and error, design innovations, common sense, and just plain luck have brought about an evolution of prisons into a system of 1,700 men responding to klaxon bells, obeying orders, and traveling in unison down a tried and true maze of day-to-day prison existence.

THEN CAME OVERCROWDED

With the arrival of that "guy" who was overcrowding us, suddenly nothing worked right. Our lives became a daily challenge to avoid injury and stay out of trouble, which left us little time to reflect on the errors of our ways. In essence, the penitentiary evolved into a ghetto.

Once its prison population exceeded design capacity, Graterford became overcrowded. This numerical imbalance forced officials to institute double-celling or barracks-styled housing to accommodate the surplus population, despite the fact that the prison's cellblocks were not built for that kind of traffic.

While much can be argued about the psychological and physical dangers of squeezing two men into a poorly lit, poorly ventilated, bathroom-sized cell, the true evil of overcrowding has very little to do with crowded living space. Human beings, if they must, can and have lived in caves and tunnels. The destructive nature of prison overcrowding stems from the fact that it came unplanned, and was imposed on a system specifically created to discourage the confinement of too many inmates in one place.

Suddenly we inmates found ourselves at odds with our own rigidly designed environment. Furthermore, while inmate populations skyrocketed, the hiring of staff to support them did not increase proportionately. In Graterford and in many other prisons, the hiring of treatment staff (e.g., teachers, counselors, vocational instructors) was in fact frozen—while an endless number of illiterate and needy inmates stormed the prison gates.

OVERCROWDING AS A PERSONAL EXPERIENCE

As an inmate confined to one Pennsylvania prison or another since 1981, I have experienced what overcrowding has done, is doing, and threatens to do. By the mid-1980s, I was fairly well into my prison routine, working, obeying, and vegetating. I had a single cell, and for better or worse the prison system was functioning at an adequate level.

Then one day, my cell door opened and another man was shoved inside. My world was suddenly turned upside-down.

My first argument with my new cotenant was, of course, over who got the top or bottom bunk. Then we fought over lights on or lights off, hygiene habits, toilet-use etiquette, cell cleaning, property storage, and whose friends could visit. Then there was missing property, accusations of thievery, snoring, farting, and smoking. As these arguments raged on every day, new ones would arise to make things worse.

Since the prison staff was somewhat taken by surprise by this sudden overpopulation, there was no time to plan or screen double celling. Inmates were shoved together solely on the basis of race, age, or cell availability. Nor did an inmate have any opportunity to screen potential cellmates. If you didn't voluntarily find someone to move in with you, one would be picked for you at random. This practice immensely compounded the problems associated with doublecelling. It was bad enough living with a stranger in such close quarters without having to worry about whether he was a Jeffrey Dahmer.

As my day-to-day struggle with my cellmate became a fact of life, I realized just how much this guy, Mr. Overcrowding, was causing me serious problems in every aspect of my prison life. As the next chapter shows, the possibility of one day waking up to a cannibal beside me, while certainly a cause for alarm, proved to be the least of my concerns.

20

Mr. Smith Goes to Harrisburg

EDITORS' NOTE

Victor Hassine shares further thoughts on crowding and how this pernicious condition not only makes daily life more difficult and dangerous for prisoners but can blind correctional administrators to the underlying faults in the prison system. Only when officials are called on the carpet and ultimately removed from the system, in Hassine's experience, do they see the problems of the prison systems in an objective fashion. By then, however, they are out of a job and unable to implement any of their newly found insights.

As I mentioned in earlier chapters, I entered the State Correctional Institution at Graterford (SCI-Graterford) in 1981. I expected to find myself in a rigid, structured environment designed to deter and punish. I hoped to discover that inmates were, in fact, being coddled in prison as the papers and TV so often reported. In any event, I believed everything was under control and that my prison home had a definite purpose and end. But within the first few weeks I realized something was very wrong. The prison was massively overcrowded. Fights were breaking out everywhere, the sale of drugs and contraband was rampant, and it seemed as if everyone was carrying a weapon.

After only three months I watched a man in the cell across from mine burn to death in his cell. The solid steel door of his cell was locked but I could see him through the fixed glass window at the top of his cell door. His muffled screams for help and his banging on the steel door could be heard as smoke squeezed out of some narrow openings in his cell. It took some time for the guards to isolate and respond to his cries. As the smoldering man was finally carried out of his cell, I remember telling myself, "I had better never need any help in this prison."

About thirty days later, with the image of the burning man still on my mind, the prison was locked down while inmates with pistols and shotguns had a shootout with state police in a botched escape attempt turned hostage taking. As the drama played out over the next few days, I stayed in my cell watching heavily armed state policemen rushing past, back and forth, pursuing armed inmates. "My God, how did these guys [prisoners] get guns?" I asked myself and that is when the panic set it.

In the months and years following the hostage crisis at SCI-Graterford, things got more violent, more uncontrolled and even more crowded. I was in such a continuous state of panic that I stopped being scared and became desperate. I lived every moment as if it were my last and I began to believe I would never survive. I watched as inmates beat and stabbed other inmates and guards alike. I also watched as guards beat inmates. I watched as gangs of inmates robbed and stole with impunity while staff smuggled in contraband for sale on the black market. Rapes were common as were sexual contacts between inmates and staff members. Then there were no less than three riots in a twelve-month period, all precipitated by electrical failures that caused black-outs on the housing blocks at times when all cells were unlocked.

In 1984, I filed a conditions of confinement suit in Federal District Court for the Eastern District of Pennsylvania, *Hassine v. Jeffes*, 896 F2d 169 (3rd Cir 1988). It was my way of banging at the window and screaming for help. But like the all-too-common nightmare scene in a low budget "B" horror movie, no one around could hear my loud cries for help. The judge listened intently (or so it seemed) to a litany of abuse and neglect, but in the end all he heard was the Department of Corrections (DOC) claim that everything was under control and that they would spend some $40 million in capital improvements to make things right. The judge accepted the DOC's promise to repair and ruled in favor of the DOC.

In the summer of 1986, three months after the trial, I was transferred across the state to the SCI-Pittsburgh. SCI-Pittsburgh was one of the first Pennsylvania state prisons forced by crowding to begin double-celling inmates in 1983. My suit at SCI-Graterford delayed doublecelling in that institution until 1988, so when I arrived at SCI-Pittsburgh it was in fact more crowded than Graterford. Also, Commissioner Jeffes had caused to be constructed a 500-cell Federal style housing unit right on the grounds of the existing SCI-Pittsburgh main yard. The plan was to move all the inmates into the new units and then tear down the old housing units to make room for a new yard. Unfortunately, the DOC never did tear down the old cellblocks, so 2,100 men lived in space designed for 1,000—with no exercise yard.

Violence and despair were a way of life at SCI-Pittsburgh, and corruption had become institutionalized. My first day at SCI-Pittsburgh I witnessed a lieutenant beat an inmate over the head with a blackjack right in the middle of the cellblock. Thirty days later there was a riot. The auditorium was set on fire, two guards were seriously hurt and many inmates were beat and/or raped. I witnessed many atrocities that demonstrated to me that human beings can very easily revert to prehistoric savagery.

After the riot, things only got worse. In 1987, I filed another conditions of confinement suit, *Tillery v. Owens*, 907 F2d 418 (3rd Cir 1990). At the Tillery trial in 1989, there was testimony revealing that crowding had produced daily living conditions so extreme that the judge found that SCI-Pittsburgh violated the constitutional ban against cruel and unusual punishment. Nevertheless, the DOC continued to claim that everything was under control. The judge appointed a master to oversee court mandated repairs that totaled more than $70 million.

In January of 1989, the random violence of SCI-Pittsburgh hit me. I was mysteriously assaulted and nearly killed by another inmate. I was hospitalized for three months and then transferred to yet another institution—SCI-Camp Hill. Camp Hill was considered the jewel in the DOC's crown. It was a fenced institution that loomed adjacent to the main offices of the DOC. In fact, one of the upper story conference rooms in the DOC had a large picture window that overlooked all of Camp Hill grounds.

It was during my first day at Camp Hill that I met Richard C. Smith, who was then the deputy superintendent of operations at the prison. He was the youngest man in Pennsylvania history to be appointed to the position of deputy superintendent. A ruddy, stocky man, he worked his way up through the ranks, starting as an entry level correctional officer I in 1977. His meteoric rise to power promised him the possibility of a commissionership sometime in the future.

I spoke, in depth, several times with Deputy Smith and he never hesitated to tell me that he neither liked me nor wanted me in his prison. He told me I was just a manipulative inmate crying wolf for attention or sympathy. Further, he assured me he ran a tight ship and he did not want me to start any trouble. He rejected my claims that it was the conditions and not me that had cost the DOC so much money in repairs, and he certainly did not want to hear my claims that the prison system was so crowded that it was effectively out of control.

Mr. Smith transferred me to SCI-Rockview in August of 1989, unwittingly sparing me the consequences of one of the greatest catastrophes ever to hit the Pennsylvania DOC. Rockview is a medium/minimum security prison that was considered at the time the Allenwood of the Pennsylvania state prison system—a comfortable place, by prison standards. As I lay in my cell still recovering from my serious injury (sustained at SCI-Pittsburgh) and adjusting to my most recent transfer, I began to think about all the prisons I'd been in and all the prison managers I'd met who, like Mr. Smith, portrayed me as the problem. I knew that until Mr. Smith, and men like Mr. Smith, acknowledged that there was a serious problem with the functioning of their prisons, they would never be motivated to fix the problems that plagued their prisons.

Nineteen eighty-nine proved a particularly disastrous year for the Pennsylvania DOC. In March of that year, a small riot broke out at Rockview, then in October a small riot broke out at SCI-Huntingdon (Pennsylvania's most secure walled prison at the time). Then on October 25, a little more than a month after Mr. Smith had transferred me, Camp Hill, erstwhile pride of the system, had the largest and most costly riot in Pennsylvania prison history. Camp Hill housed about three thousand men at the time and for four days the inmates controlled the whole institution. Hundreds of angry and desperate inmates burned down buildings and destroyed property. Many inmates and guards were savagely beaten and raped. The prison was almost completely destroyed before the Pennsylvania State Police managed to regain control.

Shortly after the riot, Mr. Smith was fired, bringing his promising career to an abrupt end. On February 21, 1990, the Pennsylvania Senate Judiciary Committee conducted an open hearing to investigate "Recent incidents at Pennsylvania State Correctional Institutions." Mr. Smith was asked to come to Harrisburg to give sworn testimony at the hearing.

In a diatribe lasting some 162 pages, Mr. Smith attempted to explain why the riot was not his fault and why his firing was not fair. Instead, Mr. Smith, for the first time ever, gave an insider's view of what was really happening in the DOC as overcrowding caused the prison system to race out of control. Mr. Smith graphically and methodically outlined incident after incident of corruption, violence, drug dealing, and incompetence of his former DOC bosses, coworkers, and subordinates. These shocking and sometimes horrifying accounts gave outsiders a real understanding of how overcrowding changes each and every aspect of a prison system. However, one should never forget that if Mr. Smith had not been fired, he would have continued to keep his secrets in accordance with some mafia-like vow of silence that binds correctional folk together. He only decided to share his experiences with the public after he felt he had been jilted.

21

Prison Rape

EDITORS' NOTE

What if the prison walls could talk? Would the corridors of a prison tell us that prisoner-on-prisoner or staff-on-prisoner sexual abuse is an exceptional occurrence or a systemic problem? Would the cells say that sexual assault is an one-time spontaneous, impulsive act or is it planned and repeated? If you could really listen, would you hear the bars tell you that any sexual act between prisoners or between prisoners and staff, whether overtly coerced or apparently consensual, is still a rape? Would the walls that shield us from prisons tell us that prison rape is not our problem?

No matter what our convictions are about the prevalence of prison rape, the fact is that rape does happen in prison. The problem of prison rape needs to be acknowledged, understood, and treated because it is a public safety matter. Take physical health for instance. Most research shows that inmates entering all levels of the correctional system have higher rates of disease, longer histories of disease, and more injuries than the general population. Every day, prisoners and staff face a risk of transmission of HIV through contact. The reality is that most prisoners will at some point be released, and our goal should be to ensure that those released from prison do no harm. Those prisoners who become sick while doing time return to society not only with a wounded heart, a perception that "I must be bad if I'm treated badly," and lack of human dignity, but with a risk of transmitting deadly diseases to their loved ones. At the end of the shift, correctional officers may bring home not only work-related stress but more important a risk of transmitting a deadly disease to family and friends.

Ignoring prison rape is pure ignorance and a recipe for the silent but deadly spread of disease beyond the walls and concertina wire fences we think—or better, hope—keep the prison separate and apart from the larger society. We think prisons are not a part of our world, but we're wrong. The problem of prison rape, moreover, goes beyond physical health concerns. Prison rape is a crime whether perpetrated by prisoners or correctional staff. The prevalence of sexual assault in prisons and other correctional facilities is not fully known nor clearly understood, but the numbers of reported assaults are high. In the collection of data from correctional facilities, the Bureau of

Justice Statistics (BJS) found 6,241 allegations of sexual violence in prisons and jails reported in 2005, up from 5,386 in 2004.* These statistics represent only reported sexual assaults. Surely this is just the tip of the iceberg.

To address the problem of prison rape, on September 4, 2003, President George W. Bush signed into law, S 1435, the "Prison Rape Elimination Act of 2003." The act requires an annual accounting of sexual assaults, an analysis of the effects of sexual assaults, and the development of information, resources, recommendations, and funding to protect individuals from prison rape. Under the law, BJS is analyzing the incidence and effects of prison rape in adult and juvenile corrections facilities including both prisons and jails. The National Institute of Justice (NIJ) has funded research in areas including the impact of sexual victimization in corrections, risk assessment and prevention, and medical and psychological effects of prison sexual victimization. The law also called for the appointment of a three-member review panel to help identify individual and system traits associated with prison rape, a National Prison Rape Reduction Commission, and finally the development of national standards related to prison rape.

The subject of sexual assault behind bars is a dark, unexplored corner of prison life that is now slowly coming to light. Historically, prisons have been exposed to periodic public scrutiny, usually after scandalous conditions are revealed in the public media. At present, the spotlight is on prison rape. Prisons are opening up the gates and exposing the problem of prison rape. Correctional facilities are forced to acknowledge the problem of prison rape and do something about it.

No one wants to face the ugly image of prison rape. We are ashamed that such a thing exists in a country dedicated to "justice for all," including our prisoners. But despite the myriad reasons to look away and ignore the problem, correctional administrators have been forced to take steps to better understand prison rape and to better protect the prisoners under their care. Prison administrators are in a difficult position. The more they hold prisons accountable for prison rape, the worse prisons and indeed the entire corrections profession looks to the general public, who only know of prisons through the popular media, which all too often exaggerates the failings of our penal institutions. We even see slogans and articles on the Internet that stereotype corrections staff and prison administration by presenting cases of sexual assault with slogans like, "Be a Guard, Get a Prisoner as a Sex Toy," or "Inmates' Coercion Makes Sex a Currency." These are gross distortions.

---

* U.S. Department of Justice. Bureau of Justice Statistics Special Report. Sexual Violence Reported by Correctional Authorities, 2005 (Washington, D.C.: GPO, 2006).

Victor Hassine offers us an insider's view that, while not minimizing the problem of prison rape, helps us place the problem in a more balanced perspective. He takes us on a journey through the pathways to inmate-on-inmate and staff-on-inmate prison rape. On this journey we are exposed to the dynamics of the prison culture and predator/victim relationships. Hassine remarks that staff prison rape is "not nearly as common as inmate-on-inmate rape," in part due to underreporting rooted in fear of retaliation. Numbers don't present the whole picture but the BJS study noted earlier reported that fully 38 percent of alleged sexual abuse incidents involved staff sexual misconduct.*

R ape is no longer a random act of violence that occurs occasionally in prison: it is now a common event behind bars, across all facilities. Few inmates today are free from the fear of rape. The strong and the weak, gang members and loners, cautious inmates and reckless ones all are potential victims of violent, uninhibited inmates in violent, overcrowded prisons. Sexual assaults are so pervasive in correctional facilities today that they have become unspoken, de facto parts of court-imposed punishments.

The culprit behind the explosion of prison rape is prison overcrowding. With overcrowding, prison rape has evolved from an unspeakable act of depraved violence into a key strategy in the fight for dominance, complete with its own sophisticated techniques. In the process, prison rapists have been elevated from the status of degenerates into shrewd predators admired for their tactics.

THE RISE IN PRISON RAPE

Since the late 1970s, the nationwide prison population has more than tripled. (In Pennsylvania the population has more than quadrupled.) Prison managers have faced the immediate concerns of housing, clothing, and feeding the flood of men, women, and even children who were suddenly being sent to prison. Meeting these basic human needs continues to be a daily challenge for prison administrators, who find themselves without the necessary resources to maintain adequate living conditions, let alone to protect inmates from each other.

In an effort to reduce the skyrocketing costs of operating overcrowded prisons, state legislatures have imposed fiscal restraints on

---

* Department of Justice. *Sexual Violence Reported by Correctional Authorities, 2005* (2006).

prison spending, often including hiring freezes. As a result, the inmate-to-staff ratio in most prisons has increased. This reduction in prison employee hiring has significantly contributed to the increase in violence that now plagues many prisons.

Administrators found themselves forced to implement untested inmate management practices and procedures to deal with overcrowding. One of the most significant and disastrous of the new policies was the practice of putting two or more inmates in a prison cell specifically designed for single occupancy.

But even with double celling, administrators could not meet the confinement needs of an ever-growing prison population. As a result, recreation areas, such as gymnasiums and day rooms, were converted into dormitories for the barracks-style housing of inmates. Once called "temporary" or "emergency" measures, double celling and dormitory housing have lasted for so long that they have become standard prison practices.

The reluctance of prison managers to abandon the practice of double celling and dormitory housing does not entirely come out of necessity. In the short run, these emergency measures greatly reduced per-inmate housing costs. If it cost twenty thousand dollars a year to confine a single person in a single prison cell, confining two people in the same cell could cut costs almost in half. In the long run, though, these savings might be illusory. Double celling and dormitory housing breed violence, disease, and lawsuits, drastically increasing prison medical and legal costs.

Once the decision to double cell was made, prison managers began to develop practical means to determine which inmates would be confined together. Again, pressure compelled administrators to take "temporary, emergency" measures that overlooked the long-term consequences of their actions. This time the order went out for inmates to find their own cellmates. Those inmates who failed to find a cellmate were randomly double celled. If an inmate refused to double cell, he was taken to the Hole until he consented.

Administrators never considered how these policies could become a boon to prison rapists. Sexual predators inadvertently were allowed to pick their victims and to rape them in the privacy of their own cells! Once he "turned-out" his victim (slang for getting the victim to submit to his fate as a jailhouse whore), the rapist was free to find a new cellmate to attack. Administrators are helpless to stop prison rapists because it is too costly to hire enough staff to watch each double cell and dormitory bunk.

The problem is compounded because victims of rape are reluctant to report the crime to authorities. This silence spares cost-conscious prison officials the expense and the burden of investigating and prosecuting incidents of prison rape. Rapists are thus virtually handed licenses for their attacks.

Recent inmate employment policies have compounded these problems. Before overcrowding, every able-bodied inmate was required to work. But when prison administrators found themselves with more inmates than available jobs, the policy of total inmate employment was modified. Current prison policy defines inmate work as a privilege that only the deserving are entitled to receive. A large percentage of inmates have been left idle and impoverished as a result of this new employment policy. The practical consequence is the creation of a large underclass of unemployed and desperate inmates, who engage in endless mischief in order to generate income and keep busy.

Prison violence, and especially rape, thrive in this climate of chronic double celling, dormitory housing, unemployment, lax security, poor facility design (blind spots) and poor management. In prisons today, rapists have their free pick of victims.

THE NEW VIEWS OF STAFF AND INMATES

It appears that prison staff members have recently relaxed their attitudes about the rape of inmates. Some staff members now seem to view prison rape as a part of the punishment risk that lawbreakers take when they commit their crimes. Others see it simply as retribution carried out on an interpersonal level if a homosexual gets raped, staff may believe that she or he deserved it.

Some officials view prison rape as a type of sexual gratification, in a violent environment where sex is usually denied. Others believe that one inmate raping another is simply a reflection of every inmate's moral depravity. Pragmatic prison officials probably see rape as an effective management tool that provides potentially dangerous inmates with sexual gratification, while at the same time pitting inmates against each other.

Whatever their beliefs, it is likely that the inability of prison staff to prevent rape has led to greater acceptance of the crime. Prison managers no longer consider the prevention of rape to be an important priority.

Among inmates, some interesting changes in prison slang suggest that views about rape have become more tolerant. The terms "pitchers" and "catchers" currently are used to refer to sex partners in prison. Because pitchers take on the "masculine" role by sodomizing other men, they consider themselves heterosexual. Derogatory names like homo, faggot, or queer now apply only to the "feminine" catchers (willing or unwilling victims of sexual predators). This change in prison slang not only protects the prison rapist/pitcher from the stigma of homosexuality, it also shows how the modern practice of prison rape has changed how inmates think.

I do not mean to imply that every new inmate in prison is going to be raped or become a rapist. Many men in prison today say that "whether a man pitches or catches, he is still playing ball," which means that they want to maintain a conventional heterosexual orientation, despite the pressures of prison life. (The primary release for these inmates is masturbation, still the most common sexual outlet in prison.) But it is true that prisoners are becoming the victims of prison rape in increasing numbers and that prison administrators appear to be unable or unwilling to bring an end to this kind of violence.

VICTIMS WHO REPORT PRISON RAPES

Inmates who have been raped by other inmates seldom report these crimes, mostly because of the way they are treated by prison officials. Prisons are not designed to administer justice; the primary job of prison administrators is to maintain order and discipline while preventing escapes. Therefore, when a victim reports a rape to prison authorities, both the victim and the rapist will immediately be locked in isolation under different statuses (protective custody for the victim; disciplinary custody for the offender). Despite these different statuses, the victim and the offender get the same basic treatment.

Prison administrators very seldom initiate criminal prosecution against an inmate rapist. Local prosecutors are reluctant to indict prison rapists unless there is overwhelming proof of guilt. The victim's word alone is rarely enough to warrant criminal prosecution. Because the victim is often a homosexual and may have been friends with the offender, the rapist's defense that he had the victim's consent is difficult to overcome. As a result, prison rapists usually suffer only prison disciplinary sanctions for their crimes.

Pending an internal investigation, both the victim and the rapist will remain in isolation. The investigation can take weeks or even months. If sufficient evidence is uncovered to support a finding that a rape occurred, then prison disciplinary proceedings will be initiated against the rapist.

Rapists are tried before a prison disciplinary hearing officer. Inevitably, the rapist will protest his innocence or claim that the incident was nothing more than a lovers' quarrel. Rapists found guilty by hearing examiners will receive several months to over a year in disciplinary custody. The length of confinement will depend on how brutal the rape was and whether there was any indication that the incident might have been consensual.

Victims who were violating prison rules when they were attacked (for example, using alcohol or drugs or being in unauthorized areas) might find themselves cited for infractions. Sometimes victims will be kept in isolation as a test of their honesty. Prison administrators believe that rape victims who are telling the truth will not protest being locked up until the incident is fully investigated. Officials consider those who complain and demand to be released from protective custody as nothing more than jilted lovers who brought false accusations against old flames to settle grudges. In any event, after reporting the rape, the victim is likely to remain in protective custody for weeks or even months.

Occasionally, either the rapist or the victim will be transferred to another prison. But more often, both will eventually be returned to the general population in the prison where the rape occurred. No matter where he ends up, the victim will have to deal with the stigma of being labeled a snitch (for reporting the rape to authorities) *and* a mark (for being raped). The victim likely will be the target of numerous other prison predators. Furthermore, the assault may become part of his "jacket" (or permanent prison record), for the world to see what another man did to him. Meanwhile, the rapist will not suffer any stigma at all, and may even enjoy an elevation in his prison status for his violent reputation.

THE TACTICS OF PRISON RAPE

The victims of prison rape are almost always inmates. Cases where prisoners rape staff members are rare, although staff sexual misconduct is not uncommon. Even during prison riots, guards are seldom raped; rapes that occur in riots generally involve prisoners taken from protective custody, especially snitches, debtors, and homosexuals. Furthermore, officials deal with prison rapes differently, depending on who the victims are. While the rape of an inmate is trivialized, the rape of a staff member is considered a serious felony.

Gang bangers often rely on rape in prison to generate fear and to maintain power over the general population. While street gangs use gunplay and murder to gain power, prison gangs use the threat of rape to dominate inmates and to ensure the repayment of even small debts.

Some prison gangs require new inmates to commit rape as a gang initiation ritual. The act of raping another inmate is viewed as a way for gang members to demonstrate courage, strength, and cunning.

Inmate-on-Inmate Rape

Strong-Arm Rape.   Strong-arm prison rape is employed by violent sexual predators. What this rapist looks for in a mark is someone who is young, attractive, feminine-looking, frightened, physically weak, and a loner or a "fish" (a newcomer to prison). Loners and fish are good targets because they have no one who will come to their defense. Victims can be heterosexuals or homosexuals, but jailhouse virgins (who've never been sodomized) are preferred because rapists can boast about turning them out.

Some strong-arm rapists stalk marks until they catch them in isolated parts of the prison. Others attack marks early in the morning, when most inmates' cells have been unlocked for breakfast. (This time is chosen because some inmates, especially fish, sleep through breakfast. If the rapist is lucky, the mark will be caught asleep in his cell, or at least won't be fully awake.) Strong-arm rapists generally act alone; those who attack in gangs enjoy watching victims repeatedly sodomized.

Most strong-arm rapists fear identification, so they often wear masks and/or ambush victims from behind. Some strong-arm rapists use blankets to cover victims' heads when they attack them (prisoners call this a "blanket party"). Others club their victims on the back of the head, knocking them unconscious to avoid detection.

Particularly violent strong-arm rapists keep their marks conscious during their attacks, sometimes challenging them to "fuck or fight," because they derive pleasure from overpowering struggling victims. The more the victim squirms or cries out in pain, the more enjoyment the rapist experiences; an unconscious victim provides little excitement. Some strong-arm rapists force marks to look at their attackers and to watch the attacks, boldly displaying their power over victims.

Extortion Rape.   Extortion rape is very common in prisons today. It is effective because it exploits the addictions of many inmates while taking advantage of the inability of officials in overcrowded prisons to control the trade in contraband.

Extortion rape is committed by common jailhouse hustlers, such as drug dealers, bookies, and loan sharks. Potential victims are the customers of the rapist's prison hustle. Even when it isn't actually practiced, the threat of extortion rape is often used by gang members and lone prison merchants as a tool to force the repayment of debts.

The rapist learns all he needs to know about his victim during their business dealings. The ideal victim for extortion rape is a drug-addicted, physically weak inmate who is unable to pay his debts and is not aligned to any prison gang. Like strong-arm rapists, extortion rapists are equal-opportunity offenders, preying on both heterosexuals and homosexuals.

The tactic of extortion rape begins when the rapist presents himself to the eventual victim as a dealer in prison contraband. The rapist typically offers to sell the mark cigarettes, drugs, or hootch at going prison rates. If the mark doesn't have the cash to pay for these goods, the jail-house hustler/extortion rapist will advance him credit, at an interest rate of two for one (meaning two dollars are owed for every one dollar that is advanced). The extortion rapist will continue to advance the mark credit for contraband, letting interest debts roll up rather than insisting on repayment. When the debts become too large to repay, the rapist asserts his control by physically beating the mark when his demands for repayment go unmet.

Assuming that the mark still cannot cover his debts, the extortion rapist will cunningly require him to perform some service to offset part of the loan. Should the mark refuse, he will be beaten again. The rapist usually forces the mark to work off his debt by smuggling drugs into the prison through the visiting room. This can be easily accomplished by putting one of the rapist's friends on the mark's visitation list. When this friend arrives, the mark will be given contraband, which he smuggles into prison by inserting it in his rectum. This is a crucial step for the extortion rapist: Not only has he forced the mark to engage in a serious criminal act, he has compelled him to penetrate his anus with a foreign object. This brings sodomy close to the victim, although he still has no idea what is about to happen.

For a while, the rapist will use the mark as a "mule" to smuggle drugs, still selling him contraband on credit. Eventually, though, the mark will be raped as a punishment for his failure to repay debts. The extortion rapist will dismiss the seriousness of the attack, rationalizing that coerced anal sex is no worse than using one's rectum to smuggle drugs.

After the first rape, many more follow. Through a combination of physical force, shame, and addiction, the mark is transformed into a sex slave. Eventually, the extortion rapist will sell the mark's body and services to anyone willing to pay.

Because they have participated in drug smuggling, victims of extortion rape seldom report the crime to prison authorities. Snitching would land the mark in protective custody, where he couldn't satisfy his addiction to drugs or to hootch. Once they have been repeatedly violated, most victims of extortion rape would rather accept their status as prison whores than face drug withdrawal alone in an isolation unit.

Date Rape. Double celling, dormitory housing, and inmate idleness have contributed to a surge in consensual homosexual activity in prisons today. This has brought about inmate courting rituals that can result in date rape.

Courting in prison occurs when an inmate contrives to be in the constant presence of a homosexual inmate. The two are seldom seen apart, accompanying each other to meals, yard, work, and anywhere else possible. The ultimate goal of the inmate-suitor is to become cellmates with his love interest, so they can live together as an exclusive couple.

The courting process is initiated in prison as a means to show sexual attraction. Courting also announces to the general population that a romance is brewing and that other suitors should stay clear. Courting serves to identify the couple as homosexual.

Prison date rapists take advantage of these courting rituals. Because they desire sexual gratification through the physical domination of victims, these rapists use romance as part of a trap designed to snare prey. Date rapists target physically and psychologically weak inmates who, they hope, won't report the crime. Unlike strong-arm and extortion rapists, though, date rapists only attack homosexuals. Prison date rapists are con artists who specialize in deception, not violent predators who work in the medium of brutality.

Often the date rapist begins to court his mark by lifting weights with him or by engaging in some other physically demanding sport. The date rapist does this under the guise of helping the mark to stay in shape or to ward off strong-arm rapists. During the weight-lifting sessions, the date rapist will demonstrate his physical superiority over the mark. This is a crucial part of the rapist's plan because it begins the process of establishing his physical and psychological dominance.

During the courting process, the date rapist will systematically isolate the mark from other inmates, looking for a suitable time and place to commit the rape. Afterwards, the mark is abandoned, while the rapist boasts about his conquest to the general population. This exposes the mark to even more danger and humiliation.

A deep sense of shame generally prevents the mark from reporting the crime to prison authorities. Even if the mark decides to report the rape, he seldom can counter the rapist's defense of consent.

Confidence Rape. Confidence rape in prison is similar to date rape because the rapist sets up his mark by gaining his trust. Unlike date rapists, though, confidence rapists derive perverse pleasure from turning out mostly heterosexual victims.

The confidence rapist usually picks his mark from among fish, who have little or no prior prison experience. The typical victim is a young, physically weak, frightened inmate, not aligned with gangs. The rapist first approaches his mark by pretending to offer assistance. Typically, this assistance involves warning the mark that other prison predators are planning to attack him. The rapist convinces the mark that he despises all forms of prison violence, and he offers protection out of his sense of "honor." The confidence rapist often will convince some of his friends to threaten the mark in his presence. Of course, the rapist will come to the mark's rescue, chasing away the attackers. This staged event not only establishes trust between the rapist and the mark, it also demonstrates the rapist's physical dominance over the mark.

The confidence rapist will claim that he is the only true friend that the mark has in prison. If the mark is a Christian, the rapist will pretend to be the most faithful disciple in the cellblock. (The rapist would claim to be Italian if the mark liked spaghetti.) This is all part of the plan to isolate the mark from other inmates so that he becomes completely dependent on the assistance and the friendship of the rapist. Gradually, the mark will become paranoid and reclusive, distrusting all other inmates. During this period, the rapist and the mark will constantly be in each other's company. Most other inmates will assume that the two are courting, although the mark won't know this because of his isolation.

Eventually, the rapist will get the mark to invite him into his cell or, better still, convince him that the two should double cell together. Once they are together in a cell, it is just a matter of time until the rapist strikes. Victims of confidence rape usually are too scared to report the attack, and even if they do report it, the rapist's defense of consent will be difficult to overcome. Of course, once other inmates learn about the mark's reputation for weakness, he will be the target of other rapists.

Confidence rape is so common in prisons today that it has inspired the conventional wisdom that convicts must immediately punch strangers in the face when they offer any form of assistance or help.

Drug Rape. This is a variation of confidence rape that involves drugs rather than fear to trap marks. Here, the rapist develops a tight drug relationship with the mark. The two take drugs together and usually traffic in drugs. A strong bond forms between the rapist and the victim, based on a common addiction and a shared financial interest.

Eventually, the rapist will convince the mark that the two should double cell together to further their enterprise. One day the mark will get so high on drugs or hootch that he passes out, and the rapist then strikes. Sometimes the mark won't even realize that the rape occurred. Those who know they've been raped rarely report the crime because prison officials will claim that they sealed their own fate by dealing drugs.

Staff-on-Inmate Rape

While staff-on-inmate rape is not nearly as common as inmate-on-inmate rape, it has devastating results because of the enormous power that prison officials wield over inmates. Staff-on-inmate rape is seldom reported because victims fear retaliation, and because staff members refuse to acknowledge the incidents.

Strong-Arm Rape. Staff-on-inmate strong-arm rape occurs when a prison staff member overpowers an inmate and rapes him. Most victims of the crime are openly homosexual. This form of rape rarely occurs in the general prison population because of staff members' fear of detection. Instead, strong-arm rape occurs in disciplinary or protective custody units, where staff members can corner prisoners in complete isolation.

These assaults appear to be the result of the sexual impulses of rapists, which suggests that some prison staff members are homosexuals. The preferred victims for these assaults are inmates who have no personal or written contact with friends or family outside the prison. Because staff members have access to personal files, they can easily identify the perfect inmate-victims.

Authority-Rape. Like strong-arm rape, authority-rape occasionally occurs when homosexual staff members are physically attracted to inmates. Generally, inmate-victims are homosexuals, but this isn't always the case.

Sometimes the authority-rapist uses his power over inmate-victims to offer privileges—preferred work details or special visitation rights—in exchange for sex. At other times, rapists deny entitlements, such as positive parole reports, until victims agree to have sex. Some offer not to write-up inmates for disciplinary infractions in exchange for sex.

In these situations, it is often difficult to know for sure if staff members are taking advantage of inmate-victims or if inmates are using sex for special privileges. Regardless of the willingness of inmate-victims, any time staff members use positions of authority to grant privileges or entitlements in exchange for sex, a rape has occurred.

Surrogate Rape.   Unlike staff strong-arm or authority-rapes, surrogate rapes aren't products of sexual drives. These rapes occur when prison staff members punish inmate-victims by having them "set-up" for rape by other inmates. Surrogate rapists approach a known inmate sexual predator, offering immunity from punishments and special privileges if he will rape selected inmate-victims. These rapes can occur in the general inmate population or in isolation units.

Surrogate rapes are seldom documented in prisons because of staff conspiracies of silence. The victims of surrogate rape are often inmates convicted for particularly repulsive crimes, such as child-molesters, or inmates who have filed official grievances or law suits against staff members.

A PERSONAL ENCOUNTER

One thing that I've learned in my many years of incarceration is that prisoners constantly search for weaknesses that they can exploit in other inmates. Since rape is a tactic that the strong practice on the weak, it should be no surprise that some prisoners use the threat of sexual assault to test the strength of others.

Over my years of imprisonment, I've been propositioned for sex several times. Brushes with sexual assault are sometimes so subtle that fish may not immediately know that they've been sexually approached. As one prisoner put it when I interviewed him for this chapter: "Every convict's been 'cracked-on' (sexually propositioned), whether he knows it or not. And any man who says otherwise is either lying or he just don't know what time it is."

I was "cracked-on" the first day that I arrived at Holmesburg County Prison (in Philadelphia) in 1980. I was terrified as I entered Holmesburg, wearing street clothes that were drenched in perspiration. I remember that my own odor added significantly to my sense of fear.

Two guards led me into a holding room, where I encountered a powerfully built inmate who stood at least six feet five inches, and who weighed at least two hundred and fifty pounds. This man's name was Sherman, and he impatiently asked me what size clothes I wore. After I told him, he disappeared silently into a hallway.

The lone prison guard who supervised the room ordered me to strip, so when Sherman returned with my jail uniform, I was completely naked. As I quickly dressed, Sherman swaggered over to me, until he towered above me. As he glared down at me, he told me in a deep, gruff voice that jail conditions were dangerous and that if I requested to be his cellmate, he would "look out" for me.

Overcoming my fear, I forcefully refused Sherman's offer. At the time, I thought that Sherman was simply trying to bully me and extort money. It didn't occur to me until later that he was pressuring me for sex. I've since learned that many sexual approaches in prison do not involve threats or violence.

I sometimes shudder to think what may have happened to me if I had been so intimidated that I accepted Sherman's offer for protection. I was strong enough to pass this test of weakness, along with others that I've endured in prison. For inmates who fail these tests, prison becomes one long ordeal after another in a never-ending nightmare. Because over 90 percent of these victims will be released back into the community, the nightmare of prison rape inevitably haunts us all.

22

Inmates and Officers

EDITORS' NOTE

Prisoners and their keepers have little in common. Yet as Victor Hassine notes, routine personal relationships between prisoners and correctional officers are an important component of the larger social system within prisons. Prisons run primarily on social control, which in turn requires relationships. When prisons are overcrowded and understaffed, social control is compromised, because the relationships that hold a prison together are compromised. When relationships among officials—line staff and upper level staff—are marked by conflict, security is compromised and prisons become more dangerous places in which to live and work. Officers may retreat, leaving inmates to fend for themselves, or turn to snitches to maintain order, encouraging inmates to turn against one another to curry favor with the staff. Either approach is destructive, setting in motion a process that corrupts daily life in the prison and promotes violence.

When I first entered prison, I was surprised to discover that there was no open hostility between guards and inmates. As a matter of fact, many inmates and guards went out of their way to establish good relationships with each other. Inmates befriended guards in the hope that they would get such benefits as an extra phone call, special shower time, or the overlooking of some minor infraction. In turn, guards befriended inmates because they wanted to get information or just to keep the peace and make it through another day without getting hurt.

From what I have observed, most guards who have been attacked were attempting to enforce some petty rule. Over time, guards have learned that it doesn't always pay to be too rigid about prison regulations. Thus, an unwritten agreement has been established between inmates and guards: Inmates get what they want by being friendly and nonaggressive, while guards ensure their own safety by not strictly enforcing the rules. For the most part, inmates manipulate the guards' desire for safety, and guards exploit the inmates' need for autonomy.

By the mid-1980s, things changed with overcrowding and the influx of new prison subcultures. Administrators could not hire new guards fast enough to keep pace with the flood of inmates, so the practice of overtime was employed. Any guard who was willing to work overtime could get it, with the result that on any given day a large percentage of guards were on overtime. This phenomenon had the immediate impact of introducing many exhausted, irritable guards into the work force, often on shifts with which they were not familiar.

These two factors virtually destroyed all sense of continuity and uniform treatment that the prison had established over the years. The most important element needed to maintain a workable relationship between inmates and staff is a continuity of treatment. Disturb the inmates' expectation of that continuity, and you destroy the delicate balance between them and the staff.

A tired, overworked guard on an unfamiliar shift tends to be unwilling to offer any assistance. Being a stranger to the unique inmate hierarchy of his newly assigned unit, he is unable to conform to longstanding customs and practices. This often spells disaster, as once workable relations between keeper and kept deteriorate into anger, distrust, and even hatred. This breakdown in relations inevitably provokes an upsurge of violence.

There is an even more insidious consequence of excessive overtime that undermines inmate and guard relationships. In every prison there is a percentage of guards who are so rigid and unpopular with inmates, or so incompetent, that they are given work assignments that keep them away from contact with prisoners, such as tower duty or the late-night shift. Any prison administrator of intelligence knows that these kinds of guards can jeopardize the tenuous order and operation of a prison. With the advent of unlimited overtime, however, these guards have found their way into the prison mainstream. As expected, their presence has further exacerbated an already tense and uncertain environment.

The overexposure of tired, irritable, overworked, and sometimes inexperienced and antagonistic guards to the population has created an inconsistent and unpredictable prison environment, especially because guards know much less about what inmates are thinking, and vice versa. With all the new inmates coming in and out of prisons every year, it is becoming increasingly difficult for the staff to keep track of who is who and who is doing what, and even harder for a prison security force trying to employ traditional investigative and intelligence methods. In the old days, everyone knew each other in a prison and knew pretty well what everyone else was up to. Not so today.

The only way the security system can effectively operate in a prison today is by soliciting the services of snitches. Guards maintain a legion of snitches and openly advertise that fact to the inmate population. To keep their informants in force, prison administrators have gone overboard to reward and protect them. Their rationale is that every informant constitutes an unpaid member of the security force that helps to compensate for understaffing. This almost exclusive reliance on informants for information and intelligence creates several conditions, including:

1. Keeping the inmate population at odds with each other over who is the informant in their midst.

2. Elevating snitches in the prison hierarchy, since they are often rewarded with the best jobs, highest pay, and best living conditions.

3. Increasing the growing antagonism between long-term inmates and parole violators, who are more likely to become informants to gain early parole and relative comfort during their brief stay in prison.

4. A proliferation of drugs entering the prison, as informants act as conduits for drug smuggling while looking for information.

5. Providing prison administrators with distorted images of inmate activity, as informants become less credible the more they are used.

This last condition often occurs because an informant is pursuing his own interests and therefore will only inform on those activities that do not affect his particular business. Such self-serving information is only as accurate as the informant needs it to be. Sometimes it is a fabricated reflection of what he knows the administration wants to hear. Thus, many informants provide the kind of information that sacrifices the truth to conform to some pre-existing view. To use a classic example of this, I knew an ambitious guard in 1983 who told me he used his overtime to ensure himself a more substantial pension benefit. (In those days, pensions were based on the three highest annual salaries rather than on base salary.) So he worked double shifts seven days a week for three years. But as a result, he became useless. He was either too listless and irritable or falling asleep all the time. To convince his superiors of his efficiency, he would reward informants who gave him information that he could use to issue misconducts. Consequently, his informants were in turn able to operate a massive drug and homosexual prostitution ring under his protection. Administrators ended up buying a nickel's worth of information for thousands of dollars' worth of corruption.

Another example involved a prison murder. One day in the yard, two inmates fought over drugs until one of them was stabbed to death in plain view of dozens of witnesses. Subsequently, the prison security officer received numerous notes from inmates wishing to give eyewitness accounts. This enabled the authorities to quickly identify the culprit. But the informants all gave self-serving details of the crime and its motives, until there were so many contradicting versions of what happened that all their testimony was rendered worthless. Without enough evidence, the state was forced to offer the murderer five to ten years in return for a guilty plea. Such a sentence for a murder committed in a public prison yard is so lenient that it could be considered a license to kill. This failure of justice on the part of the prison administration was precipitated by its exclusive reliance on unreliable informants.

The end result is that today's prisons have become even more violent. Inmates do not trust each other, because informants call the shots and even initiate or encourage most of the crimes they report. Guards are overworked and increasingly alienated from the mainstream of prison life. And finally, a new breed of criminals—young, violent, ignorant, drug-addicted, and completely self-absorbed—is pouring in and leaving even the most veteran inmates and staff scared to death.

23

In Search of the Convict Code

EDITORS' NOTE

"Honor among thieves" is a romantic notion sometimes applied to convicts. Based on his experiences, Victor Hassine holds few illusions about the prison as a place or about inmates as a community. He finds no credible code of conduct but much posturing by inmates, who assert their dignity and honor in a world where these traits are virtually nonexistent. He makes the insightful observation that calling oneself a convict is like covering oneself with tattoos; it suggests a fierce identity but often is in fact a mask to make oneself a less likely target for predators.

Criminologists have studied the convict code and described it as a powerful force in prison affairs. Hassine's observations suggest, however, that this line of research may be futile. The real codes of conduct, he argues, are imported from the outside world, as suggested in the seminal work by John Irwin (see The Felon*), then translated into the coin of the prison world (as explored by Hans Toch,* Living in Prison*). Something resembling a convict code, which is unique to prison, only exists when officials have lost control of the prison and a "Kingdom of Inmates" has been established. This is not to say that inmates don't share an understanding of the prison world that allows them to communicate with one another, when necessary to the exclusion of staff. Prisons have various cultures within them, and inmates are aware of those cultures in varying degrees; staff members, for the most part, are left out of these worlds and the exchanges that occur within them. Hassine's point is that codes of conduct in prison are fragile, sometimes ambiguous and always situation bound. For any outsider, it is difficult to ascertain whether pronouncements about a prison code of conduct are real or fictitious.*

He had his hands cuffed behind his back as he was shoved along by two flanking prison guards, a third walking in front of him and a fourth trailing behind. This was a common sight in prison, so aside from looking to see if I recognized the man bound for the "hole," I went about my business. Moments later, I heard him shout to anyone who might be listening, "That's right, I ain't no inmate—I'm a convict, motherfuckers! You can't just treat me any way! I'm a convict!"

On hearing this proud announcement, I was able to conclude (quite accurately as it turned out) that this man probably had some inmate trouble over a debt or a possible retaliation, so he committed a public infraction calculated to make himself look "tough." Perhaps, he provoked a fight with someone or threatened a guard, making sure that he was caught and taken immediately to the hole, where he could safely await a transfer to another prison, far away from his troubles. Then, as soon as he arrived at the new prison, he would display the misconduct report he had received to every convict he could to mislead them into thinking: This was a tough, stand-up kind of guy.

One class of convicts, those who at every opportunity vehemently proclaim their staunch adherence to the "Convict Code," are predatory informants. They spend each day soliciting inmates to trust them or getting them involved in illegal activities so that they can harvest information to sell to prison staff. These predators often brandish a stern, lawless version of the Convict Code to lure new arrivals and gullible convicts into a false harbor of trust, tricking them into thinking they are safe to reveal confidences, plots, and secrets.

When I first arrived into prison, one of the initial conclusions that I reached was that the existence of the much touted Convict Code of conduct was only an ennobling myth used to affect and obscure the true nature of a convict's intentions or character. My prison experiences have taught me that honor and human decency are learned and that these fragile things need constant relearning and reinforcement; that no lofty sense of humanity automatically substitutes our selfishness with some inherent dignity that requires us, even under the harshest of circumstances, to behave as "noble beasts" ultimately bound to do the "right thing."

When that escorted inmate loudly proclaimed himself a convict, he was actually using a shorthand expression to identify himself as an adherent to this fictitious Convict Code of honor. Every time a fellow convict tries to convince me that he is a proponent of this code of conduct, I have no choice but to assume that he is trying to deceive me. Contrary to common knowledge, most inmates and the majority of prison staff who participate in this collective ruse publicly claim the existence of a Convict Code, abided by since bygone days, even though they know that it never existed.

To test my understanding of the Convict Code, I drafted a questionnaire and distributed it to twelve of my fellow inmates, all of them varied in age, sentence, race, and experience in prison. Though I am familiar with each of them, I never before spoke to them about the Convict Code. The following are their individual responses:

Convict Code Questionnaire Results

		1 Inmate Code: Yes/No	2 Difference Convict/Inmate: Yes/No	3 Code Followed: Yes/No	4 Conditions: Too Hard/ Too Easy/OK
Age Sentence Time in	32 Life 2 yrs	Yes	Yes	No	OK
	37 15–20 yrs 15 yrs	Yes	Yes	No	Too Hard
	40 Life 2 yrs	Yes	Yes	No	Too Hard
	76 15–40 yrs 3 yrs	Yes	Yes	No	OK
	34 Life 10 yrs	Yes	Yes	No	No Answer
	30 13–29 yrs 10 yrs	No	Yes	No	OK
	41 7–14 yrs 2 yrs	No	No	No	OK
	20 2.5–10 yrs 3 yrs	No	No	No	OK
	40 4/5–10 yrs 8 yrs	Yes	Yes	No	Too Hard
	25 Life 6 yrs	Yes	Yes	No	No Answer
	22 5–10 yrs 2 yrs	Yes	Yes	Yes	OK
	24 1.5–5 yrs 3 yrs	Yes	Yes	No	OK

DESCRIBE WHAT YOU THINK THE CONVICT CODE IS AND WHAT IT MEANS?

"It means to distinguish the oppressors from the oppressed."

"At one time, yes, there was. It involved the cooperation of everyone, including guards to protect what rights inmates had. I say guards, because if they tried to involve themselves in taking away what freedom we had, their lives were either threatened or taken without hesitation. And if you even appeared to be part of what these guards represent, the same would happen.

"Before all these rules were in place, the D.O.C. [Department of Corrections] would think twice about taking away something that would threaten us as a whole, because it would cause even greater problems for them."

"(1) Not to be a rat. (2) Watch those backs who would watch yours. (3) Reputation of not being chumped out is important. (4) Not associate with people who always talk to guards. (5) Keep your enemies closer than your friends."

"The code I was taught isn't really followed anymore but consists of, basically, if you want to stay outta trouble, don't gamble, do drugs, and don't mess with queens. Mind your own business and don't trust anyone. A lot of people in new jails such as this don't really follow any code. Now the code is basically do your programs and try to get out on your minimum."

"If you are a convict, you are an inmate of the state. The guards and any other staff that are part of your incarceration are looked at through my eyes as nothing more than white supremists, the convict code is that inmates are suppose to see anything that doesn't involve you and keep your mouth shut if you do. The code also enforces. If you're caught snitching, you get what's coming to you because nobody likes a snitch. Don't fuck with faggots or do drugs and you'll be alright. The Convict Code has changed and now people want to do their time and get out."

"The code is, stay with your own. Never be a rat."

"The inmate code is not one of intrinsic honor, it is relating more to respect and straight forwardness. One does not snitch, back bite, or fraternize with officials in a congenial or brotherly way.

"Institutions are only comprised to or in regards of what caliber of convicts it houses. Inmates that are passive aggressive, passive, and subservient in nature, are the prime recipe for officials to take back all of the basic human rights that we, the older convicts, have fought for in the past.

"I must say in closing that in regards to the Convict Code in the past, there was not a high degree of respect, honesty, or unity then. However, compared to today's standards, we were true fighters. *Respect* and *unity* are the key words here."

"Don't snitch on other convicts."

"Don't snitch; don't borrow; don't mess with homosexual; don't 'see' anything (be a witness); don't 'hear' [anything]; don't 'say' [anything]; don't gossip; watch who you walk with; don't debate PRS (politics, religion, and sports); stay away from people who talk a lot; don't trust the system (DOC, U.S. government, prison staff and policies, medical services, etc.); don't trust most of what you hear or see and research everything; don't talk with prison guards; don't disrespect anyone."

IS THERE A DIFFERENCE BETWEEN A CONVICT AND AN INMATE? IF SO, EXPLAIN WHAT IT IS?

"Semantics."

"Well, for starters, convicts were there for one another. I guess what I'm trying to say is there was a sense of honor among one another. There was no such thing as a snitch, and if you were one, you would be "taken care of." I could remember a time when my uncle made prison, in his words, look like hell, because he would explain how not only were you to prove that you were a man but you would also have to be a survivor.

"Inmates, on the other hand, have no honor, no respect. Their very existence evolves around mimicking their "so-called friends." But if their friends are involved in anything that could jeopardize their parole, they back down, especially if it involves something that will benefit everyone. These are not men, these are children."

"A convict is a person who, even while incarcerated, has the same criminal thinking that he had when he committed the crime he or she did.

"An inmate is a person who in some way has been rehabilitated and thinks different."

"A convict is one who repeatedly gets locked up over a number of years and adjusts well to prison. An inmate is one who not only adjusts well to prison but also staff members."

"I wasn't sure, so I looked both words up in my dictionary. I realized that there is a difference in the two words.

"I know now that I'm both, I was convicted by the courts and now I'm an inmate of the state. I was a convict, a person that committed crimes until I was arrested and found guilty in court, and now I'm serving time as a inmate."

"The difference is, a convict stands up for change. An inmate just goes with the flow."

"A convict is someone that demands respect from prison officials and will not tolerate pitting one convict against another. Many convicts have some sort of unity when injustice occurs by the hands of prison officials.

"An inmate is or are people that will conform or work with prison officials in efforts of causing anarchy among other prisoners. Many inmates commonly refer to the theory 'get down first.' And it is that thought process which I believe is destroying the very fabric of the basic liberties, and rights that many convicts in the past have sacrificed life, limb, and their dignities."

"In the old days, convicts looked out for each other."

Nine of the twelve convicts surveyed claimed that there was a "Convict Code," and ten agreed that there was a difference between being a convict and being an inmate. Only one out of the twelve, however, stated that he believed the code was actually followed. Those who did not believe a Convict Code was followed in practice were in fact indicating that they did not believe such a code existed in the prison world, despite claims to the contrary.

Consider the disparity in the various descriptions of the Convict Code and the differences in describing the terms *convict* and *inmate*. Apparently, not only do most convicts take no stock in an actual Convict Code but none seem to know what the code really is, was, or should be. This lack of common understanding may not have anything to do with the inherent uncertainties found in an oral code supposedly handed down over the years by mostly illiterate convicts. It may instead reflect a common understanding of the Convict Code as a myth—an ideal—for them to freely recall and recount in any way that best serves their individual interests. To prisoners, the Convict Code is a living thing meant more to create and express a sense of belonging than to dictate actual conduct.

In reality, convicts coming to prison bring with them a moral and ethical code of conduct that they learned and developed from their individual street experiences. For example, members of the Mafia bring with them a Mafioso's code, street-gang members bring their own gang code, and drug addicts bring a junkie's code of conduct. When a convict enters prison, he naturally gravitates to others who are or were part of his gang or community on the street, i.e., his homeys. In doing this, his code of conduct is likely to be similar, if not identical, to the one he must abide by within his new prison community. If a convict arrives in a prison that has none of his homeys, he will gravitate to the group that exhibits the most familiarities then adopt that group's code as his own. So in truth, prison populations do not have any single, common Convict Code but instead a collection of unique codes derived from various distinct prison groups.

As in the outside world, moral and ethical practices in a prison group are learned and acted on as a means of maintaining group identity, integrity, and cohesiveness. Thus, to the extent that prison managers are able to control the development of these groups, they can also control the code of conduct convicts are likely to adopt. When officials lose control, as when a "Kingdom of Inmates" emerged in Graterford (see chapters 5 and 22), something like a Convict Code reigns or at least receives consistent lip service.

The least effective method for preventing the adoption of an unwanted Convict Code is to punish individual prisoners for practicing such a code of conduct, since this does nothing to prevent their group from doing the same. To prevent the practice of undesirable codes of conduct, a prison administration must develop, support, and fund voluntary convict groups that attract membership and teach a more acceptable code.

The question remains, why do convicts and staff alike continue to proclaim the existence of a nonexistent Convict Code? When a convict declares adherence to some presumably noble Convict Code, he is actually declaring affiliation to a mythical group of tough, honorable convicts. To most prisoners, group identity and affiliation are a matter of survival. The more successful one is at convincing others that he belongs to a larger group, the more likely he will be able to remain off a prison predator's short list of intended victims.

A convict who declares adherence to a Convict Code or claims to be a convict rather than an inmate is a variant akin to the common prison practice of having tattoos with grotesque images of violence and death. Many convicts tattoo themselves to falsely suggest that they are part of some outlaw gang, since gang members often use tattoos to identify themselves. Displaying such an affiliation is meant to ward off prison predators. Similarly, convicts perpetuate the myth of a Convict Code as a means of suggesting affiliation with a strong, tough, and lawless group.

Staff members, on the other hand, use the myth of a Convict Code to justify their belief in their superiority over prisoners and their assumption that convicts deserve the inhuman treatment they receive. After all, staff may consider convicts to be "noble beasts" but in the end analysis, they know that beasts are beasts—not human beings. So, while a convict describes the Convict Code in a way that elevates him in the eyes of his peers, prison staff view the Convict Code in a way calculated to distance and dehumanize convicts. For example, when a convict states that the Convict Code requires him to mind his own business, he is describing a stoic adherence to brave, fearless practicality. But when guards or officials explain this same version, they portray convicts as so despicable that they will tolerate lawlessness even when it is in their power to prevent it. In the staff's eyes, the stoic convict thus becomes the cold-blooded thug.

When I find myself in a prison where convicts perpetuate the myth of a Convict Code, I know that I am in a relatively safe environment where the various convict groups have been allowed by prison staff to develop and practice their own unique inmate code. In violent and unsafe prisons, convicts must believe in and actually abide by a common code of conduct as a mutual defense against the dangerous consequences of anarchy. (As a case in point, see my discussion of the Kingdom of Inmates in chapters 5 and 22.) To explore the hypothesis that safe prisons do not promote a binding code like that at Graterford, I asked a third question of my respondents:

WHAT DO YOU THINK IS THE WORST PART ABOUT DOING TIME?

"The constant attempts at brainwashing and debasement."

"Not having one ounce of freedom."

"The hardest part is being away from those you love. Not being able to be present in their good times and bad. Life is a one-way ticket, and you can't go back to whatever you missed."

"The worst part of doing time is being away from loved ones. And the feeling of helplessness when tragedy happens or when trying to handle business on the street."

"The worst thing about doing time is being disrespected and treated like animals, cattle, mentally fucked by people that have issues and personal vendettas towards inmates."

"Being lonely."

"The hardest part is not being with loved ones. Also, the loss of basic freedom and, last but not least, being forced to live under such abnormalities."

"Separation from loved ones."

"Being here. Dishonor."

"I feel being separated from my family is the hardest part and I don't feel the D.O.C. puts enough effort into keeping us close to our families. We need more family-based programs."

"So far away from home."

"I think the worse thing about being locked up is if you have kids. It's having them grow up without you around and knowing who they daddy is. That's the worst thing for me, while doing time."

None of the respondents ident ified violence as the worst part of prison life. This is a great change in thinking from my days in Graterford, where the threat of violence was a part of everyone's nightmares. In relatively safe prisons like this one (Rockview), convicts feel little need to follow or even pay lipservice to a common code of conduct. In my survey, seven of the twelve respondents stated that prison conditions were OK and, accordingly, eleven out of twelve said the code was not followed. These results would have been unthinkable in Graterford.

A Hitchhiker's Guide to Prisons, Part I
A Study in Fear

EDITORS' NOTE

People develop a sharp sense of the world as it affects them. Eskimos are thought to have many names for snow, the French as many names for love. According to Victor Hassine, prisoners too have a finely attuned sense of one particular word—fear—that in prison follows highly identifiable patterns of change over time and circumstance.

The hitchhiker unlucky enough to land in prison has entered a kind of twilight zone in which fear is the center of existence, the engine of the penal universe. Fear in prison takes many forms: Fear that is overt, fear that is covert, fear that is planned, fear that is unplanned, fear that is physical, fear that is psychological, and fear that builds you up or tears you down. If the essential dynamic of prison life is fear, as Hassine argues, prisoners must adapt, control themselves, and control the environment. If they are lucky, and if the prisons that house them are well run, then they will settle down and open up to the possibility of change. (The prisons discussed by Hassine have very different ecologies, offering different adjustment opportunities and challenges. See Toch, Living in Prison, *and the next two chapters in this book.) Hassine relates here how offenders cope with fear, and how officials might convert a danger zone into a place where new lives can be forged without fear.*

> Crreeekk! Ch-ching-ch-ching! Ring!
> Mumble, mumble, mumble.
> Dim, dingy, hot, humid, and foul smelling.
> Slam!

No matter how often I enter a prison—for initial commitment, court return, or interprison transfer—I always experience a visceral, gut-wrenching reaction once I have stepped inside and heard the sharp, metal-against-metal report of the entrance gate slamming shut behind me. Even prior to my incarceration, when I routinely entered prisons as a criminal justice intern or law school graduate, the moment I was locked inside I experienced the same uncomfortable fear that I feel today as a prisoner.

In fact, prisons are uniquely designed to instigate fear in so many creative ways that fear has become a kind of language on its own, silently but relentlessly commanding specific inmate conduct and behavior. Prison designers and managers have developed a precise and universal alphabet of fear that is carefully assembled and arranged—bricks, steel, uniforms, colors, odors, shapes, and management style—to effectively control the conduct of whole prison populations.

Every time I look up at stacked coils of glistening razor wire atop fences around me, for example, I am being told, *DON'T TRY ANYTHING—YOU'RE SURROUNDED!* Fear is reinforced by the redundancy of steel gates and bars that warn, *THERE IS NO WAY OUT!* Unnecessary strip-searches and pat-downs that are repeated obsessively are actually reminders: *AT ANY TIME WE CAN DO ANYTHING WE WANT WITH YOU!*

The use of prison architecture to communicate fear and force to influence behavior is nothing new and certainly no secret. Consider the dark, powerful stone edifices and sinister, castle-like outlines of early nineteenth-century prisons. No one would dispute that their foreboding exteriors were meant not just for security but as a warning: *STAY OUT OF PRISON!* Such Gothic-styled fortresses were designed to serve in part as menacing billboards to frighten people into obeying the law.

Surprisingly, even with this close, historic relationship between prison architecture and the communication of fear and force, the creators of these designs seldom if ever examined the provoking effects they have on the prison population itself. Consequently, their influence is rarely credited for a fight in the yard, a rape, a suicide, a riot, or for that matter, even well-behaved inmates. Prison managers, therefore, freely explain away violent events as random or unique acts based on personal circumstances in an effort to avoid official responsibility for the fear-suffused environments they create.

My experience, however, has been that little occurs in a prison that is random or unique, and that nearly all extraordinary prison events and behaviors are common, predictable responses to the instigation of fear. Inmates are human beings who possess a biology, physiology, and psychology evolved from a keen sensitivity to danger, including the innate ability to manage or avoid things that frighten them. During my two decades or more of incarceration, little in my actions was not an instinctive response to the presence or absence of fear within my environment. The overwhelming effect of a prison's many fear-based systems weighs so heavily on inmates that, in my view, it decisively influences their conduct and behavior years after they have been released from prison.

ENGINES OF FEAR

American prisons are virtual engines of fear, driving the conduct and behavior of everyone confined in them—staff and inmate alike. Criminal justice experts and the public at large generalize about prisons in terms of extraordinary incidents that periodically occur, such as rapes, assaults, riots, suicides, and murders. Relying on preconceived notions, they make assumptions and choose recommendations for prison management from a narrow understanding of prisons based on the sum of these incidents. In reality, such incidents account for a tiny portion of the drab, day-to-day prison experience.

Every aspect of prison life is measured and managed to prevent the occurrence of anything extraordinary. As a result, our prison is not simply a cage of stone and steel but an impermeable wall of rules and regulations grounded in fear and reinforced with hundreds of staff members specifically trained to make sure that we obey every rule. To draw an accurate picture of prison life requires looking beyond its sensational occurrences and focusing instead on its dully oppressive, fear-suffused mechanical functions on a daily basis.

An honest examination of prison management would reveal that one of the great dangers of prison life is the maddening repetition of its daily routine. Too much reliance on routine can leave staff and inmates unprepared for the eventual occurrence of an extraordinary, sometimes violent event. A small minority of inmates undoubtedly needs to be restrained and controlled with strict, redundant, often dehumanizing fear. At the same time, responsible prison management should also address the following concerns: How do harsh, fear-generating systems affect the vast majority of well-behaved inmates; and do such systems, designed to correct a small minority, actually increase crime and violence within the greater prison population?

Surprisingly, the ubiquitous effects of fear-generating systems on a general population have never been studied to determine the change they produce in the majority of inmates. How prudent would it be if the medical profession suddenly required all its patients to take powerful, potentially harmful anti-cancer medication to treat the very few that might one day develop the cancer? Similarly, should prison managers be allowed to subject whole populations to the harsh, uncertain effects of artificially induced fear to prevent misbehavior and violence committed only by a very few inmates?

TOUCHED BY A PRISON

Personally, I am strongly affected by a prison system that intrudes itself directly into my awareness. Three ways by which this can occur are through a prison's design, its population and staff, and finally its administration.

The sights, smells, touches, sounds, and tastes of a prison are so terrifying that simply coming into contact with its physical components continues to have the most profound effect on my day-to-day conduct and behavior. These sensations also affect the way I feel about people and circumstances.

I have never fully overcome my fear of the prison environment, but I have managed to cope with it. However, this toleration does not include the prison environment's second intrusion: fear generated by contact with the inmate population and the staff. Waking up every day to find myself completely surrounded by unreliable strangers and superficial friends, many of whom try to appear menacing and dangerous, is an extremely unsettling, stressful experience that has affected me deeply.

In addition to fears triggered by the prison's design and its inhabitants, I must cope with the crushing weight of its administration. Living under the thumb of an indifferent, punitive, arbitrary, and tedious bureaucracy with an obsession for rules and punishment is the stuff of nightmares. Furthermore, prison administrations strive to separate, alienate, humiliate, and minimize inmates, a process that greatly magnifies all other generated fears.

The multiple levels by which the prison world intrudes itself into my psyche have frustrated my efforts to initiate any thought or action that is not first filtered through these engines of fear. As a result, my behavior at any given time is largely predicated on strategies that I have developed to cope with prison's most frightening experiences.

FEAR THROUGH PRISON DESIGN: POLICE LOCKUP

When I was arrested in 1980, I was transported by squad car to a local police station, an unimposing, two-story, white-washed cinder-block structure that included a lockup unit of less than twelve cells. The police lockup, commonly referred to as the "Drunk Tank," had no food service, clothing issue, or shower facilities and served only as a temporary detention facility for those awaiting booking and transfers to a city or county institution. Detention time in this lockup seldom lasted more than a few hours, forbidden by Pennsylvania law to exceed twenty-four hours.

A police lockup is the initial entry into the American prison system and by design subjects detainees to a barely tolerable degree of captivity. In my case, I was unaware of the full impact of initial detention because of my preoccupation with my arrest. The public nature of the arrest process—flashing lights, loud sirens, and an overpowering paramilitary police presence—had me so frightened and confused that I simply did not have the emotional reserve to muster a response to being locked inside a cell. My solitary confinement in that cell actually afforded me some quiet relief from the distress and anxiety caused by the trauma of my arrest. By design or coincidence, the greater fear of arrest far outweighed the lesser fear of captivity.

To further quell resistance to the saddle of captivity, the entry process of local lockup is designed to allow detainees to feel as if they still have one foot planted in the free world. Although a Drunk Tank cell seems like any other jail cell, its surrounding environment still has the smell, touch, and unthreatening appearance of an office. During my stay there, I was able to entertain the notion that, despite my captivity, I was still free.

The Drunk Tank was air conditioned and well ventilated, so my nose was spared the smell of unpleasant odors. As I was the only person in the lockup, I did not have to deal with overcrowding or the sight of hostile, unfamiliar faces. The ceilings were low, the lighting bright, and the colors contrasting and varied. In the background were the muffled sounds of office activity rather than the roar of prison life. All these conditions helped to alleviate my fear of captivity. The fact that I was spared a strip search and allowed to wear my own clothes was perhaps the most significant calming factors.

CITY AND COUNTY PRISONS

After several hours in police lockup, I was transported to the Bucks County prison/jail. This detention facility had the unmistakable appearance of a place that I absolutely did not want to venture into. Nicknamed the "Pine Street Motel," it bore the street-front appearance of a dark, ancient brownstone castle surrounded by a twenty-foot perimeter wall. This jail and prison held both pretrial detainees and convicts sentenced to less than two years of incarceration.

Handcuffed and flanked by two police officers, I was escorted into the interior of the castle. My perspiration and heartbeat increased as I penetrated deeper into the mouth of this monstrous prison, and I finally began to feel the mounting fear of my impending captivity.

I sensed a change in the atmospheric pressure and humidity, as I approached a rectangular cage of steel bars in the heart of the castle. This cage was the initial holding cell where all new arrivals, returns, or releases were collected, pending the processing of paperwork that would authorize their transfer to the prison population or release back onto the streets.

Several feet in front of the holding cage were the administrative offices, visibly in operation behind half walls mounted by transparent glass partitions. On opposite sides of the cage were half-lit corridors of mysterious doors and gates that greatly contributed to my fear, as I pondered their unknown purpose and destination.

Inside the cage were rows of long, narrow, backless wood benches worn smooth by decades of use and anchored to the dirty, concrete floor by steel bolts. Men in prison uniforms sat on these benches, eyeing my arrival with hard stares that unsettled me and invoked exaggerated imaginings of menacing, sadistic guards. I was convinced that I was surrounded by the most desperate, dangerous men on earth. Like myself, however, they were simply awaiting the processing of their paperwork.

Once inside the holding cell, the police officers who escorted me removed my handcuffs and disappeared behind the glass partitions. I sat on a bench farthest from the others, numb with fear, trying to collect my thoughts as I waited anxiously for whatever would happen next.

For hours, I just sat there, watching and listening to the casual daily activities of prison life. Before me, convicts, prison guards, and policemen calmly and indifferently went about their business as if I were not there. In this beehive of activity, the prison world around me seemed to grow larger than life, and I felt less and less significant, as if my identity was slowly being leached out of me. I imagined myself as some observer of a movie unspooling before me. This defensive detachment from reality, combined with the monotony of idle waiting, infused me with a sense of calm. Hence, I was able to rationally input and process information about my surroundings.

WHAT I SAW

First came the visual image of captivity: dark, dirty, scarred floors and walls; dusty, dim lighting fixtures dangling from cathedral-high ceilings; shadows from poor lighting that made distant details hard to discern; a drab colorlessness and harshness to everything in sight; the steady flow of strangers pouring in and out of corridors like some ant colony; the constant presence of stern, uniformed police and prison guards; and the unkempt, disheveled appearance of uniformed inmates. All these images were disturbingly unfamiliar. They were not only future signs of my fate but fixed environmental conditions that could not be escaped or altered. I felt hopelessly trapped.

WHAT I HEARD

Then came prison sounds to accentuate the severity of these images. A prison's "voice" is a cacophony of interminable, tortuous noises layered together at a constant pitch as pervasive as the air: loud, irritating, vulgar, and out of tune, all trapped by prison design and replayed as fragmented echoes throughout the prison.

The first layer of prison noise is a collection of constant mechanical droning from machines, motors, and engines. Layered over this is the higher pitch of sounds and voices from human activity. The final layer of noise—the loudest and highest pitched—permeates from a prison's operation: the intermittent slamming of gates, rattling of chains, and the screams of bells and whistles. This noise not only hurt my ears but interfered with my normal ability to hear sounds that were important to me.

WHAT I SMELLED

Like most built before the 1950s, the Bucks County prison had no ventilation system. Odors remained trapped inside until they found escape through open windows. Because the walls, floors, and ceilings consisted of porous stone or concrete, they were embedded with decades of decaying dirt, fungus, and bacteria that released putrid-smelling gasses to further foul the prison air.

Aggravating this condition were old, filthy mops used to clean floors, given that the Bucks County prison did not have a laundry system capable of routinely cleaning mop heads. As a result, mopping prison floors repeatedly every day to provide unskilled work to inmates actually increased the spread of dirt, fungus, bacteria, and odors throughout the prison.

Worst of all was the unmistakable stench of human waste. Like most prisons in the United States, Bucks County was overcrowded. At the time of my incarceration, in fact, it was about 300 percent over design capacity. Plumbing and waste treatment systems were grossly overtaxed and constantly broke down. On any given day, there would be an eruption of raw sewage or sewer gasses somewhere in the prison. This produced a nauseating smell that, combined with all other odors, created a noxious stench from which there was no relief. Though I eventually grew accustomed to the prison's odors, they still caused me great discomfort. At times when I breathed, I could taste the fouled prison air at the back of my throat.

WHAT I COULD FEEL

My first tactile sensations on entering the county prison were the ambient temperature and the atmospheric pressure, both unique to this artificial environment. Because the Pine Street Motel was not climate controlled, heating and cooling was supplied by a primitive, inefficient system of cast-iron steam radiators and adjustable windows. The temperatures and atmosphere created by this air system were then trapped by the walls and ceilings of the prison.

Due to the county prison's massive building design and lack of air circulation, hot air would rise up to the tall ceiling area and force cold air down to the occupied spaces at ground level. On the unseasonably warm winter day of my arrest, the holding cage was chilly and damp. Had it been summer, the place would have been hot and humid. Only on temperate spring days, when all the windows were opened, would the ambient temperature be within the comfort zone.

While I sat squeamishly in the holding cell, bombarded by frightening sights, sounds, and smells, I was shivering cold in my jacket and tie. The damp, clammy thickness of the interior's stuffy winter atmosphere nearly stifled my breath.

HOW I WAS TREATED

Despite my low-grade state of alarm, the long hours of waiting in the holding cell allowed me to settle down and feel more like my normal self. A prison's architecture of fear has its limitations: The longer I was submerged in the prison environment, the better my coping instincts adapted to it and enabled me to tolerate its fear-inducing agents.

The balance between the hostile environment and my fear management strategies was soon upset when I finally experienced the full force of the fear generated by the prison's administration. After my paperwork was completed, I became the official property of the prison staff. The district attorney had requested that I be transferred to the Philadelphia County prison, one of the oldest, most violent county penal institutions in the state and possibly the country. The law permits the housing of detainees in any facility, so long as it meets constitutional standards. Therefore, district attorneys often influence prison assignments to punish uncooperative defendants, often to encourage confessions or guilty pleas or to expose detainees to jailhouse informants.

Despite my familiarity with the system, I never suspected anything sinister about my transfer. At this point, I was taken out of the holding cell by four officers and accompanied into a small bathroom. Crowded shoulder to shoulder with them, I was ordered to strip naked. The strip-search that ensued provoked a rush of overwhelming fear so distressing that I could actually smell the secretion of fear mingled with my sweat. More than anything else, this routine administrative procedure made me feel like an *inmate*. Two of the officers were Bucks County prison guards, the other two Philadelphia County sheriffs assigned to deliver me to the Philadelphia County Prison at Holmesburg. I was ordered to get dressed then I was again handcuffed.

Thus began my transfer to Holmesburg, all performed with such dispatch and indifference that I knew with certainty now that I was nothing more than property—a prisoner of less importance than the paperwork that identified me. I remember thinking at the time that this transfer was to my benefit, since I was leaving a small, old jailhouse that looked, felt, and smelled like a dungeon, destined for a major cosmopolitan facility that certainly had to be less hostile. How wrong I was!

PRIMAL FEAR

An outsider's knowledge of prison structures, rules, and regulations, no matter how comprehensive, reveals only what ought to be, not what is in prison reality. To fully understand the prison experience requires a personal awareness of how bricks, mortar, steel, and the endless enforcement of rules and regulations animate a prison into a living, breathing entity designed to manipulate its inhabitants.

The life-giving force of a prison is its inhabitants. Like blood, they course through the flesh and bone of a prison, stimulating its pulse. The nature of this pulse is established by the collective state of mind that exists within the prison population. Daily prison life is driven by the behavior of its inhabitants, whose actions are driven by fear. The amount of fear within its physical and operational body determines the mental state of a prison.

Experience has taught me that fear always initiates some form of agitation within me. This agitation then triggers actions meant to reduce its intensity by reminding me to develop and apply fear management strategies. There are five distinct states of agitation that can be developed after a fear response. These five states identify the steady reductions in agitation, as fear becomes tolerated through personal management. The highest magnitude of agitation, always reached immediately after becoming afraid, is the "Fearful State," followed in succession by lesser levels of agitation: the "Adaptive State," "Rebellious State," "Compliant State," and "Institutionalized State." These responses to fear are explained as follows:

1. *Fearful State.* This is the most energetic and volatile level of agitation, reached on initial incarceration or submersion into any new prison environment as the result of a spontaneous fear response. If prison violence is the focus of one's fear, then it will be in this state of agitation. Everything—sounds, sights, smells, textures, and people—seems unfamiliar. New inmates will remain frightened, paranoid, and defensive until they can grow accustomed to the environment. The more complex, unstable, unusual, foreign, violent, and dangerous the environment is perceived to be, the longer it will take new inmates to cure themselves of the Fearful State.

Only after new inmates begin to adapt to the environment can their level of agitation be expected to decrease. If after this is accomplished, however, they are moved to a different environment (even one they adapted to in the past), then their level of agitation once again elevates to the Fearful State and remains there, until they have re-adapted.

2. *Adaptive State.* Once new inmates have grown accustomed to a prison environment, they become much less fearful and their level of agitation drops. They can then begin to critically access their surroundings and modify their conduct and behavior to better adapt. The Adaptive State activates "nesting" instincts. New inmates in this state maintain a high level of caution while they set about "digging in." Generally, adaptations at this level of agitation are limited to unalterable factors that affect daily life, such as fixed environmental conditions and the people who share the environment with them. Accordingly, new inmates remain compliant, obeying rules and regulations while they nest and develop survival strategies.

The level of stability, complexity, and danger that exists within the environment greatly affects the length of time that new inmates will remain in this state before they can step down to the next level of agitation.

3. *Angry/Rebellious State.* After new inmates successfully adapt, nest, and perceive that they fit in, they grow less afraid and more comfortable. This translates into feelings of greater safety, allowing them to assess conditions within the environment that include the more restrictive administrative and operational structures.

During this state of agitation, they begin to feel secure enough to express resentment and even resist environmental conditions that they perceive to be arbitrary or unfair. They often test the confines of the environment to learn the limits of their ability to affect it. Their acquired familiarity with the environment enables them to challenge the environment in a way that does not overstep its boundaries. The need to resist or challenge experienced by new inmates who have arrived at this state is actually a delayed reaction to the loss of liberty and control over their own lives.

This need is often expressed as misdirected anger arising from the lingering fear of their initial submersion into the environment. Since the architecture and people of this new environment are constants that cannot be changed, much of their misdirected anger is aimed at the administrative and operational structures, simply because these constructs appear to be vulnerable. During this state of agitation, new inmates can be expected to receive the greatest number of misconduct citations for infractions of the prison's rules and regulations.

4. *Compliant State.* Eventually, most new inmates learn to adapt to fixed environmental conditions as they discover that resistance to administrative or operational structures is futile. Once this awareness is reached, they will reduce their level of agitation by adapting completely to all aspects of the prison environment.

Complete adaptation requires the newcomer to divest himself of all preexisting strategies. Feelings of anger and fear over environmental conditions are replaced by feelings of resignation. Completely adapted new inmates cease their resistance against the environment and concentrate all their efforts on maintaining and exploiting the status quo.

At this level, anger and resistance are seldom directed at the environment but instead at anything that threatens its stability. New inmates now feel safe and secure enough to exploit whatever benefits exist in the environment, so that real learning and even reform can take place, if opportunities are available.

This level can be considered the *rehabilitation window.* It should be the goal of prison managers that their prison populations reach the Compliant State as soon as possible. To maximize the effectiveness and length of the rehabilitation window, prison managers must maintain the status quo, keep their prisons safe from violence and agitation, and provide an adequate number of reward-based educational programs. Material changes in a prison environment that interfere with the perception of safety and stability can throw a prison population out of the rehabilitation window and back into the Fearful State.

5. *Institutionalized State.* This is reached once new inmates resign themselves to complete dependence on the prison system. To attain this state, they must convince themselves that the normal administration and operation of their environment provides the only means for survival and sustenance.

In this state, prisoners actually become numb to fear. They do not exert any effort to either challenge the environment or maintain the status quo. Instead, they minimize their needs so that they are satisfied by whatever they can receive with the least amount of effort. Reaching this lowest state of agitation can be accelerated through the use of psychotropic drugs. Any reduced state of agitation below this level can only be achieved through illness or death.

The Institutionalized State is the least preferred state within a prison system, as it creates lazy, unproductive prisoners who become an enormous and continuing drain on resources without any positive results. Once released into the free world, the institutionalized often remain dependents and wards of the state.

In Pennsylvania, most inmates are eligible for release to a halfway house at the conclusion of their minimum sentences. They can then expect to spend at least one year in a halfway house before becoming eligible for parole in the free world. The anticipated change of environment from prison to halfway house normally triggers a fear response that reverts inmates back to the Fearful State. However, if the prison system has been successful at keeping its prisoners for long, uninterrupted periods of time in the rehabilitation window, then their adjustment will be quick (given a safe environment) and they will return rapidly to the Compliant State.

When inmates are finally released from the halfway house to the community, they once again experience a fear response. Because of their periods in the rehabilitation window in both prison and halfway house, however, they can quickly adapt to the new free-world environment and step down to the Compliant State. In the free world, released inmates should be better equipped to exist in the rehabilitation window if they have a good job, adequate housing, and community support, the surest sign of adaptation.

HOLMESBURG PRISON: THE WHEEL OF FEAR

Holmesburg Prison was designed by the Quakers in the mid-to-late 1800s and reflected the *state-of-the-art architecture* of its time. The Quakers had earlier developed the concept of the penitentiary, expressed through the construction of Eastern State Penitentiary, the first one ever built. "Old Eastern," as the antiquated and now retired prison came to be called, was built in the vicinity of rapidly growing Philadelphia in the early 1800s. It continued to operate as a state institution until 1969, when it was finally closed and later converted into a museum. Holmesburg Prison, an offspring of Old Eastern, mirrored its design, purpose, and operation.

The Quakers made no secret of their belief that crime was the work of the Devil, operating through the acts of misguided humans. To these Quakers, lawlessness had to be discouraged by putting the fear of God into the hearts and minds of all those tempted to do the Devil's work. As a result, penitentiaries were designed to frighten and punish sinners, at the same time schooling them in the strict ways of righteousness. The fear and punishment components of the Quakers' penitentiary system were expressed primarily through architecture, while the religious programming component was accomplished through daily inmate management.

By nightfall, I was finally transported to the Philadelphia County Prison at Holmesburg, nicknamed "The Burg." Emerging from a squad car, I stood handcuffed and helpless before the old prison's monstrous yet magnificent, dark stone walls. The gloom of that moonless night seemed to possess its stone and steel, awakening in me a sense of sinister foreboding.

Like many others in my circumstances, I would come to realize that confronting my fears meant abandoning the tillage of my past and the vistas of my future to address a present reality surrounded by threatening new possibilities. As the Burg's entrance gate slowly opened to swallow me up, I began to lose all hope with each step into the prison's belly. Only my fear and shame remained, guiding me through what I knew would be the worst, most terrifying ordeal of my life.

With Old Eastern and The Burg, the "enlightened" minds of the nineteenth century had sufficiently mastered the alchemy of fear to reach out over a span of 150 years to frighten the hell out of me with their horrific creation.

Architectural Elements of Fear

The Shape of Fear. The Burg was the shape of an octagon, at the center of which was a twenty-five-foot-tall, circular, single-story building with an arched ceiling, commonly referred to as the "center" or "control." Radiating out from the center were eight rectangular cellblocks, measuring about 450 feet long by 45 feet wide. These were circumscribed by a huge stone wall of 35 feet that connected to each of their outer extremities. From an aerial view, The Burg resembled a gigantic spoked wheel with a rounded hubcap.

Viewed from an outside street level, The Burg's many deflecting angles concealed its overall shape. The first time I saw the prison from this point of view, I was troubled by the fact that I could not fathom its appearance on the inside, as if confronted by a huge stranger wearing a mask.

Inside, each cellblock had two rows of cells running lengthwise, separated by a fifteen-foot-wide, unobstructed walkway. Each row of cells contained some sixty-five cells that measured about seven feet by fifteen feet (see Figure 24.1).

Originally, none of the cells contained running water. Sometime in the mid-1900s, each cell was equipped with toilets and sinks with hot and cold running water. Their entrance doors also used to be solid without any openings. By the time I had arrived, tray slots had been inserted into the doors. I could look out my cell-door slot to see the cells directly opposite mine.

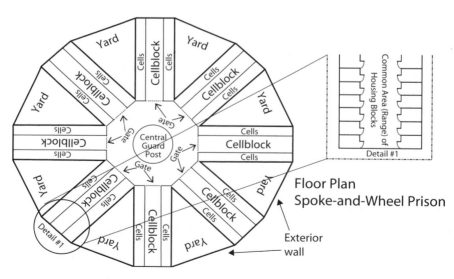

Figure 24.1 Holmesburg Prison Floor Plan

The Color of Fear.   Constructed entirely of dark stone, The Burg was a depressing world of grays and blacks, its bleakness magnified by an absence of windows. A primitive system of skylights served as the only source of natural light throughout the whole prison, each cell with one skylight and the center with a ring of them lining the rim of its ceiling.

Electric lighting was another adverse factor. The inadequate number of light fixtures in The Burg produced a perpetual gloom of shadowy, colorless twilight. On my arrival there, this constant dimness not only deepened my depression but also obscured and distorted my vision, increasing my sense of vulnerability.

Fear in the Air.   The Burg had no air exchange or circulation systems. The extremely high stone ceilings, vaulted in the cellblocks and arched in the center, trapped warm air twenty to thirty feet overhead and forced cold air to dominate the floor level. The result was a stagnant atmosphere that created a perpetually chilly, thick, smelly, and bone-aching dampness.

The Sound of Fear.   The vaulted stone ceilings also served as sound-conducting and amplification systems, causing even low-level sounds to be heard throughout the cellblocks and the center. All prison noises traveled up and along the ceiling to eventually empty out into the cavernous center. When The Burg was first built, inmates were required to serve their sentences in total silence. In this way, its system of vaulted and arched ceilings actually served as an audio-monitoring system that enabled guards stationed in the center to hear every word and sound made by inmates anywhere in the prison.

The Daily Bow Down.   One of the best examples of the Quakers' attention to detail was the unique construction of each cell's entrance. An elevated stone platform at the foot of the entrance forced an inmate to step up onto it then step down into the cell. The height of this step-up was precisely measured to ensure, that a man of average height or taller had to bow his head each time he passed through the threshold of his cell; in a sense, designed so that he must bow in submission on every entrance to and exit from the cell.

No Sleep for the Frightened.   Through out my five-month stay in The Burg, its collection of fear-inducing elements prevented me from a single peaceful night's slumber. It was always too cold, too hot, too humid, or too noisy to sleep. The perpetual shadow world that surrounded me kept me nervously awake, worrying about unseen dangers lurking nearby. As a result, I remained irritable and confused due to chronic sleep deprivation.

Consequences of Progress. The Burg was designed for single-cell occupancy under conditions of silence and solitary confinement. One of its original intentions was to enable one prison officer posted in the Guard's Station at the center to see and hear everything in all eight cellblocks. Consequently, the effectiveness of The Burg's penitentiary system depended entirely on the enforcement of silence and an unobstructed view of all cellblock walkways, so that a minimum number of center guards could easily oversee the inmates and control their activities.

By the time I had arrived, the "Open Range System" (ORS) was the preferred inmate management system in Pennsylvania prisons. ORS allowed inmates out of their cells for at least ten hours a day to socialize, exercise, or participate in rehabilitation programs. The ORS also included the double celling of inmates and an end to forced silence.

To accommodate this new system, the walkway of each cellblock was converted into a makeshift dayroom and recreation area accessible to inmates outside their cells. This resulted in cluttered walkways and noise pollution, completely frustrating the audio/visual monitoring systems at the heart of The Burg's purpose and design. As a result, the prison that I entered had many unintended fear-inducing elements caused by its antiquated technology that clearly contradicted its intended use.

Skylights. The Burg's skylights, although once considered innovative by contemporary standards, were crude and defective. They allowed inmates to occasionally benefit from natural light, but they also caused rainwater and melting snow to drip down into cells. What little heat managed to find its way into a cell would ultimately escape through the glass of the overhead skylight. While I was in my cell, day or night, awake or asleep, I was constantly rained on and a puddle of water always collected on the cold stone floor.

Insects and Rodents. The dampness and darkness of The Burg made possible an infestation of roaches and mice that had lasted for generations. The upgrading of cells to include running water exacerbated the problem with a dramatic increase in water leakage. The invasion of these insects and rodents was a nightmare like none I had ever encountered. They were fearless and huge, especially roaches that were often more than two inches long and ran on their hind legs to escape. Being awakened by a roach or a mouse crawling over me was as common as their bites on my body.

Blind Spots. With double celling and the application of ORS, walkways became overpopulated with inmates. Each housing block contained between 250 and 300 inmates. During "block-out" periods when inmates were allowed out of their cells, it became impossible for prison guards to observe or hear what was going on in the cellblocks. For a good portion of each day and night, the activities of the vast majority of inmates were completely invisible to the prison staff. Whenever one or two inmates stood at the cellblock entranceway, a routine requirement while waiting to report for work details and appointments, prison guards in the center were rendered blind to everything behind them.

Because of the dense mass of inmates on walkways, roving prison guards could never see more than a few feet in front or behind themselves. As a result, they seldom ventured far from the entrance gates where center guards could visually confirm their safety.

The first time I ventured along one of The Burg's crowded walkways, it became fearfully apparent that if I were attacked by an inmate, no guard could possibly detect it or hear my cries for help. As a consequence of this glaring inability to police the cellblocks, I not only felt threatened but I frequently heard screams for help or witnessed violent attacks on these mobbed walkways.

Prison Gangs.   Once every newcomer to The Burg realized that prison guards could not protect them, it became necessary to seek one's own protection. The easiest, quickest, and most effective way to accomplish this was to form alliances with other inmates. The necessity of such alliances usually led to membership in a prison gang.

Under these circumstances, every act of inmate violence threatened a potential gang war. Predictably, The Burg served as an arena for the daily occurrence of multiple gang wars, varying in duration and degrees of violence. This fact earned The Burg the notorious distinction of being rated one of the country's most violent prisons, as well as the nation's capital of prison rape.

The Prison Population

The idea of being surrounded by strangers automatically creates an element of fear, especially when those strangers are convicts. The Burg, nevertheless, was designed as a total-isolation, "super-max" prison where inmates could never see the occupants of adjacent cells. Under such circumstances, the emotional impact of an inmate population would have normally been neutralized, since all its members were completely hidden.

The Quakers, however, were able to extract an extra measure of fear by converting the neutrality of an invisible inmate population into a reliable fear-inducing element. They achieved this by requiring inmates to leave their cell wearing a hood over their head (hence such slang terms as "hood" and "hoodlum"), so they could not see nor be identified. Thus, these *hoods* were left to wonder who was on either side of them. In addition, the ranting of unseen inmates driven to madness within their cells lent a further element of fear.

Following the Quakers' lead, contemporary prisons have learned to use different aspects of a prison population to generate fear. Fundamentally, four such aspects in a prison population can instigate fear in individual inmates: (1) population density; (2) population composition; (3) continuity of a population; and (4) physical appearance of population members.

Population Density. Living amidst a crowd of strangers forces an inmate to be physically closer to people than his concern for personal safety would normally allow. This promotes fear because crowd density affects his ability to see what is happening around him.

Under ORS, inmates spend most of their day pressed shoulder to shoulder against one another in the narrow walkways or confined together in an undersized doublecell. This extreme population density was further aggravated by the foul scent of body odor, uninvited touching, and excesses of noise.

Composition of the Inmate Population. The demographics of a prison population (average age, offense types, past histories, time in custody, etc.) set the tone for the whole prison. For example, a population of white-collar convicts over the age of thirty-five looks and acts much differently than one composed of street-gang members under twenty-five.

Many inmates in The Burg were, like myself, only recently removed from the free world. To the "Old Heads," we were "Young Bucks still shitting street food." That is, we were still experiencing social withdrawal and had not been confined long enough to passively surrender to captivity. Resistance to initial captivity was so predictable that the prison phrase "bitting" (doing his "bit" or full sentence) was coined to express it. "He hasn't started 'bitting' yet," one inmate might say to another to explain the agitation and impatience of a new prisoner.

Life in The Burg is always feverish and hyperactive, reflecting the street behavior of its inmates. Only the prison walls could contain this constant buzz of intense excitement that seemed to border on mass hysteria.

Continuity of the Inmate Population. The thought of living in close quarters with strangers who may soon be one's neighbors, acquaintances, or even friends is less of a fear factor than living among strangers whom one can never hope to know. As one gets to know fellow inmates, confinement within a general population that remains relatively constant for long periods of time helps to facilitate one's eventual recovery from the fear of initial incarceration.

The Burg, however, had a transient general population that consisted of convicts serving less that twenty-four months, parole violators confined for weeks or months, and pretrial detainees committed for days or weeks. This hodgepodge population of "short-timers" turned over so quickly that it was impossible for inmates to know their neighbors well enough to feel safe. For me at the time, it was like being confined in a subway car during rush hour, mobs of strangers getting on and off the train at every station.

Appearance of the Inmate Population. First impressions are the ones that count, this is also inherently true of an inmate community. A prison population that is generally well-groomed, adequately clothed, and healthy in appearance seems much less stressful to a newcomer than one full of dirty, unkempt, pallid-looking convicts.

The Burg was so overcrowded and antiquated, processing so many convicts for commitment and release that access to adequate clothing, laundry, shower, and medical facilities was virtually impossible. As a result, its population looked much more menacing than it really was, because most of its members were unable to exercise good hygiene or grooming, often forced to wear worn and dirty clothes. In addition, many of the mentally ill remained untreated, walking around cellblocks with crazed, unwashed appearances.

The Prison Administration and Fear

Management by Accommodation. Everyone in The Burg, including the staff, were concerned about their own safety. Because prison guards on the front lines never ventured far from a cellblock's entrance gate, they rarely enforced the rules against inmate violence. As long as they themselves were not assaulted or endangered, all cellblock activity was negotiable, resulting in prison management by accommodation.

Such accommodations included allowing contraband into the institution, turning a blind eye to gang activity, and tolerating violence. Consequently, the response of guards to threatening situations was virtually indistinguishable from that of convicts. This behavior did not stem from corruption or greed but from a state of extreme, unrelenting fear that had made accommodation a necessary tool of survival.

Rules and Regulations. The Burg, like all other prisons, provided a long list of rules and regulations. But overcrowding, understaffing, and high inmate turnover made it difficult to maintain a routine system of informing inmates of these rules and regulations. The Burg's administration instead relied on inmate word-of-mouth and experience to instruct new arrivals. Even if they issued each inmate a rulebook or conducted orientation programs, it would serve little or no purpose because most of its rules and regulations were rarely if ever enforced.

Inmate Employment and Treatment Programs. In The Burg, most convicted inmates who could work remained idle because, as a result of severe overcrowding, the demand for employment far exceeded job availability. The same applied to pretrial detainees because technically they were not yet wards of the state and could not be assigned to a work detail. Furthermore, treatment programs for family visitation, education, medical care, substance abuse, and the like were very limited due to understaffing and lack of space. Prison managers allowed this to persist, since they believed that inmates would not be confined here long enough to benefit from employment and treatment programs. Necessity forced them to instead focus their attention and resources on maintaining a balance between new arrivals and discharges, while making certain that inmates kept their court appointments.

The Burg that I experienced during my incarceration was a world of daily administrative tolerance to extreme overcrowding, idleness, violence, and inmate self-policing; a crucible of violence, anarchy, and fear for both the keepers and the kept. My initial exposure to this old, dark, hostile, overcrowded institution was frightening enough. But once I realized that prison guards had tacitly ceded control of the prison to the toughest, most vicious inmates, my fear turned to panic. I found myself so terrified that the prospect of facing a capital murder trial seemed to be my least concern.

The Burg's Performance

The combined effect of constant fear and extreme idleness prevented me from ever fully adapting to the prison environment in The Burg. I was always too disoriented to think clearly. Every time I would begin to adapt, some new cause for fear would force me to "step up" to the Fearful State. As a result, I was never able to step down to any less agitated level of behavior.

The Burg only released its inmates to the streets or to other state prisons, therefore having no impact on behavior in halfway houses. No matter what new environment they entered, however, most of them were still reeling from their previous habituation to extreme fear. After five months in The Burg, I was transferred back to Bucks

County Prison to attend my trial. Even after I had been out of The Burg for weeks, I was unable to step down from my Fearful State, despite the more pleasant conditions in the Pine Street Motel. In my view, any release from conditions in The Burg inevitably retards one's ability to gradually step down to a lower level that supports productive adaptation and improved behavior.

GRATERFORD PRISON: THE TELEGRAPH POLE

Graterford was designed to be a prison work camp, not a penitentiary—a major distinction from The Burg. To accommodate the policy shift from salvation to the production of free labor, Graterford had to be spacious and massive rather than streamlined and compact. Operating a work camp required plenty of land, living space, staff, and equipment to compel convict labor into the production of surplus goods and services necessary to render the prison economically self-sufficient.

The notion of making people *pay* for their crime was rooted in a self-serving assumption that human action is motivated by some innate greed that determines social and economic *costs and benefits.* Under this model of human behavior, the prevention of crime was simply a matter of training convicts in the relative costs and benefits of particular acts; the greater the disparity between cost and benefit, the more effective the conditioning. Accordingly, Graterford was designed and operated with the belief that the threat of slavery would produce good citizens, since its cost to the convict exceeded any potential benefits of crime.

The only difference between Graterford and an ante-bellum plantation was that Graterford's free labor was provided by convicts rather than slaves, and that its earnings went to a state government rather than to a private plantation owner. By the time I had arrived there, slavery had been abolished for over one hundred years and "Jim Crow" had been dead for at least a generation. But slavery was still entrenched in Graterford's bricks and mortar. Only severe overcrowding managed to transform the prison from a cost-efficient plantation into an unmanageable, overcrowded warehouse that could not earn its own keep.

The Prison's Architecture

Shape. Whereas The Burg was circular and compact, Graterford was long and massive with blocks and corridors of great distance that impaired visibility and created blind spots (see Figure 24.2). Though its spacious size made me feel small and insignificant, Graterford's

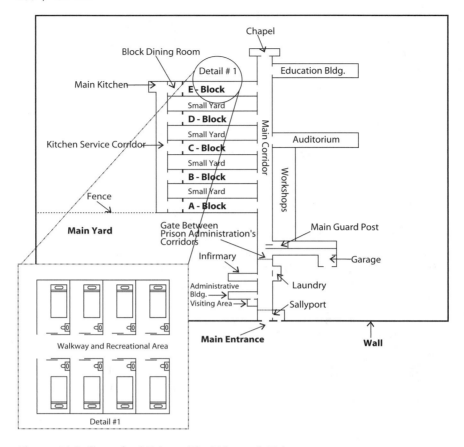

Figure 24.2 Graterford Prison: The Telegraph Pole

vastness helped me to overcome fear caused by the extreme, continuous crowding in prisons like The Burg. Gone was the sensation of feeling penned in with hostile strangers.

Lighting. Each cell had a window that could be opened or closed by its inhabitant, providing plenty of sunshine and fresh air. This meant, of course, a cold cell in the winter. But the ability to regulate light and air made conditions tolerable. A skylight ran the length of each cellblock, so the walkways that were used as dayrooms were well lited during the day.

Heating. Each cell was dry and equipped with a small radiator that, oddly enough, was mounted at the ceiling over the toilet. Despite the inefficiency of this design, these heaters kept Graterford's cells much warmer than those in The Burg.

Colors. Although the predominant colors in the prison were grays, each cell door was painted a light aqua-blue. Inmates were also allowed to paint the ceiling of their cells a powder-blue. The contrast of these spots of color in an otherwise drab prison rendered Graterford more lively, commodious, and accommodating than The Burg.

The Prison's Population

Population Density. Although Graterford had a larger general population than The Burg, its spacious design allowed much more room between each inmate. This reduced the fear associated with being in close proximity to strangers, which in turn promoted uninvited physical contacts. In Graterford, I always felt that I could keep a safe distance from danger. During general line movements, however, Graterford's main corridor was as densely populated as any walkway in The Burg, although this situation was intermittent and avoidable when necessary.

Composition of the Inmate Population. About 80 percent of Graterford's inmate population consisted of African Americans from the Philadelphia area, who were over the age of twenty-five. The vast majority of its population, therefore, were actually "homeys" who belonged to one Philadelphia neighborhood gang or another. This common kinship gave Graterford a familial atmosphere that embraced everyone in the population, regardless of race or origin, thereby rendering violence less visible and life more tolerable.

Graterford's large percentage of non-white staff is also worth noting. The prison had the highest number of minority prison staff in the state, more so than all other Pennsylvania prisons combined. Most of the staff were from the Philadelphia area, so the racial and geographic commonality between inmates and staff contributed greatly to Graterford's neighborhood feel.

Continuity of the Prison Population. Graterford was a *long timer's* prison, most of its inmates serving sentences with minimums exceeding five years. At the time of my initial entry, it had the largest population of lifers in the state. As a result, cellblock neighbors tended to stay neighbors for years. My first fears associated with Graterford eventually matured into the comfort of familiarity—knowing everyone, including those whom I needed to avoid.

Appearance of the Prison Population

The inmates of Graterford appeared typically intimidating, as did most maximum-security prison populations, but what distinguished them from The Burg's population was the relative absence of the mentally ill. These men were housed in a special unit and kept apart from the general population. As mean, tattooed, angry, and unkempt as the men of Graterford may have appeared, they never seemed as dangerous or desperate as the men of The Burg.

The Prison's Administration

Graterford, despite its bubbling turmoil that characterized maximum-security prisons, never came close to the potential for violence in the Burg. Its prison practices, programs, and policies had evolved to constrain violence with simple administrative initiatives never implemented in The Burg, which accounted for The Burg's noticeable difference in its degree of violence. Although design and population demographics may determine a prison's *range* of violence, the *degree* of violence actually experienced in a prison is fixed by its managerial operation. Policies, practices, and programs that proved effective in keeping Graterford well below its threshold for violence are discussed later.

Single Celling. During my residency, the general population at Graterford remained single celled. Later, the prison adopted a policy of double celling, with drastic results. The profound effect that double celling had on one particular housing block was made clear to me every time I walked by E-Block and noticed the comparative fear and chaos that reigned over it.

When I first arrived at Graterford in 1981, E-Block was the initial intake unit that had begun double celling in response to a dramatic increase in prison commitments. Yet, the four other housing blocks remained single celled. The comparison between E-Block and the others was like night and day. E-Block was by far the most violent and out of control, with incidents of aggression far exceeding those of all the other cellblocks combined. In 1988, all of Graterford converted to double cells. To regulate the violence incident to double celling, prison staffing had to be greatly increased and major structural changes had to be made to each of the cellblocks.

Full Employment and Wages. Graterford hosted the factories that manufactured all uniforms, shoes, mattresses, and textiles used in prisons throughout the state. As a result, every inmate who wanted a prison job could easily get one. Many of the manufacturing jobs paid bonuses based on production. Skilled workers who were willing to work two eight-hour shifts per day could earn hundreds of dollars each month in wages.

As a general policy, any inmate requesting a prison job was given one immediately. The only waiting list for employment was for high-paying, skilled jobs. Not only did this full-employment policy keep people busy and prevent poverty-related misconduct, it allowed inmates to form a working-class community whose members freely interacted and bonded on the job. Consequently, a great deal of violence was averted, simply because men chose to avoid conflict to keep the jobs that offered them social and financial benefits. Graterford's policy and ability to keep the whole prison population employed helped inmates better tolerate deprivation, overcrowding, and violence. The opportunity for meaningful employment, furthermore, offered a powerful incentive to resist violence, disorder, and despair.

Treatment Programs. What I remember most about Graterford was not its violence and despair but the friendship and sense of community that existed there. For many years after I was transferred out of Graterford, I missed that community spirit and wished I could rejoin the fold from which I had forcefully been separated.

Although my desire to return to an ostensibly dangerous and frightening prison may seem irrational to the reader, this demonstrates the overwhelming power of the human need to belong. At Graterford, I felt so attached to family and friends that I was willing to risk my life by ignoring, tolerating, and even resisting the prison's extreme conditions. In the end, Graterford was a less violent place to live in, because its *community dynamics* offset its objective dangers. These community dynamics are based in part on family visits, rehabilitation programs, and the ubiquitous presence of volunteers.

Family Visits. General population contact visits at Graterford were an administrative priority. The visiting room stayed open from 8:00 AM to 8:00 PM, seven days a week. It was small and always crowded, but the prison staff was generally nonintrusive and friendly with visitors, so that visits were as pleasant as possible. Because sanctions for misconduct citations included suspensions of contact visits, most inmates tried harder to stay out of trouble to maintain their visiting privileges.

In addition to family visits, there were banquets and award ceremonies sponsored by inmate religious and social organizations to which family members were invited to attend. During these events, prison policy allowed and encouraged inmates to freely interact with family members. Since these events always occurred inside the prison itself, family members were given an opportunity to inspect the inmates' habitat, which helped to ease tension with the prison staff and encouraged the staff to maintain a clean, humane prison.

The primary concern of prison guards during family visits was the smuggling of contraband and inappropriate behavior. Contact visits, however, were such effective incentives for good behavior that they easily outweighed other security concerns. The visiting program at Graterford was designed to join staff, inmates, and families together into an extended prison community. Their involvement in this community promoted an interest by everyone who had to live in, work in, or visit Graterford in overcoming the unnecessarily dangerous elements of prison life.

Programs. As with its visitation policies, Graterford actively encouraged inmate participation in education, recreation, and religious programs. What these programs lacked in staffing and financial allocations were made up for in their outreach and accessibility. The prison school, chapel, and gym were open and available to all inmates from morning activities at 8:00 AM until cell confinement at 9:00 PM.

Classrooms were used for basic literacy as well as college-degree programs. There were no eligibility requirements or restrictions. If an inmate wanted to participate in a school program, he simply acquired a pass to the school and enrolled in the appropriate class.

Religious programs were even more accessible and extensive. Every conceivable religious denomination conducted worship services in Graterford's chapel. Any inmate who wished to go to the chapel at any time needed only to ask his block officer or work supervisor for a pass. At least one chaplain was always on duty, and no one was ever turned away.

Those programs provided not only religious, educational, and recreational activities but a place where an inmate could retreat to scream, cry, complain, or just recover from the harsh conditions of prison life. Educators, chaplains, and recreation supervisors tried not to be disciplinarians and often won friendships with inmates. Whether by temperament or direction, these staff members went out of their way to ease the burden of fear that weighed so heavily on each inmate. Their programs provided an oasis of humanity, community, and caring in a prison specifically designed to filter out such social amenities. There is no doubt that these "kinder and gentler" aspects of Graterford rendered it a much safer place for both staff and inmates.

Volunteers. In Graterford, inmates' need for chaplains or teachers far exceeded the latter's availability. Prison managers, therefore, actively solicited the assistance of volunteers and volunteer organizations to supplement the religious, educational, and recreational staff.

Prison managers realized how important treatment programs were to the safety and well-being of both staff and inmates. Graterford had thus become a Mecca for community-based volunteer programs operating inside the prison. Every week, hundreds of volunteers entered the prison to teach, pray, counsel, and console its convicts. As a result of this openness, prison staff and inmates were always on their best behavior, given this exposure to the public at large. Volunteers also contributed a level of dedication and purpose that salaried staff members simply were not willing or able to match. Volunteer participation in Graterford's treatment programs rendered them more dynamic, effective, and genuine.

During my incarceration in Graterford, I would awaken every morning in a cold, dark, lonely cell, greeted by the sights and sounds of captivity, indifferent guards, and intimidating neighbors. But then I would go to the chapel, education building, or even the gym, where I could talk to a volunteer or staff member who treated me as a friend rather than as a subordinate. Such small human comfort was all I needed to encourage myself to continue trying to be a productive member of society. In truth, I would do anything to maintain a bond between myself, my family, and my friends, so I always tried hard to resist violating the rules or succumbing to prison violence.

An interesting footnote to Graterford's voluntarism: One of the most active, dedicated volunteer organizations operating in the prison was the Pennsylvania Prison Society. This volunteer organization was originally founded by the Quakers to manage the operation of penitentiaries throughout the state, starting with Old Eastern. Eventually, state government took over the management of its prisons and penitentiaries, and the Prison Society became a watchdog group overseeing the humane treatment of inmates. When I first arrived in Graterford, volunteers from the Prison Society were actively seeking an end to practices and conditions that the Quakers originally introduced when they built and operated Old Eastern and The Burg.

Through correspondence, I was once asked by a renowned psychiatrist specializing in the treatment of extreme violence what I believed was the *x factor* that enabled me to remain a productive member of society, despite my prolonged incarceration under harsh, violent conditions. After a year of considering this complex question, I discovered the simple answer. Throughout my prison experience, I had managed to maintain strong ties with family, friends, and volunteers. As a result, my behavior conformed to their expectations of me, because I wanted to remain in good standing with my chosen community. If I had not been able to maintain these "free-world" ties, I would have most likely attached myself to some prison gang and conformed to its requirements rather than to that of society. Hence, I realized that the x factor was my ability to remain rooted in a community that had expectations of me unaffected by the hardships and violence of my prison environment.

A prison's ability to reduce violence within itself and the community beyond its walls depends on its efforts to keep its inmate population rooted in the greater community. More prison guards, isolation units, and increased deprivations that impair inmates' abilities to maintain family and community ties contribute significantly to the development of prison violence.

Graterford's Performance

Unlike The Burg, Graterford's progressive conditions allowed me to step down my fear level below the Adaptive State to the Angry/Rebellious State. However, Graterford was still too violent to allow me to step down through the rehabilitation window to the Compliant State. Every time that I managed to safely function in Graterford's mercurial environment, some new wave of violence, management upheaval, or physical plant breakdown would occur to rush me back into the dysfunction of the Fearful State.

I spent most of my five-plus years in Graterford lingering in the Angry/Rebellious State, due principally to the extreme violence I experienced in The Burg. As a consequence, I soon found myself resisting my confinement by cooking hamburgers in the major's office, buying "swag" (contraband) sandwiches and services, filing law suits, and basically trying everything I could to safely test the limits of my imprisonment.

The extensive periods of time that I spent in the Angry/Rebellious State led me to receive many misconduct citations for infractions of prison rules, as I slowly, painfully measured the narrow boundaries of my prison home. Although most of the violence and disorder associated with the Fearful and Adaptive States are inmate on inmate, the resistance and violence of the Angry/Rebellious State are almost always directed against the administration and staff. This style of learning, through resistance and misbehavior, typifies a condition that is constantly troublesome to prison administrations and staff.

The perpetual state of anger and disobedience I embraced at Graterford turned me into a chronic complainer and risk taker. Because of my legal training, much of my complaints were expressed in the form of formal grievances and law suits challenging conditions of confinement. Those who could not resist with pencil and paper did so with fists and shanks. Despite the general population's low percentage of literate men, however, most of my fellow convicts in Graterford overcame their illiteracy to supplement their misbehavior with the filing of grievances and lawsuits. Although conditions in Graterford certainly warranted and even demanded these legal actions, the mind-set of the Angry/Rebellious State was more in the form of pay back or revenge than justice.

A final casualty of Graterford's violence was the halfway house program. Eligibility for admission into a halfway house required that an inmate be misconduct free for at least nine months prior to application. Since inmates in the Angry/Rebellious State tended to receive a lot of misconduct citations, many inmates at Graterford were unable to qualify for the halfway house program. This, in turn, resulted in the release of many inmates directly into the community without proper supervision or support. Those who did manage to find themselves in a halfway house prior to release often discovered that the fear and anger they had been accustomed to in Graterford retarded their ability to successfully adjust to this new environment. As a result, many of them were returned to Graterford for violating halfway house rules.

The only opportunity that most Graterford inmates had to feel safe enough to step down to the Compliant State came only after their release into the community. Because these inmates left the prison fearful and unprepared for the free world, they tended to remain in the Fearful State much longer than necessary, thus slowing their successful reintegration into the community at large. Generally, for an inmate to remain in the rehabilitation window of the Compliant State after release to a halfway house or the streets, he must receive family or community support in the form of money, housing, employment, and positive reinforcement. Many of Graterford's inmates lacked most if not all of these support elements. The lingering residual anger and resistance they took with them to the streets usually resulted in their return to Graterford for parole violation or some new crime.

A Hitchhiker's Guide to Prisons, Part II
The Big House: What Goes 'Round Comes 'Round

EDITORS' NOTE

This chapter and the next are continuations of the "Hitchhiker's Guide to Prisons." In this chapter and the next, Victor Hassine does what no other inmate author has done, namely, to walk the reader through the range of prisons he has lived in and to compare and contrast them in terms of living conditions, social climate, administrative organization, and the experience of prison as punishment. Social scientists know that prisons have different ecologies; the bricks and mortar and razor wire fences may be the same for all prisons but the internal worlds can be as different as night and day. One reason for such differences is that prisons are built at different times with different designs and different goals (or at least different understandings of punishment and treatment). Yet those prisons live on into different eras and must be adapted to different purposes as generations of administrators and prisoners pass through them. Regrettably, the original failures and shortcomings of penal institutions typically become magnified over time because of what might be called "historical drag"—the original purpose and design places sharp limits on what is possible, try as we might to "retrofit" our prisons to reflect other hopes and aspirations. Prison history is thus a history of individual prisons and their often troubled evolutions over decades and in some cases centuries. This is "prison history from the inside," to quote Hassine, and it is a history that would remain unwritten were it not for Hassine's insightful examination of his own prison life.

I didn't know it, but I'd never been in a Big House until I'd arrived at Western Penitentiary, originally built in 1827 and then converted into a Big House between 1878 and 1892. Like most other people, I'd thought Big House was a euphemism for prison, never suspecting it was actually prison slang for a particular design of prison. I also never suspected that one day, I would arrive at the Big House, an exile of Graterford violence finally coming around to me.

It was Summer 1986, and as usual I had reported to my cell in Graterford for the final 9:30 PM count. As was the practice, a bell sounded to announce count while all four hundred cell doors on the block were levered open to allow block officers to manually lock each inmate in his cell. (In more modern prisons, especially super-max prisons, this and many other activities related to prison management and movement are automated.) This was a tedious and frustrating chore as hundreds of raucous inmates reluctantly returned to their cells to be locked in for the night. Once the count bell was sounded, it took block officers at least twenty minutes to lock everyone in their cells. Because my cell was deep in the interior of the block, my door remained unlocked for at least ten minutes until a prison guard eventually locked me in.

I was seated on the edge of my bed, waiting for the guard's arrival, when suddenly, an inmate pulled my cell door open, rushed in toward me, and threw the contents of a large bowl at my face. The stranger's bowl was filled with a sticky substance, possessing the consistency of very thick oatmeal. The homemade concoction was actually a mixture of caustic acids, bleach, ammonia, oatmeal, and glue, designed to adhere to flesh so that the acids could inflict maximum pain and permanent chemical burns. My face and eyes were targets of the flesh-eating mud, which could burn and blind me into defenselessness.

Luckily, things didn't turn out the way my attacker had planned. Quick reflexes, honed by years of captivity, allowed me to turn my face away in time for the acid to strike only the top of my head. Made too thick, the acid clung to my thick, curly hair and did not seep into my scalp or ooze down to my face very quickly. Instead, when I flicked my head to face my attacker, much of the clumpy acid fell from my head, leaving only a stubborn patch still sticking to my hair. Eventually, a small amount did finally drip down to my left eye, which I had closed in time to protect my eyeball.

With one good eye, I jumped up from my bed and charged head on into the man who had tried to blind me. I could feel the acid beginning to burn my skin, and I knew I was in a fight for my life. Because I was bigger and heavier than my attacker, our collision bounced him back. It was evident from his expression that he had not expected me to resist. This element of surprise gave me a momentary but critical advantage.

My primary objective was to prevent the attacker from using a shank that I was certain he possessed. I hoped to accomplish this by muscling him out of my cell and into the tier where friends or prison guards could quickly come to my aid. My plan failed when our collision drove him against a wall rather than out the door. Fearing my attacker had cohorts to assist him, I instantly executed Plan B: I pulled my door locked. Now it was a fair man-to-man fight with me possessing the dual advantages of momentum and home turf. One-eyed and scared, I fought for my life.

We fought for the longest ten minutes of my life, during which time I threw at the trapped and armed attacker (he did have a shank) my TV, radio, and everything else I could get my hands on. Finally, I overpowered and disarmed him, pinning both his arms against the floor with my knees. This allowed me one free hand, which I used to stick my thumb into one of his eyes. The man, still resisting, was calling for someone's help, and I could hear somebody pounding on my door, trying to get in.

Now, I had a decision to make: What do I do to the man who had just tried to blind and maybe even kill me? Still thinking rationally, I decided it was fairest and safest to subdue him by using the goo, the chemical blob with which he planned to disable me. So, with my free hand, I grabbed a handful of muddy acid, still clinging to the top of my head, and spread it generously on the attacker's face. The man immediately started to scream and demand I get off of him because I was hurting him. Me hurting him! The shear nerve of his demand so angered me that I quieted him by shoving some of his acid paste into his own mouth.

Guards finally arrived to take the screaming and spitting intruder out of my cell. Meanwhile, I was locked in my cell with my left eye swollen shut. During the fight I felt nothing but now, in its aftermath, I felt like my face, head, and eye were on fire. So I immediately diluted the acid's potency by washing my face with water from my sink. I couldn't open my eye, so I couldn't tell if it was blind. About an hour later, I was taken to the infirmary where nurses flushed out my eyes with warm water. But the swelling didn't go down, and I still couldn't open my eye. It would take a nervous two weeks before I learned that I could still see through both eyes.

From the infirmary, I was taken to solitary confinement, where I remained for several months while prison officials investigated the incident and decided what actions needed to be taken. One month

into my isolation, the superintendent came to visit. We were well-acquainted and shared a very good relationship. He had come to inform
me that his boss, the commissioner of corrections, had ordered that I
be transferred to another institution. I couldn't believe it. I had been
attacked and yet I was the one being transferred!

"[Because of] the admissions by the Graterford Administration regarding the
impositions that have been placed upon inmates as a result of severe overcrowding, we are reminded of Coleridge's verse:

> As he went through Cold-Bath Fields he saw
> A solitary cell;
> And the Devil was pleased, for it gave him a hint
> For improving his prisons in Hell.

Coleridge, S. T., The Devil's Thoughts, in *Poetic Works* (E. Hartley ed. 1978)."

In *Hassine v. Jeffes*, 846 F3d 169 (3rd Cir 1988).

"Why am I the one being transferred?" I asked.

"Well, let's put it this way. I've never had a problem with you. In
fact, I appreciate the lawsuit you filed against the prison because it has
gotten me all the money I need to try and fix this place. I never got any
money for capital improvement before. Unfortunately, for you, there
are some who took your lawsuit more personally, and well, they want
you out of here," the superintendent confided.

"What do you mean?" I asked, actually knowing the answer.

"Well, let's just say, someone feels you had been treated pretty good
over the years, and you have betrayed all the trust and privileges you
have received," he answered.

A month before the attack, I had sat for trial in federal court to litigate
a conditions of confinement suit that I had filed against Graterford and
the Bureau of Prisons (*Hassine v. Jeffes*; see box) In the suit, I asked that
double celling in Graterford be stopped until such time as the prison was
repaired and staffed to a degree that rendered it legally safe and clean.

Only a few weeks before my attack, I had asked the presiding judge
if he would allow me to cross-examine a witness—particularly one
of the prison's expert witnesses scheduled to testify about the safe
conditions in Graterford. Remarkably, the judge agreed, but he conditioned his approval on the witness being the deputy superintendent
of security—the once major of the guards who had been my former
employer and was still my strongest staff supporter.

I should have declined the offer, but I desperately needed to feel like
a lawyer, if for only a moment. Desperate needs make for bad decisions
and so I decided that I could cross-examine the deputy superintendent

without offending him or injuring our relationship. So I cross-examined the deputy and, of course, I was wrong.

> "The best way to survive in prison is to remain anonymous."
>
> Old Jailhouse Wisdom

In November of 1986, the day before a scheduled hearing for the lawsuit, I was transferred to Old Western—The Big House. The transfer placed me as far west in Pennsylvania as the Bureau of Prisons could send me: More than six hundred miles away from my family and, coincidentally, outside the jurisdiction of the federal judge deciding my case. This left me too far away for regular family visits and no longer a party in my lawsuit.

My move to the Big House was the first, but certainly not last, reminder of prison managers' disdain for inmates who publicly complain about prison conditions or treatment. I remained in solitary confinement longer and was transferred farther away than the inmate who attacked me. As measured strictly by punishment, filing a lawsuit, challenging the conditions of confinement in a prison is a more serious offense than a violent, unprovoked criminal act meant to blind and possibly kill another man.

In the end, my lawsuit succeeded in delaying double celling in Graterford until after 1988 and required the Department of Corrections to spend more than $45 million in capital improvements to the prison—including the establishment of the State's first privatized prison Mental Health Treatment Unit. It also led to prison managers labeling me a "troublemaker" and over the years transferring me to no less than seven different Pennsylvania State prisons. But my keepers' intolerance of my criticism ultimately led to more successful conditions of confinement lawsuits and my writing of four editions of the book that you are now reading, all of which confirm what has consistently been revealed to me over twenty-five-plus years of incarceration: Cruelty and unfairness are self-defeating; in the end, they make problems worse, not better.

PRISON HISTORY FROM THE INSIDE

The way I see it, the most significant aspect of the penitentiary system was its innovation of collecting criminals, in a central secure location, for the express purpose of plying them with a specific and uniform process designed to produce a desired end product. In this context, penitentiaries, past and present, are little more than processing plants housing assembly lines that receive inmates, make them into commodities, and then uniformly subject them to various punitive and reformative treatments that are calculated to convert criminals into something more useful or at least less noxious.

In the early nineteenth century, New York's Auburn prison operated under a penal philosophy in stark contrast to the Quakers'. What was different was its purpose. Where the Quakers employed their penitentiary assembly line to deliver isolation and religion for the purpose of producing reform, Auburn penitentiary's more cynical "congregate system" operated to deliver forced hard labor and brutal physical punishment for the purpose of manufacturing fiscal self-sufficiency. In New York, where criminals were deemed unworthy or incapable of reform, should brutal conditions and forced labor happen to result in rehabilitation, well, that would be just an unexpected benefit.

Prison purpose always dictates prison design. The Quakers' penitentiary assembly line emphasized the minimal and efficient use of staff to deliver their chosen recipe for reform. Ultimately, the spoke-and-wheel prison design proved ideal for such an assembly line, since it facilitated and greatly reduced the cost of delivering religion and isolation to inmates doomed to perpetual confinement.

Constitution of the United States of America

THIRTEENTH AMENDMENT, SECTION 1: SLAVERY ABOLISHED

"Neither Slavery nor involuntary servitude, except as a punishment for crime whereof the party shall be duly convicted, shall exist within the United States, or any place subject to their jurisdiction."

Meanwhile, a prison assembly line designed to exploit convict labor takes a different form. This assembly line needs significantly less square footage of convict living space because an inmate will be forced to labor out of his cell most of the day, only sleeping in the cell at night. Smaller cells are the result. Savings realized from building and maintaining smaller housing units can then be used to maintain a larger prison work force, dedicated to maximizing the exploitation of unpaid inmate labor, which is to say, slave labor. Consequently, Auburn-style prison structures could be built small and up, rather than long and wide.

A traditional Auburn-style penitentiary consisted of a rectangular containment building, more than five stories high, encasing five tiers of very small cells (three and a half by seven feet), each tier of cells stacked one on top of the other. Once inside a cell, an inmate could not see other cells or inmates. Such a design is perfectly suited for slave quarters.

Sing Sing, New York's most famous Auburn-type penitentiary, was built on a grand scale. In keeping with its cynical penal philosophy, inmate laborers were pressed into service building what would ultimately become their own slave quarters. Sing Sing boasted two giant Auburn-style cellblocks with an equally tall administration building sandwiched between them. For purely aesthetic reasons, the street-facing side of Sing Sing was provided with columns and other stylish design elements that, from a distance, gave the administrative building and two attached cellblocks the appearance of a large, multiwinged mansion, hence the term "Big House." Note that the main house on slave plantations was traditionally called the "Big House."

WESTERN PENITENTIARY

Western Penitentiary's construction in the Big House fashion represented Pennsylvania's surrender of its singular commitment to the prison purpose of reform and the adoption of the less enlightened prison purpose of fiscal self-sufficiency. Its two-cell blocks were of Auburn style and built in succession with the first (North Block), containing five tiers of 128 (six feet wide by six feet deep) cells per tier. When North Block was finally occupied by inmates, the cells proved to be too small for human habitation. (The average size of prisoners had grown over the preceding century; so too, perhaps, had expectations about what constituted a decent penal living arrangement.) Therefore, the second cellblock (South Block) was redesigned to contain 100 (seven feet wide by eight feet deep) cells in each of its five tiers.

When I entered the Big House, I had no awareness that I was to live in what was intended to be slave quarters. Nevertheless, I felt as alone as I ever had before, as I walked along the narrow corridor that separated the containing structure from the interior five tiers of cells, on my way to a tiny cell on North Block. Instead of fear, I felt anger and frustration, fueled by my longing to return to Graterford: the physical and emotional home of my family and support.

My separation anxiety caused me to romanticize Graterford's violence and uncertainty while disdaining the relative calm I intuitively sensed in the Big House. It seems that Graterford, inch for inch the most life-threatening real estate in Pennsylvania, had somehow conditioned me into a violence and fear addict, accustomed to life on red alert.

Western's Lighting

Western was always dark and gloomy, much as one would expect from a prison built to house inmates slated for slave labor. Light fixtures were dated and provided shadowy and uneven lighting. Poor lighting made anything requiring vision to be difficult and uncertain. It was hard to read or write in my cell. The walkways on the block and outdoors, leading to other buildings behind the wall, were shadowy and scary, like walking at night on a poorly lit street in a rundown neighborhood.

"The evidence indicates that the architecture of the cellhouses and the physical layout of buildings and other structures contribute to the violence and illegal activity by inmates. [citations omitted] The architecture of cellhouse one and seven, which was designed for a less mobile prison population, does not provide adequate visibility for guards to properly monitor from secure vantage points inmate movement within the cellhouse."

Ramos v. Lamm, 639 F. 2d 559 (D. Colo. 1979).

Circuit Judge Hollway writing for the Court and describing Old Max, the state's Big House penitentiary.

The lighting made it difficult, most of the time, to see or identify people or things near me. Blind spots, created by poor lighting, abounded on and off the blocks. This permitted many "war zones" where anything could and often did happen. Danger was not only hidden around every corner but hidden in plain view, in the open.

Beside the increase in potential for violence and criminal activity, lighting establishes mood and feelings. It was hard to stay focused or positive at Western because I was always distracted by shadows and what I couldn't see. I was always edgy and vulnerable.

I hated Western, and much of my anger was stoked by the perpetual gloom surrounding me. It was as if I were stuck under a dark rain cloud for the three years that I lived in Western. My negative feelings, caused in large measure by poor lighting, greatly contributed to my deciding to spend my time in Western by filing and helping others to file lawsuits against staff and the prison administration.

Cell lighting is wholly inadequate in double cells. Only one double lamp fluorescent unit is mounted above the upper bunk. The inmate controls the on/off switch, located outside the cell, from inside by pulling on a string....

> In addition to causing eyestrain, the inadequate lighting impedes the inmate's ability to clean thoroughly and move about safely.
>
> *Tillery v. Owens*, 719 F. Supp. 1256 (W.D.Pa. 1989).
>
> Chief Federal Judge Cohill writing about Western penitentiary.

The darkness at Western left me apathetic about myself and my safety. I realize now that I had been experiencing depression from separation anxiety and prison conditions. In my case, depression translated into a compulsive animosity and a desire to get even. It's sad to think that by merely providing adequate lighting, Western could have saved prison managers and me a whole lot of unnecessary problems.

Blind Spots

Western penitentiary was extremely effective and efficient—as sleeping quarters for inmate slaves. However, converting its use into an open-range "rehabilitation" prison with little or no supporting structural modifications proved counterproductive; design elements discouraged rather than accommodated peaceful inmate interaction outside their cells. Western, in purpose and outcome, can be defined by its misuse, which made it little more than one big "blind spot." That is to say, its rectangular multitier design made it impossible for cellblock staff to observe or supervise inmate activities without jeopardizing their own safety. Every one in the Big House—staff and inmate alike—had to fend for themselves.

> As has been detailed, the architecture and layout of the facility make it virtually impossible to provide security. There are innumerable blind spots which permit assaults, stabbings and rapes to occur without surveillance. The design and staffing of all major housing units contribute immeasurably to violence between inmates, often leading to severe injury and death. Prisoners have been brutally injured in every major living unit, including the "protective custody" units. What nooks, crannies and cells are not concealed are cluttered...
>
> No matter what physical changes are made, the grossly inadequate staff could never cure the problem. The staff which does exist is largely preoccupied with self-protection and maintaining control of the prison.
>
> *Ramos v. Lamm*, 485 F. Supp. 122 (D. Colo. 1979).
> (discussing adverse effects of blind spots in a Big House prison)

Life in Western was like living in a blind alley full of dangerous, armed strangers. Like everyone else, I adjusted to life in the blind spots. Looking back, I can see that Western's effect on my conduct and feelings was profound. Everyone at Western who was not a victim had to be, or appear to be, a violent and potentially lethal thug.

The need for Big House inmates to act tough tainted every aspect of the prison's efforts to reform convicts. An inmate at work, school, or therapeutic program had to somehow act tough and dangerous before his peers while, at the same time, convincing a supervising staff that he was trustworthy, nonviolent, and ready for release. Deception through effective development and maintenance of dual contrasting personalities was necessary for survival since, at the end of each and every day, inmates had to return to an unsupervised cellblock where people would be waiting to victimize them if they detected weakness in the form of nonviolent attitudes.

Therefore, a Big House used to rehabilitate inmates actually causes them to act and appear more dangerous and violent than they actually are. It also teaches inmates how to suppress and disguise their gentler feelings. Certainly, most men in Western were not violent predators, but due to the prison's design, everyone was prepared to violently defend against a minority of men who could act without consequence or mercy.

The housing areas are severely understaffed. Approximately 741 inmates reside in the South Bloc with at most seven corrections officers assigned to the bloc at any time. "Blind spots" abound throughout the block where incidents, including rape, assault, cell theft, cell arson and drug use may occur unknown to the corrections officers. The shower area is one of the most dangerous areas; no corrections officers control this area on a full-time basis....

The effects of weapons availability combined with the lack of adequate staffing are apparent—assaults, rapes and cell thefts are frequent. Even though the number of reported inmate assaults does not appear extraordinary given the number of inmates housed at SCIP, in light of circumstances there, we believe that the unreported occurrences far surpass those reported. We note that being branded a "snitch" may have serious consequences to the inmate's health. Therefore, SCIP inmates that fear for their safety may forfeit their shower and exercise privileges to avoid confronting other inmates when no corrections officers are present.

Tilley v. Owens, 719 F. Supp. 1256 (W.D. Pa. 1989).
(discussing blind spots and their consequences at Western Penitentiary)

Blind spots affect prison staff as well, by making them feel frightened and vulnerable. Staff's response to unavoidable blind spots is often very much like that of the inmates; they act tough and violent to reduce the risk of being jumped in a dark alley. In Western, this meant that staff did not enforce rules as much as they made certain that they were safe from harm.

To enhance their safety, prison staff allowed, inmates to attack and victimize each other. Many of us believed that staff sometimes encouraged inmates to prey on one another. Why? Because if violent predators had enough vulnerable inmates to prey on, they would not need to victimize staff.

Allowing, if not encouraging, inmate violence to flourish was not simply an unintended response to prison violence but an unwritten, well-established, and practiced policy of prison staff. Given prison design and staffing limitations, there really as no other way for staff to effectively protect themselves from Western's ever-present blind spots. So, if they couldn't stop violence, then all that was left to do was to direct it away toward someone else. In this case, that someone else was me and all the other inmates.

The Curious Case of the Missing Tape

Western's practice of transferring rather than suppressing violence damaged the physical and emotional well-being of both keeper and kept and numbed their ability to distinguish right from wrong. For example, sometime after filing my conditions of confinement suit against Western Penitentiary, I was summoned to the Restrictive Housing Unit (RHU) to represent an inmate charged with misconduct. In those days, prison misconduct hearings included a truth-finding component, and inmates charged with misconduct were permitted an opportunity to prove they were innocent of the charges. (In contrast, contemporary prison misconduct hearing processes tend to be purely dispositional in nature; i.e., guilt is presumed upon issuance of a misconduct report, and a misconduct hearing is conducted only to determine punishment.) Many inmates were illiterate and needed help in these hearings. I was often called on, without notice, to represent one inmate or another at a misconduct hearing. This time an inmate in the hole had requested that I represent him against a charge of fighting with another RHU inmate.

Most of the time, my representation did little to affect outcome, but by promising not to appeal a decision—thereby reducing paperwork—occasionally I was able to persuade the hearing examiner to be lenient in punishment. So, when I arrived at the RHU's hearing room, I anticipated the usual guilty verdict accompanied by a bit of haggling over severity of punishment. However, this time things went very differently.

When I met with the inmate who had requested my assistance, I recognized him as someone I had known at Graterford. He looked as if he'd just lost a barroom brawl and was very anxious to speak to me. He excitedly explained that he had been brutally attacked by another inmate and that the guards had orchestrated the attack.

I presumed the incident had been videotaped in accordance with a recently passed direction requiring RHU officers to videotape all Extraordinary Incident reports, so when it was time to address the hearing examiner, I requested the videotape of the incident be viewed and admitted as evidence. Clearly annoyed by my invoking a little known or used prison procedural rule, the hearing examiner telephoned someone to arrange for the videotape to be brought to him. After fifteen uncomfortable minutes of silently sitting in the hearing room, a uniformed prison guard delivered the requested videocassette.

The hearing examiner loaded the videocassette into a VCR, and the RHU inmate, his escort, the hearing examiner, and I impatiently waited to view its recorded contents on a nearby TV monitor. Frankly, I thought the film footage would be of little value to the charged inmate, because I reasoned that RHU officers would never voluntarily provide incriminating evidence at a misconduct hearing.

The playback began with the unsteady sight and echoing sounds of a tall and muscled RHU inmate, standing in his cell, screaming and cursing at the camera and corrections officers who were standing in front of him, on the other side of his closed cell door. Prison guards were ordering him to turn around and place his hands on the wall in the back of his cell so that he could be hand-cuffed.

The enraged inmate was not cooperating and responded by threatening, "I'll fuck up anyone who comes into my cell."

The inmate looked like he could do someone serious harm before being subdued. And, after tense moments of orders being ignored, the voice of someone in authority, outside camera view, ordered corrections officers to "get the other guy over here!"

Soon my RHU client, with hands restrained behind his back, appeared on the TV monitor, being escorted to the front of the angry inmate's cell by two corrections officers. My client could be heard repeatedly begging, "You can't put me in there—dude's crazy!"

Then we all watched as the angry man's cell door was thrown open with my client, hands still cuffed behind his back, being pushed into the cell and the cell door quickly being shut and locked. The angry inmate, a man of his word, immediately began punching and kicking the helpless inmate who was soon knocked to the floor under a rain of savage blows to his body.

Then the voice in authority could be heard demanding, "Okay, go in there now and cuff 'im up while he's busy with the other guy."

With this, the hearing examiner quickly turned off the playback as everyone in the room stared dumb-founded at the TV monitor. The only sound in the room was the voice of the RHU inmate repeatedly proclaiming, "I told you that's what happened!"

The hearing examiner ordered the guard escort to take the RHU inmate outside the room and instructed me to stay in my seat. Then, when only the hearing examiner and I remained, he leaned forward toward me and almost whispered, "Look, I didn't know anything about this. I'm just doing my job and following orders. I have to find him guilty because they told me to, but I want you to know I had nothing to do with this."

I was still stunned by what I had seen, and the hearing examiner's attempt to distance himself from the role that he was playing in this brutal crime made me angry and eager to expose his complicity.

"That's the same thing the Nazi's said after World War II, and look what happened to them! If you don't report this and throw out the misconduct, you'll have an opportunity to explain how you were just doing your job when you're in front of a judge," I warned, stern and serious.

The hearing examiner had to find my client guilty of fighting with another inmate, because the RHU officers had no other way to explain my client's need for medical attention, following the savage beating that he received.

"I have to do what I was told. I'm sorry. There's nothing I can do," responded the hearing examiner, visibly distraught over the possibility that I might be able to bring the incident to the attention of a judge.

As suspected, I contacted the lawyers litigating my conditions of confinement suit to report the incident. This initiated the filing of a law suit, on behalf of the injured RHU inmate, seeking an investigation and monetary damages. About a week or two later, the videotape of the incident mysteriously arrived, through the mail, at the offices of the injured inmate's lawyer.

The lawyer came to visit me at the prison shortly after, viewing the videotape. He was excited because the film footage evidenced serious criminal and civil liability on the part of prison officials, including the hearing examiner. This meant that there would likely be a large monetary civil settlement, as prison administrators paid, with taxpayer money, to shield the offending prison staff from the civil and criminal consequences of their crimes.

Unbelievably, the lawyer informed me that he would have to return the videotape to prison officials so that he could officially receive it through the law suit—to protect its forensic value by insuring its authenticity. I begged him to keep it or send it to the judge first or at least make a copy of it. But the lawyer believed that copying the tape without permission was illegal, and the only way to authenticate the evidence was to have it sent to him from prison officials. He insisted that I shouldn't worry, because when he returned the videotape, he would include a cover letter stating that he was aware of its content, and if it disappeared, he would inform the judge and seek a criminal investigation into its disappearance.

In the end I was right; after the videotape was returned, the prison's legal counsel responded to a formal request of its production by declaring that the videotape had been accidentally destroyed. The injured inmate's lawyer complained to the judge but to no avail: Without the videotape or a copy of it, there was no proof that any crime or civil tort had occurred. Business as usual at Western could continue unobserved until another guilty conscience decided to "blow the whistle." Until then, directing inmate violence toward other inmates would simply be moved outside camera view.

The Big House survived the prison reform movement that took hold in the 1960s and 1970s. Like hooded Southern night riders, our Big House prisons clandestinely and brutally made certain that liberating convict slaves within their confines would only lead to other forms of oppression—namely, the violence, and disorder I have described in this chapter.

So there I was in a slave camp, sandwiched between frightened and indifferent staff and inmates, while surrounded by uninhibited, violent predators with license to prey on me. What else could I do? I had no choice—but to sue the Department of Corrections in federal court.

Colors

In keeping with its design demands, colors in the Big House were expressly limited to unrelenting dark, dreary, and dirty brick and mortar, and painted metal in earth tones: a world of dark brown, charcoal, and black. Colors affect a prison environment by influencing mood. That's not to say that seeing any one color made me happy or sad regardless of other environmental conditions. It is the combination of colors and where they appear in relation to other colors that can add dimensionality and depth to small and crowded places. Color greatly affected my feelings of security, making me feel safe or frightened, and this was done by their ability to brighten or darken areas. Colors that extend vision created warm and good feelings, while colors that reduced visibility created fear, depression, and uncertainty.

At one time, an under-sized recreation yard provided green that offered a blessed relief to the monotonous, gloomy cemetery hues of everything else in sight. But when I arrived at Western, the yard had been commandeered for the construction of a new 500-bed housing unit. So, not only was I without a recreation yard, but I was also completely surrounded by stern and merciless colors, engineered to support the status of "slave," which not only kept me fearful but also kept me resentful of my masters.

Heating and Cooling

By design, big houses do not offer heated individual cells. Instead, they use large radiators or forced-air blowers, mounted on the ground level to "area heat" the whole cellblock. For cooling or heat retention, there are many columns of floor-to-ceiling pull windows, which can be opened or closed, as needed, using a long pole affixed with a hook.

Western's housing units were so old that they did not have air circulation or exhaust systems, so the heat from its huge, forced-air blowers would invariably rise and collect at the top of the cellblock. And, because cold air sinks, the low lower levels of the cellblocks harbored all of the displaced cold air. Therefore, every cell in Western was either too cold or too hot because of poor heat distribution, a condition shared by all big houses. I was locked on the top range, and the heat in both summer and winter was so stifling at times that I had problems breathing. Meanwhile, at the same time, on the bottom ranges, inmates had to sleep year round in their long-johns and winter coats to stay warm. Extreme temperatures resulted in chronic sleep deprivation from many sleepless nights. Consequently, much of my mood and behavior were influenced by the effects of sleep deprivation rather than prison rules and regulations.

Wildlife Behind Bars: Insects, Rodents, and Birds, Birds, Birds

Insect and rodent infestation was part of the Big House experience, since its design was meant to keep convicts in but not keep vermin and other creatures out. And, because Western was well over a hundred years old, an ecosystem had developed within its walls and structures that supported insect, rodent, and avian life. Inside the mall-like housing units, completely ignoring human inhabitants, swarms of rodents and birds feasted heartily on an abundance of big, juicy insects of all kinds. Meanwhile, the insects thrived on the waste and droppings deposited by the human, rodent, and bird population. As interesting as this may sound to evolutionary biologists, the daily effect was quite disgusting.

Big House jail birds, insects, and rodents were so fully adapted to prison that they lived and died within the housing units without venturing outside. Because of this virulent infestation of bugs and critters, my life in Western was rendered more miserable and unsafe. The added danger was the result of the disease and bacteria that the swarms of Big House wild life spread on me, my clothes, my mattress, and anything else that they could crawl on, fly over, or nest in.

The birds were a particular nuisance. They flew overhead, day and night, with cheerful abandon, chirping and screeching as they buzzed past my head, threatening me with their droppings. Living in Western was like living in an aviary that was never cleaned. Never. While I eventually adapted to my life in a giant bird cage, coexisting with insects and animals distanced me from civilized life. I felt less attached to the people and world on the free-world side of my prison home, and more alienated from those humans who did not have to share my primitive lifestyle. Much like nomads might disdain the life and culture of town and city life, I became hostile to the free world that I longed to re-enter. This emotional disharmony turned me bitter and resentful.

Gangs

Gangs in Western were dramatically different than those at Graterford. Graterford had dozens of gangs that had migrated into the prison from the countless Philadelphia neighborhood street gangs. Pittsburgh, from which most Western inmates were drawn, had a much smaller citizen population than Philadelphia and, therefore, had far less street gangs that could stream into its prison.

Also, Pittsburgh's white and African American communities were much smaller and less fragmented than were their counterparts in Philadelphia. Therefore, white and black Pittsburgh convicts tended to stick together, based entirely on racial affiliation rather than neighborhood loyalty. There were few intra racial turf battles in Western, except with Graterford convicts who, like me, were transferred to Western for disciplinary or administrative reasons. Graterford convicts in Western stuck together because the native Pittsburgh staff and convicts would shun, distrust, and, when possible, mistreat "The Trouble Makers" from the east. This forced Graterford transplants to overlook their neighborhood differences and join together. Therefore, in Western, there were fundamentally only three gangs: Pittsburgh white convicts, Pittsburgh black convicts, and Graterford transplants.

While the majority of the prison population at Western was black (about 60 percent), because the black convicts were divided into

Pittsburgh (Burger) and Graterford (Philly) convicts, its three controlling gangs were numerically even. This numeric balance made Western less subject to gang violence than Graterford. Western was an ultra-violent prison, for the reasons I have indicated, but the numeric balance between dominant gangs kept turf and gang violence at a minimum. Most violence at Western, as I noted earlier, was the results of predatory attacks on the weak and nonaligned convicts.

Also, the prison staff constantly encouraged and even created animosity between Philly and Burger convicts in a never-ending effort to divide and conquer. The vast majority of prison staff were white; while the black gangs in Western bickered among themselves, the white convicts enjoyed the favor of the staff. As a result, Western had a much more "white racist" feel to it than did Graterford, where the overwhelming black prison population made white racism impossible and allowed black racism to thrive (a little noted feature of many contemporary prisons).

White racism at Western was openly practiced. White staff and convicts routinely used the term niggers, and white inmates had the best jobs and were the most likely to be recommended for parole. Overt favoritism, combined with the friction within the black population, resulted in an uneasy balance of power under which the white inmates benefited the most.

While I certainly appreciated Western's less violent prison environment, my increased safety was offset by the blatant racism that I daily had to endure from staff. (I am not black and I was considered a minority by the white officers and even some of the white inmates.) This racism heightened my anger against staff and the society that permitted and even institutionalized such mean-spirited behavior. For this reason, to this day, I consider Western as the most evil prison that I have ever been housed in.

THE PRISON POPULATION

Population Density

Big House prisons were designed to squeeze as many bodies in as small a sleeping space as possible. This, of course, is the logic of any setting designed to serve as slave quarters. Consequently, Western forced me to live almost shoulder-to-shoulder with nine hundred other men who shared my double-celled housing unit.

It's difficult to convey in writing the discomfort and distress of having to live in such close quarters with so many strangers: Never being able to be alone or escape the aggravating odor of hundreds of unwashed and sweaty men who surrounded and brushed against me; all of us contending for space in an environment overrun with vermin and other disgusting creatures. Human density of this extreme kept me in a constant state of agitation and distress as my primal survival instincts were triggered by a flood of noxious and unfamiliar human and animal scents. It was the designed density of Big House prisons that made Western naturally hostile to positive reform and left me feeling as if I lived in a crowded elevator that I could never escape.

Continuity and Composition of Inmate Populations

Unlike Graterford, Western wasn't a reception and classification prison, so men assigned to live behind its walls usually remained to serve their sentences, often long sentences. This kept the population stable in terms of a low inmate turnover rate. My neighbors remained my neighbors for years.

Also, the average age of inmates in Western was over thirty-five years old. This mature population was an important factor in suppressing prison violence and disorder. Older inmates had the most influence in the inmate population, and they were able to keep the young bucks in check. If Western had a younger inmate population, life there would have been a daily bloodbath.

The relative numeric balance between the competing White, Black Philly, and Black Burger inmates in Western is what kept the general peace and enabled coexistence in this very crowded prison. In the end, it was the composition of the inmate population that contributed the most to stopping Western from becoming a killing field of cramped and angry men.

Appearance of the Inmate Population

Because of its maturity, Western's inmate population tended to remain employed and encouraged a work ethic. A fully employed inmate population meant that Western's inmates could earn disposable income through inmate wages. Some of this spending money was used to purchase clothes (at the time, inmates in Pennsylvania were permitted to purchase clothing; today they can't; they must wear uniforms). As a result, Western's inmates were relatively well-dressed. In fact, dressing well imparted an elevated status within the inmate population, which in turn motivated inmates to be well-dressed and groomed. This was all part of the work ethic maintained by Western's mature prison population. The well-dressed inmate population offset some of the stress and anxiety generated by Western's extreme inmate density.

THE PRISON ADMINISTRATION

Prison Management: Laissez-Faire Plus Exploitation

It may come as a surprise that a prison, originally designed to support convict slavery, could retain much of its intended purpose, despite more than one hundred years of evolving modernization. Maybe it's back-to-back and high-stacked cells made the men within resemble caged zoo animals, creatures on a par with slaves. Maybe the unmanageability of the crowded cellblocks masked the inmate's human faces to outside observers. Or maybe it was the ghosts of dead convict slaves, tortured souls who had once lived in Big House bondage and who now refused to let their agony and misery escape the brick and mortar that they themselves were never able to leave. For whatever reason, in the end, the Big House has resisted every attempt to transform it into anything other than some form of slave camp.

When the open range system made its way to Western in the late 1950s, inmates were allowed to congregate freely on the prison yard, here called a range. Supervision and control of Western's tightly packed prison population became impossible. Prison guards could not police the dense mass of inmates without placing themselves in harm's way. As a result, Western, like other Big House prisons that adopted an open range system, developed a laissez-faire prison management style.

Instead of patrolling the prison's cells and common areas, uniformed prison staff observed inmate traffic from a safe vantage point. If a disturbance was spotted, an alarm would sound and a cohort of prison guards, colloquially called the goon squad, would be dispatched to the area to end and contain the commotion. This approach is by definition reactive and hence precludes the possibility of preventing or forecasting disorder. Further limiting the effectiveness of such a policing system is the fact that Big House prisons are riddled with blind spots and poor lighting, so that only a fraction of daily prison disturbances can ever be observed or detected. Out of their cells, Big House inmates are pretty much on their own.

It was this same kind of overcrowding and lack of inmate supervision that contributed to the creation of Graterford's Kingdom of Inmates and, predictably, a similar kingdom developed in Western. Although the inmate kingdom in Graterford was an unintended consequence of a failed inmate management system, Western's inmate kingdom was the product of design: a laissez-faire prison management system.

As we know, an inmate kingdom, however it emerges, produces a set of distinctive administrative practices and procedures. These were seen at Graterford and at Western. In particular, inmate rules and regulations were passed on inmate to inmate, through experience, rather than through some form of published manual or orientation. So, like most other Western inmates, I generally learned prison rules and regulations once staff caught me committing an infraction. Compliance was less important to me than learning how to do things without being detected. Rules and regulations meant nothing; it was all about staying under the radar.

While Graterford's and Western's overcrowding and inmate kingdoms led to adoption of similar inmate policies and practices, two key factors resulted in very different consequences that made Western less violent (at least in terms of gang violence) but more oppressive than Graterford. The first difference was staff stability in terms of staff turnover. Graterford's staff turnover rate was very high, resulting in a constant and large-scale replacement of staff, which greatly diminished the continuity of goals and directives, enforcement, and management. New prison staff often results in new, personalized and hence unpredictable ways of doing things.

In contrast, Western's staff was one of the most stable in the state's prison system. Western's staff tended to stay on the job until retirement, lending a great deal of continuity to enforcement and implementation of prison management directives. The long tenure of Western's staff had everything to do with the fact that the prison had continuously operated as a maximum-security facility for over 100 years. Following five generations of evolution, prison employment at Western had become handed down, first from father to son, then more recently from fathers and mothers to sons and daughters. Prison staff who weren't related by blood were related through marriage or intimacy. By the time I arrived at Western, prison staff had become so "familial" that almost every staff member was related to one or more other staff member by blood, marriage, and/or intimacy. Nepotism at Western led staff to treat each other like family members rather than coworkers or supervisors.

Western's familial prison staff tended to ignore central office rules and regulations in favor of developing and applying unique local family prison rules and regulations. In Western, if a staff member liked an inmate, then the whole family of prison staff would like the inmate. Of course, if a staff member didn't like an inmate, then none of the staff liked that inmate. Free of central office rules and regulations, Western's staff was able to lavish rewards on its favorite inmates. These rewards included contraband, preferential treatment, and even sex. "You make my life easier, and I'll do the same for you," was Western's standing rule for each day of its family-run, laissez-faire prison management system.

Western's prison management system conditioned most inmates to do whatever was necessary to curry the favor of prison staff to receive contraband and other special staff favors. Therefore, the Kingdom of Inmates that evolved in Western eagerly courted the approval of prison staff, unlike its counterpart in Graterford, where inmates sought to challenge staff. Consequently, there were very few inmate-on-staff disturbances in Western.

The second distinction in Western's management style was the institutionalized monetary exploitation of its inmates. Western's maverick family of staff developed and enforced their own "inmate purpose," which did not include rehabilitation or reform. Western's staff decided to pursue the more practical goal of personal enrichment. The only way that I can describe this management style is by presenting you with examples that represented business as usual in every department in Western, at least during my tenure there. Be advised that what follows are things I've observed first hand or are common knowledge among the inmates of Western.

Medical Department

Nursing staff freely dispensed prescription drugs to favored inmates. In turn, those inmates traded away their right to expect adequate medical care in return for the free narcotics that they received. By providing inmates with unrestricted access to drugs and even sexual favors, nurses were able to avoid doing their jobs. In addition, these same nurses would then sell the prison's medical material, equipment, and medication to stores and individuals outside the prison. Because little actual medical treatment ever took place at Western, there were always a lot of medical supplies to sell on the open market.

Doctors in Western would freely authorize minor surgical procedures for inmates to collect referral fees from the treating specialist or hospital. This legal but ethically questionable practice led to the absurd outcome that Western's inmates were able to receive exotic knee and leg surgeries more readily than they were able to receive day-to-day medical treatment. The exploitive medical practices resulted in Western's having the highest inmate death rate of all the Pennsylvania adult corrections facilities combined.

The medical department had become so corrupted that in 1990 a federal court ordered a complete restructuring of Western's medical department and placed it under court supervision.

Education Department

Western's education department staff would share an annual budget allotment that totaled about two thousand dollars per teacher per year. These full-time prison teachers would then be expected to use their budget allotments to purchase books or other teaching supplies. Instead of purchasing teaching supplies, however, they spent most of their budget buying electronic devices (TVs, VCRs, radios, etc.), which they would simply take home. Meanwhile, their inmatestudents were required to bring their own paper and pencils to class because none had been purchased for them.

I worked in the education department as a teacher's aide, and when I discovered what was happening, I reported it to the superintendent. Shortly afterward, I was summoned by the school principal and instructed not to return to work anymore. However, I was told that I would continue to collect my full wages at the top pay level. In Western it was easier to pay me not to work than to discipline me for reporting the truth. The experience of Western's staff had been that like them, most inmates followed their financial interests; therefore, they felt sure that I would take the money and not complain. At Western it was never personal; it was only business.

For several months, I received payment doing no work, but once it became clear that I was proceeding with my conditions of confinement suit, I was fired, and my paychecks were discontinued. However, after months of receiving financial reward for doing nothing, I must reluctantly admit that I had developed a sense of entitlement to the unearned income. I ended up filing a series of grievances, trying to force the prison administration to resume paying me for doing nothing. I even toyed with the idea of including a claim for back pay in my conditions of confinement suit. Incredibly, in my grievances, I proudly admitted that I was being paid for doing nothing! My perverse argument was that because I was doing what I was asked to do, I felt that I was being wrongly punished for no good reason.

It seems outrageous now, but the management policy adopted by Western staff had a habit of making the absurd seem reasonable—which led to unwanted consequences. In this case, Western had conditioned me to believe that I deserved and even had a legal right to be paid for doing nothing. And, I would suggest that almost every inmate in Western eventually developed this destructive sense of entitlement of which many ended up taking with them to the streets.

Food Service

After staff salaries, food service is the most costly prison expenditure. With millions of dollars a year going to feed its inmates and staff, Western's food service was ripe for exploitation. In the mid 1990s, Western's food service supervisor was dismissed for operating a catering business out of the prison. Using free inmate labor and prison-purchased food, the food service supervisor filled catering orders received by a catering company that was owned and operated outside the prison.

The prison catering business had been operating for years before it was finally halted. To appreciate the full extent of the administrative tolerance of this exploitive enterprise, keep in mind that catering supplies and finished products had to flow freely in and out of Western—a maximum-security prison. This could not have been possible unless the prison security staff did not perceive it as a security risk and allowed it to happen.

Visiting Room

In 1986 Western built a new visiting room. It was twice as big as the older one and much more pleasant. Included in the visiting room was a bank of vending machines that charged sports stadium prices for vending machine food, snacks, and soft drinks. Oddly enough, there were no water fountains in the visiting room.

The vending machines were offered by a social organization that was founded, operated, and governed by Western's administrators and employees. As might be expected, the prison administration gave the employees organization exclusive license to operate a vending concession in the visiting room. In turn, the employees organization contracted with a private vending company to equip, stock, and manage the visiting room's vending concession. The vending company paid the employees organization thirty thousand dollars per year, plus a percentage of gross proceeds for the right to do business in the prison. The employees organization was free to spend the monies they received from the vending company as they saw fit.

To enhance the profitability of their enterprise, the prison administration suspended the practice of allowing the family members of inmates to bring picnic lunches with them for prison visits: a practice that was, at the time, routine and well-established in every other prison throughout the state. In addition, prison officials purposely decided not to install a water foundation in the visiting room so that visitors would have to purchase a soft drink or bottled water from a vending machine when they became thirsty.

When I learned that Western was forcing me to purchase vending food in lieu of receiving cherished family picnic visits to financially enrich themselves, I couldn't believe it! I filed a complaint with the prison administration, seeking reinstatement of picnic visits and the installation of a water fountain. The response was quick: I was found guilty of circulating a petition and sanctioned to 180 days in the hole.

A federal judge ultimately reversed the prison's decision, and a subsequent complaint to the Pennsylvania's Auditor General led to an order directing prison officials to immediately halt the illegal practice of allowing a private social organization to conduct a business on prison property. Also, the Department of Health directed that two water fountains be installed in the visiting room.

Western's original design was meant to facilitate the exploitation of inmates. Its practice of inmate exploitation had survived for over one hundred years and indicates how difficult it is to end an entrenched institutionalized practice. In fact, the only change in Western's purpose has been a shift from the exploitation of inmate labor to the exploitation of inmates' goods and services, a process that has only been moderated by the external authority of the courts.

Despite the pervasive nature of Western's exploitive practices, prison staff were deeply offended by the suggestion that they were illegally exploiting inmates. To them, their acts were merely a continuation of a prison management system handed down to them by their parents and grandparents. In fact, Western's staff found it odd that anyone would object, since staff and inmates alike shared in the bounty of the exploitation.

To me, it was as if I was listening to slave masters explaining to the world how slavery was actually as much a benefit to the slaves as to the slave owner, since the slaves seemed happy with their lot. My experience at Western taught me that even in these modern times of progress, enlightenment, and liberty, the institution of slavery has remained with us and is only a prison away.

Western's Performance

The living conditions, blind spots, and overcrowding that contributed to making Western a violent prison also made it unlikely that most of its inmates could get access to rehabilitation programs. Admittedly, Western had less gang violence than Graterford, but nevertheless, the Big House model at Western proved hostile to efforts at rehabilitation. Although Graterford had me always fearful, all the time, Western had me feeling secretive, bitter, and angry. It was this bitterness and anger that made it more difficult for me to think about anything other than getting back at the prison administration. The last thing on my mind at Western was becoming a better citizen. I viewed every day at Western as a gauntlet in which I had to dodge individual predators, luking in the shadows provided by blind spots, and self-serving staff members, blind to the harms they inflicted by enforcing a regime of sheer exploitation that defined Western Penitentiary.

The reason for my bitterness and anger was the blatant practice of exploitation at Western. Although conditions at Graterford were, in some ways, more desperate and unpleasant, at least I knew or felt that these failings were not the product of willfulness. Staff and inmates at Graterford were the victims of crisis management, and if there was an invisible hand guiding circumstances and prison conditions, the hand did not belong to prison staff or administrators. At Western, I knew that the prison staff and administration purposely exploited me and manipulated inmates into confrontations in furtherance of a scheme to profit financially from my misery and hardship.

An exploitive prison management system might result in less violence but will always offset that benefit by creating resentment and anger that preclude any success at rehabilitation. This is because bitter and resentful inmates will not surrender to the leadership of the cause of their hostility. Only "prisonization"—internalizing prison values, not free world values—can result from an exploitive prison management system.

So, although the structure of Big House prisons make rehabilitation more difficult, it is the inherent culture of exploitation that makes rehabilitation impossible. On a personal level, my stay at Western marked a time when I had become most like a desperate convict. I received very few visits from my family, and so I joined my fellow convicts in a bond of hatred toward the prison staff and administration. If anything, Western made me a criminal, not only in my actions but also in my hate-filled heart.

The lesson of Western is a very important one, and one that we must keep in mind as our journey through the universe of prisons leaves the past and moves on to the present and future. Exploitation of inmate populations has become the norm. This exploitation is more subtle than in times past, but the end result is always the same: A slave will always hate his master.

A Hitchhiker's Guide to Prisons, Part III

The Contemporary Prison: Yesterday, Today, and Tomorrow

EDITORS' NOTE

This chapter, as indicated in the title, is a continuation of Hassine's original and impressive "Hitchhiker's Guide to Prisons." It represents the mature reflections of a man who has seen all prisons have to offer, starting with the oldest facilities and working his way to modern prisons, and has lived to tell us firsthand about the deceptive differences and lingering continuities of penal institutions. Hassine himself best describes the nature of this chapter when he observes the following: "The order in which I was submerged into my new prison habitats [over the course of my imprisonment] has provided me with a historic overview of the various prison models. This intimate contact with prison-past and then prison-present has left me able to discern the structural and operational distinctions between the earliest and newest incarceration systems. So, despite the obscuring mist of evolutionary change, I can clearly identify the elements that control the scope, nature, and consequences of contemporary prison management models." Prisons past determine the shape of prisons present and yet to come, and no one sees this sobering reality more clearly than Victor Hassine.

In 1989, I was transferred to a prison operated by Superintendent Joseph F. Mazurkiewicz (Doc Joe), who held a Ph.D. degree in psychology, and happened to be the leading and most respected prison manager and reformer in the state. Doc Joe understood that people needed to feel safe before any attempts to reform them could be expected to work. As a result, his prison, Rockview, maintained a therapeutic environment while being managed as the safest prison in the state.

The safety I experienced at Rockview quickly transformed—or more accurately, reconstituted—me by vanquishing the fear that had taken possession of me. I am not exaggerating. The change I experienced was real. And, not only had I been changed, but other men, whom I had known as "violent men" in other prisons, were now well-behaved in this more peaceful prison.

Once I was secure in my safety, all the thoughts and energies I had previously devoted to avoiding violence were now available for use in more creative and worthwhile endeavors. Shortly after my arrival at Rockview, I began writing about my prison observations and experiences. As research subjects for my writing projects, I interviewed countless numbers of inmates and prison staff about such topics as prison rape, crime, prison management, and prison life. Eventually, I turned my attention to prison violence.

When recalling those early prison years, it's hard for me to believe that I was the person who had acted so desperately and irresponsibly. But, in a way, it really wasn't me. It has become obvious to me that fear is much more than merely the condition of being afraid. It is a catalyst for the emergence of an altered state, which disables higher—more rational—thought processes to install, as Lord of one's psyche, a paranoid primitive thug whose intentions are unable to extend beyond the moment.

I had been housed at SCI-Rockview for more than ten years since my transfer from Western Penitentiary when, in November of 1998 at about 6:30 in the morning, two prison guards appeared at my cell. Because of our many years together in the prison, these men and I had developed a mutual friendship so I was able to accurately interpret their uncharacteristic sternness as an indication of some unpleasant purpose.

"Hassine, the major wants to see you right now," informed one of the officers.

"Don't ask us any questions. Let's just get going," ordered the other guard, anticipating my response to their presence.

"This is going to be a bad day!" I thought to myself as I reluctantly walked to the major's office, flanked by silent escorts.

The major, a short, slender man in his fifties, was unique among Pennsylvania's uniformed prison staff: As a teenager, he had been sentenced to serve five years in Graterford for participating in an armed robbery. A few years after his release from prison, he had been hired as a prison guard by a Pennsylvania prison system, at the time strongly committed to the rehabilitation model and eager to have an ex-con prison guard serve as a flesh-and-blood example of an inmate transformed into a law-abiding citizen. To myself and most every other Rockview convicts, the short ex-con major was a powerful and

constant reminder of hope in an increasingly hopeless prison environment. However, to many of his coworkers, he was more "ex-con" than
major.

"What's up, major?" I asked in a tone, reflecting our casual
relationship.

"You need to pack up your stuff. You're being transferred today,"
the major matter-of-factly explained as he held a cup of coffee in one
hand and took a drag from a cigarette with the other.

Their job completed, my escorts left the room but not before wishing
me good luck in a mumbling, low-pitched monotone that men often
use when they, awkwardly, try to express fondness toward another
person.

"Where am I going?" I asked.

"I can't tell you," the major responded and then sipped from his hot
cup of coffee.

"Why all the drama?" I probed.

"I don't know, Vic. The first I heard of it was this morning. You
know things have been changing pretty fast since Superintendent
Mazurkiewicz retired. I've never had a problem with you, but I don't
call the shots. This came from way over my head. There's a whole lot
of guys we need to get rid of before shipping you out. But what do I
know?" the major responded, reflecting some of his own frustration
and uncertainty over changing times.

The optimistic social mood that had led to The major's hiring had
evaporated, and recent changes in laws had made it impossible for
an ex-con to ever again be hired as a prison guard in Pennsylvania.
This new public sentiment must certainly have left the major feeling unwanted and insecure rather than a shining example of prison
reform.

DOC JOE

Rockview was Pennsylvania's premiere rehabilitation prison for the
more than thirty years that Doc Joe had been its superintendent. Doc
Joe, the last of the state's great prison reformers, was hired in 1955 as
part of an ambitious effort to reform Pennsylvania's harsh and brutal
prison system. His first job was to create and operate an educational
program in Old Eastern Penitentiary. A deeply religious man, Doc Joe
was convinced that prisons should be used to reform convicts, and he
dedicated his career to changing a cruel punishment-based prison system into a national model of prison rehabilitation. By the time he retired

in 1997, Doc Joe had played a leading role in making Pennsylvania's prison system one of the most effective and respected rehabilitation models in the nation.

"When I first came into the system, one of the first things I was asked to do was participate in a frontal lobotomy; in those days it was state-of-the-art science, and many believed it would cure criminality. It was a terrible experience for me. I helped perform four lobotomies my first day: only one showed minimal positive benefits," Doc Joe once recalled after I asked what it was like when he first started at Old Eastern Penitentiary.

Doc Joe used his formal training, strong management skills, and firm belief in rehabilitation to develop and operate Pennsylvania's first prison school and counseling, psychiatric, and vocational programs. He helped implement the Open Tier System statewide and fashion the first prison therapeutic communities. These were only some of the innovations that Doc Joe introduced into Pennsylvania's reluctant and punitive prison system.

Rockview, a Big House prison, was Doc Joe's proudest achievement. He gradually converted the one-time labor camp prison into a sophisticated and well-integrated rehabilitation-based prison that effectively used its primitive structures and design to support a successful reform-based prison. Doc Joe was able to do this by insisting that all inmates and prison staff meaningfully participate in the rehabilitation process so that everyone in Rockview had a stake in the outcome of its treatment programs.

Rockview's success was reflected in its standing as the cleanest, safest, and most cost-efficient prison in the state. That success also included the career achievements of the major, who was hired as a result of a corrections philosophy that Doc Joe helped create and enforce.

Then in 1994, the newly elected governor of Pennsylvania, Tom Ridge, narrowly won election as the result of a single event: A lifer, released from Doc Joe's prison, had within six months murdered at least four women in New York. Candidate Ridge had promised that if elected, he would see to it that "Life Means Life" and that "Do the Crime—Do Hard Time" would be the motto of his administration.

If nothing else, Governor Ridge was a man of his word. Immediately after taking office, he drastically reduced funding for prison rehabilitation programs, including educational programs. In Addition, he caused to be implemented practices and policies that returned Pennsylvania's prison system to the singular business of disabling and punishing criminals. Pennsylvania's prison system was now at the mercy of politics and politicians.

The major and I were victims of the profound changes that affected his free world as much as my prison world. In Rockview, the full force and madness of that change came soon after Doc Joe had retired. One day, all of the beautiful trees, plants, and shrubs, introduced into the prison decades earlier to soften the harshness of its appearance, were cut down and removed. These elements of nature had suddenly become security risks. Razor wire, new gates, and fences took their places. Then came the requirement that outside work details be supervised by mounted and armed prison guards: a sign not seen in a Pennsylvania prison since before the reforms of the 1950s.

After a decade in Doc Joe's prison, I had settled into a safe and stable prison environment that sheltered me from the social and political upheaval taking place in the free world. Of course television programs and print news warned me about the changes taking place, but while living in Doc Joe's prison, these changes were too abstract for me to fully appreciate.

In Rockview, time seemed to stand still, and I felt securely anchored to the rehabilitation-based prison environment. Doc Joe's world had caused me to develop a naiveté that led me to believe that I would always find myself living in one rehabilitation-based prison or another. It was soon after Rockview's defoliation and occupation by mounted and armed prison guards that, surrounded by the pervasive smell of horse manure, I was summarily transferred from Pennsylvania's prison past and forced to face a brave new prison future. Prison future, however, was looking and smelling like the return of Pennsylvania's harsh prison past.

THE PAST AS THE FUTURE

First I landed in Holmsburg Prison, one of the oldest and most dangerous county prisons in the nation. Then I was moved to Graterford, a 1934 version of a super-max prison. Next I landed in Western, a century-old prison that marked Pennsylvania's departure from a correction-based penal system. In 1998, I was transferred to SCI-Albion, which had been newly constructed in 1994. Albion boasts of state-of-the-art technology and design and operates under newly minted notions of the nature and purpose of adult corrections. What an eerie feeling it was to enter Albion, having just been plucked from prison-past and suddenly planted in some futuristic prison world.

The order in which I was submerged into my new prison habitats has provided me with a historic overview of the various prison models.

This intimate contact with prison-past and then prison-present has left me able to discern the structural and operational distinctions between the earliest and newest incarceration systems. So, despite the obscuring mist of evolutionary change, I can clearly identify the elements that control the scope, nature, and consequences of contemporary prison management models.

My insight has little to do with intellectual ability. You see, all existing prison systems are nothing more than extensions of an entrenched originating prison bureaucracy. Therefore, the potential for change in any prison system is limited by the inherent nature of its founding bureaucracy. And, despite popular belief, contemporary prisons are not new institutions rising atop the ashes of discarded older ones. Actually, they are merely the new growth of a maturing but still operating originating bureaucracy.

Despite dissimilar design and appearance, super-modern Albion is structurally and operationally a composite of Holmsburg's, Graterford's, and Western's prison management systems and models, but with a new coat of paint. For this reason, understanding the nature and consequences of contemporary prison models requires a careful examination and evaluation of their past originating penal system. In terms of evolution, a prison's past is also its future.

This understanding is often overlooked. As a result, many contemporary prison managers find themselves entangled in the fruitless practice of reinventing the wheel, as they attempt to develop and operate new prison management models, only to discover that they must revert to "the old way of doing things" because their prisons are still tightly tethered to the limitations and capacities of their originating bureaucratic substructure.

SCI-Albion

SCI-Albion was conceived and eventually constructed following the convergence of tumultuous events that occurred in Pennsylvania in 1989. Early in that year, the conditions of confinement suit that I had filed against Western Penitentiary was won. Then severe overcrowding led to prison riots in SCI-Rockview and SCI-Huntington. Finally, a four-day-long prison and hostage takeover completely destroyed more than 50 percent of SCI-Camp Hill.

Moved to action by the prison riots of 1989, the legal team, which had successfully litigated the conditions of confinement suit against Western, filed a conditions of confinement suit against all of Pennsylvania's adult corrections facilities. The lawsuit was resolved with a consent decree in which the Department of Corrections, amongst other things, agreed to build six new one-thousand-cell, state-of-the-art prisons.

In 1990, the governor of Pennsylvania appointed a new commissioner of corrections, Dr. Joseph D. Lehman (current commissioner of corrections for Washington State) to oversee reforms to the state's overcrowded and riot-torn prison system and to negotiate and enforce the consent decree. Between 1994 and 1995, SCI-Albion, and five other identical one-thousand-cell, prototypical prisons came online in accordance with the consent decree. Commissioner Lehman made certain that the new prisons (six in all) were designed and constructed to accommodate an aggressive inmate rehabilitation model. To me, after having been stuck in Pennsylvania's prison past for almost two decades, the result was breathtaking.

Like most other modern prisons, Albion is secured by a thirty-foot high, stainless-steel mesh perimeter fence topped with thick curls of stainless-steel razor wire. Therefore, I was greeted to Albion by the wide if cold grin of its glittering silver-on-silver woven metal fence topped with a tinsel-like razor wire. The transparent fence artistically framed and highlighted the prison scenery, which was clearly visible through its mesh. And instead of being scared and intimidated, as I had been when I first entered Holmesburg, Graterford, or Western, I remember feeling curious and even excited about exploring the beckoning prison I was able to spy through the pretty perimeter fence.

Albion was an ocean of plush green fields of grass with handsome geometric outcroppings of earth-toned brick buildings of various shapes and sizes. The buildings were generously spaced so that the deep green of the grass, the proportionate lines of the buildings, and surrounding cerulean blue of the sky combined to create an eye-pleasing and harmonious vision of tranquility that evoked safety and relaxation.

All of the Albion's buildings are climate-controlled, well-lit, spotlessly clean, and color coordinated. There are security cameras everywhere and blind spots nowhere. There are eight separate general population housing units of only 128 cells each, three separate dining halls and two huge recreation yards.

Each housing unit has shower stalls, laundry facilities, a spacious day room (with cushioned chairs), two TV rooms, and large windowed cells. Each recreation yard has a paved quarter-mile running track, basketball courts, a baseball diamond, and lots of green grassy landscape. There is also a large gym complex with a full indoor basketball court, two weight-lifting rooms (with free weights, treadmills, and universal machines), a barber shop, classrooms, and administrative offices.

There is as well, a large education complex with classrooms, conference rooms, administrative offices, and vocational training rooms. Many of the rooms have banks of desk-top computers for student use. There is a separate psychology department with individual counselor's offices and group meeting rooms. And there is a spacious interfaith chapel staffed by three full-time chaplains.

If I had predicted in 1980 that one day I would be housed in a prison that featured the living conditions of Albion, I would have been considered crazy and probably prescribed psychotropic medication. Suffice it to say, strictly in terms of living conditions, being housed in Albion was like living in some on-campus college dormitory.

Rest assured, however, that Albion was no college campus. With its large inmate population of 2,300 men, the prison was crowded and uncomfortable. Every inch a very secure and controlled prison, Albion didn't look or feel like an old-fashioned prison because its architecture created an illusion that made its hard and gritty daily grind of prison outwardly appear natural and even benign. This manufactured effect is comparable to that of a store-bought ant farm: The visible order, regularity, and routine of the seemingly content ant colony fails to expose the violence and crushing hopelessness the trapped ants are actually forced to endure. Albion is a crowded and violent place and, in many ways, more hopeless and indifferent than any prison that had ever housed me.

How did Albion, built with such high hopes and good intentions, come to be a failed prison? I believe it is because of the profound disjuncture between its design and operation. Although Commissioner Lehman specifically designed Albion to accommodate a rehabilitation model, Governor Ridge, after forcing Lehman to resign in 1994, went about implementing policies, procedures, and practices directed at undoing or neutralizing many of the prison's reform-minded design elements. In a great twist of irony, Albion—which had been built to correct problems associated with failed attempts to modify Pennsylvania's old punitive prisons into accepting rehabilitation programs and elements—was now having its rehabilitation design modified to accommodate antagonistic punitive programs and elements. In the end, operating Albion in a manner contrary to its design mandates will ensure that prison's failure for the same reasons and in the same way that the old Spoke and Wheel, Telegraph Pole, and Big House prisons failed when they tried to accept incompatible reforme elements.

The New-and-Improved Belly of an Old Beast

All contemporary American prison systems are defined and, therefore, limited in scope and operation by core elements of what might be called their "prison assembly line" system. A prison's assembly line system includes the following components: inmate collection, inmate containment, inmate management, and end-product production.

Inmate Collection.   This element refers to the system prisons use to collect convicts. The practice of collecting all the convicts of a region into one central location was an innovation when the Quakers first developed the penitentiary system. That innovation was actualized in the form of a huge singular stone structure within which the multitude of Philadelphia's convicts was collected. Subsequently, all competing penitentiary systems, including the Auburn type, followed the practice of gathering convicts in one secure structure, regardless of plans for the handling of the contained inmate mass.

As the number of convicts grew, the single-structure collection system proved impractical and even dangerous, especially when the open tier system allowed inmates relatively free movement on the tiers at certain times of the day. The mammoth size of Graterford and its inherent inability to safeguard its inmates or staff demonstrated the need to reduce the size of a convict mass collected within a single structure. Smaller prisons have since become the norm in American corrections.

Albion prison reflects the contemporary approach of collecting inmates in relatively small housing units to ensure safety and manageability of both staff and inmates. Each of its ten separate housing units consists of two evenly sized and separate "pods." Each pod contains only 64 cells so that its maximum housing capacity is 64 single-celled or 128 double-celled inmates per pod. Therefore, a housing unit's design capacity is only 128 to 256 inmates, with its independent pods ensuring that a disturbance in one cannot spread to the other or to another housing unit.

Inmate Containment

Inmate containment systems refer to the secure perimeters of a prison. The Quakers' containment system, for example, was a thirty-foot high, dark stone wall that enclosed its spoke-and-wheel prison design. Modern containment systems have become much more complex and specialized. Secure, steel mesh fencing has replaced stone containing walls. Moreover, the security level of a contemporary prison is formally determined by its perimeter fencing. Generally, inmate containment systems are either single, double, or triple fences; the greater the number of parallel perimeter fences, the more secure the prison.

A minimum security prison compound will be enclosed by no less than one twenty-foot steel mesh security fence topped with razor wire.

A medium security prison compound will have at least two parallel running security fences spaced ten or more feet apart. In addition, medium security fencing can be electrified and/or have pressure-sensitive alarms installed beneath the ground between the fences. Maximum security prison compounds must be enclosed by electrified double fencing equipped with a pressure-sensitive alarm system. Additionally, maximum security containment systems will include extra perimeter lighting and double-dense razor wire along the top, bottom, and on the ground between the double fencing. Some super-maximum security prison compounds will also have a triple security fencing system.

Steel mesh fencing makes the convict world transparent to outside observers. Accordingly, the visible structures of contemporary prison compounds are designed to appear pleasing to the eye and, even, to resemble a landscaped college campus. Therefore, contemporary prison containment units not only serve to enclose inmate populations and establish a prison's security level, they also serve to assure onlookers of the humane, embraceable, and perhaps even pleasant conditions within a prison campus.

This move away from the old style of impenetrable, scary, stone-walled prison containment systems and toward visual transparency is a significant and consequential, yet often overlooked, departure from the past. Transparency allows and indeed encourages free-world observers to believe that contemporary prison environments operate like college campuses and, therefore, fit naturally within the fabric of a free society. In this way, prisons can be more readily accepted as necessary and even congenial features of a healthy, free community.

Inmate Management. A prison's inmate management system consists of the conditioning regimen that it imposes on its convicts during their term of incarceration. The purpose of a management system is twofold: establish control and deter re-offending upon release. Prison management, defined in this way, is imposed upon inmates through the actions of prison staff.

Originally, penitentiary management systems were simple. Walls, cells, and bars were designed to provide most of the security needs—in terms of preventing escapes and disturbances—so uniformed prison guards were responsible only for the day-to-day management of inmates. Specifically, inmate management required prison guards to (1) open and close steel gates and cell doors (to allow inmates to go to work, meals, or any other permitted locations), (2) police inmate behavior, (3) supervise inmate work details or recreation, and (4) administer corporal punishment.

In Auburn-style prisons, management systems were designed to press inmates into hard labor. Therefore, the duties of uniformed prison guards centered on managing inmate labor. The intended purpose of these management systems was twofold: primarily to deter re-offending by disabling inmates with harsh, forced labor and, secondarily, to economically exploit inmate labor to offset incarceration costs.

Meanwhile, Quaker-style prisons used their uniformed prison guards to manage prisoners through an imposed regime of bible study, forced silence, and isolation, for the singular purpose of deterring re-offending by conditioning inmates into Christian piety. Common to Auburn and Quaker-style prisons was the promise of brutal corporal punishment for those who disobeyed or resisted authority. In actuality, both Quaker and Auburn management systems were punishment-based with the withholding of punishment being the only earthly incentive for good behavior.

The limited nature of prison guards' duties in early prison management systems earned them the nicknames of turnkey, screw, and lock keep, which accurately described the scope of their duties. But despite limited and often brutal interaction with convicts, mutual self-interests allowed friendly relations to develop between keeper and kept. Friendly relations with prison staff allowed inmates to gain better jobs and living conditions (e.g., less punishment). Meanwhile, prison guards sought friendly relations with inmates (usually the leaders) to establish a safe, easy, and stress-free working environment. Mutual self-interest defined inmate/staff relations.

Social Distance.   The degree of familiarity between keeper and kept can be measured in "social distance." The greater the social distance between staff and inmates, the less friendliness and personal contact exists between the two. It is not the strength of the master/servant relationship, existing in all keeper/kept environments, which determines the breath of social distance. In a prison environment, social distance between keeper and kept is set by its management system's reliance upon inmate/staff cooperation. The greater the perceived need for cooperation between prison staff and inmates, the narrower the social distance is between the two. Consequently, social distance defines the day-to-day "inside feel" of a prison's environment, which can range from calm and engaged to turbulent and antagonistic.

In the developmental period of early prisons, convicts, and their turnkeys shared a need for mutual cooperation, so their social distance was narrow—in fact, so narrow that harsh conditions and brutal treatment did not prevent a dysfunctional yet genuine friendliness from developing between the two. And as any prison guard will tell you, it is this "friendship of mutual interests" that keeps resentful inmates and outnumbered prison staff safe and tolerant of each other.

In contrast, contemporary prisons have complex management systems, which have arisen to accommodate the late 1950s shift from punitive to rehabilitative prison models. Today's prison management system divides prison staff into two distinct categories: security and treatment staff.

Social Distance—Security Staff. Prison security staff consists of the uniformed officers who police inmates' behavior, movement, and activity and administer punishment. Security staff duties include locking inmates in their cells, counting inmates, citing inmates for rule infraction, breaking up and preventing disturbances, and controlling inmate movement.

Since uniformed prison guards are no longer required to press inmates into labor or manage their work assignments, very little personal contact between security staff and inmates is required or occurs. Security staff officers have fundamentally become disciplinarians and therefore do not need or expect cooperation or friendliness from their inmate charges. In fact, because uniformed prison guards are now primarily responsible for policing inmates and detecting their rule infractions, the performance of their duties requires them to maintain a cynical view of all inmates as likely rule breakers. Therefore, in contemporary prisons, the social distance between uniformed prison guards and inmates is extremely wide. Their mutual hostility and dislike is undiluted by any meaningful mutual self-interest.

Social Distance—Treatment Staff. Meanwhile, contemporary prison treatment staff members are associated with the broadly defined goal of rehabilitation, and include teaching, medical, counseling, psychological, and vocational treating personnel who, by design, do not participate in policing or punishing day-to-day inmate activity or conduct. These nonpunitive roles are meant to facilitate positive reform through the development of congenial and cooperative relationships. Where uniformed prison guards no longer need or expect an inmate's cooperation, a prison teacher, nurse, or counselor depends on it.

Accordingly, the social distance between treatment staff and inmates is meant to be as narrow as possible to support the mutual cooperation needed to facilitate the delivery and reception of what are essentially rehabilitative treatment staff services. However, because contemporary prisons have dramatically shifted away from rehabilitation and toward punitive prison models, a great distancing between inmates and all prison staff—both custody and treatment—has resulted.

Social Distance—Tension Between Security and Treatment Staff. Some healthy tension between prison security and treatment staff is expected and actually intended to establish a passive checks-and-balances system between the two (as treatment and security staff compete for resources and support from prison managers). Security staff, who collectively are clearly the dominant force in contemporary prison treatment systems, often see treatment staff as "inmate lovers" who coddle inmates and are regularly deceived (conned) by them. Contemporary prison administrators greatly favor punishment over reform, and therefore tend to tip the inmate treatment scale in favor of security staff. This, in turn, has caused treatment staff to become less attentive and more suspicious and authoritarian toward inmates in an effort to align themselves closer to the dominant security staff's expectations.

The tension between security and treatment staff has turned contemporary prison environments into battle fields of hostility as a result of the resentment, suspicion, and even indifference of the security and treatment staff toward inmates. Also, the resentment of security staff toward treatment staff has made matters worse by causing treatment staff to further distance themselves from inmates.

Social Distance: Social Distance and Re-Offending

Inmate behavior following release from prison depends, in large part, on the habits developed through years of day-to-day existence and conditioning in a prison environment; repetition and habituation results in responsive and reactive thoughts and actions to become programmed. The one thing prison experts and administrators agree on is that a prison's environment is the most influential conditioning element affecting an inmate's future behavior. Therefore, a prison's environment is the essence of every prison's inmate management system.

The social distance between prison staff and inmates greatly influences the nature of a prison's environment and, therefore, also of its management system. Since contemporary prisons maintain a great social distance between (a) security staff and inmates, (b) treatment staff and inmates, and (c) security staff and treatment staff, the affected prison environment features a hostility, suspicion, and polarization that actively suppresses the treatment side of a prison's inmate management system.

Contemporary convicts, in the absence of any incentive to cooperate with treatment or security staff, are steeped in a prison environment that trains them to be completely dependent on an authority system whose agents resent, distrust, and even despise them. On release from incarceration, ex-cons—who have spent years and even decades in this toxic environment—invariably take their learned reactionary hostility, distrust, and vengefulness toward authority back with them into the free world, where they not only continue to practice their learned behavior but also teach it to everyone they are able to influence.

The great social distance currently maintained between inmates and prison staff is often explicitly encouraged by correctional managers and indeed by the general public mood of "lock 'em up and throw away the key." The criminogenic consequences of this brutalizing prison environment are rarely considered, despite their profound culumlative effect both on the offender and the free world community to which he returns.

End-Product Production. Prisons can be seen as institutions that seek to manufacture an intended end product. Historically, the only intended end product of America's prison systems had been a "law-abiding ex-convict." There were only two kinds of law-abiding ex-convicts a prison could attempt to manufacture: One conditioned to embrace a law-abiding lifestyle or one so physically and mentally disabled that re-offending is highly unlikely.

A prison's end product is determined by its controlling penal philosophy. A belief that convicts are inherently good and capable of transformation into law-abiding citizens is expressed in the operation of rehabilitation-based prison systems. The belief that inmates will always be criminals is expressed in the operation of disabling-based prison systems.

The evolution of American prison systems has been controlled by an ongoing struggle for dominance between the penal philosophies of nature and nurture (disabling versus rehabilitation). This inability to agree on a unified guiding philosophy has resulted in a compromise that today has a prison's management system operating both reform and disabling processes. Punitive work camp prisons (like Western and Graterford) have been modified to include educational, medical, counseling, and other treatment programs. Meanwhile, correction-based prisons like Albion have been modified to include punitive work details, isolation units, and other disabling processes.

Combining correction and disabling programs within a single prison has hindered a prison's ability to consistently produce either a disabled or rehabilitated law-abiding ex-con. In my opinion, this is because these incompatible processes diminish each other's ability to operate effectively; rehabilitation programs soften disabling processes while disabling programs neutralize rehabilitation processes. In the end, prisons operating both disabling and rehabilitating processes are transformed into arbitrary and even random punishment institutions that uselessly operate costly rehabilitation programs, knowing their effectiveness will be totally neutralized by disabling practices.

Contemporary prisons have attempted to remedy the incompatibility between their correction and disabling-based processes by simply altering their intended end product to reflect what a hybrid prison assembly line can, with certainty, be expected to produce. Accordingly, prisons today only seek to manufacture a compliant convict who remains stable enough to adapt to indefinite incarceration without causing a disturbance—in other words, a "warehouse stable inmate," or more cynically, a "warehouse friendly inmate."

Prisons no longer endeavor to produce any sort of law-abiding ex-convict. Reigning criminal justice models actually anticipate re-offending by ex-convicts and continuously instigate the passage of new criminal statutes and sentencing guidelines aimed at permanently subjecting convicts and ex-convicts to close supervision or incarceration (consider Three Strikes, Megan's, and other mandatory sentencing laws).

To accommodate the change of the intended end product, prisons no longer find it necessary to press inmate labor. This is because forced labor disturbs the preferred tranquility of a warehouse prison. Also, outside inmate work details introduce needless security risks and costly supervision.

Since contemporary warehousing prisons have no forced labor to economically exploit, they have developed an ingenious and successful process of drawing financial gain directly from the incarceration process itself. Prisons are now operated to provide government-funded job opportunities to unemployed blue collar workers who have been displaced by our nation's shift from an industrial to a service-based economy. Economic gain results from returning the unemployed to work and, therefore, to the tax rolls. As a result, prisons are now built in high unemployment areas where they are greatly desired, appreciated, and encouraged to expand.

Also, communities and private companies generate additional income and jobs by providing goods and services to prisons and prisoners. In turn, prisons tax these service providers by charging them an annual percentage of gross revenues, which amounts to a fee for the privilege of doing business. This novel process of taxing private service providers to offset prison costs has led to the outsourcing of many prison operations as a way of increasing a prison's tax revenues. For example, there are prisons today that have outsourced and taxed their commissary, medical, inmate phone, inmate cable, psychiatry, transport, counseling, food, and even prison security services. Many prisons have become de facto partners of their service providers.

As a result, incarcerating more citizens for longer periods has been made economically beneficial, which, in turn, has led to business and job-starved communities actively lobbying for continued growth of the prison industrial complex. But in actuality, the financial benefit of taxing prison services and growing prisons is illusory because prison service providers factor the "cost of doing business" tax into what they charge prison managers for goods and services. Therefore, taxpayers end up paying grossly inflated prices for diluted goods and services as the excise tax that prisons enjoy proportionately increases the cost of the goods and services that they must buy.

The change in the intended end product has profoundly altered the nature of America's prison systems. Successfully promoting a cynical view of convicts as incorrigible has led to lessening citizens' expectations from their prison managers. Instead of demanding more safety in the community, citizens are content to clamor for harsher retribution. Instead of expecting fewer prisons, citizens are content to grow prisons to create jobs and increase financial gain. And instead of expecting improved social tranquility, citizens are content to live in a fragmented society of free versus warehoused citizens

Prisons have become profitable human warehouses. The scope of their use has been encouraged to broaden to include the incarceration of social misfits as well as common criminals. Today, the vast majority of prison inmates are mentally ill, drug addicts, homeless, juvenile delinquents, or physically disabled (without medical insurance) who in the past were not considered career criminals. Social cleansing, not deterrence, has become a prison's "raison d'etre." Therefore, the number of social outcasts and nonconforming citizens, rather than common criminals, is currently responsible for establishing the number of prison cells that must be built.

A Revolution Not Televised. Albion is so well-designed, aesthetically pleasing, and so tranquil, and comfortable in appearance that its physical aspects have overshadowed all debate over its socio-environmental consequences to inmate and free-world populations. Any criticism of Albion's conditions is likely to be dismissed as ingratitude or excessive liberalism. Certainly, anyone who has ever experienced life in an older penitentiary would find it hard to find anything to complain about, and that is precisely the prison's most effective growth element. Contemporary prisons' conspicuous displays of comfort and beauty have led the general public to embrace the building of many more prisons, to hold many more inmates for many more years.

Consider these facts: In 1994 when Albion and its five sister institutions came online, to ease prison overcrowding, the total number of inmates in Pennsylvania's adult corrections facilities stood at 26,000. Without serious incident, public outcry or environmental impact considerations, in just twelve years, that population has risen to over 43,000, while all indicators of prison overcrowding have continued to rise.

This trend of rapid prison expansion has also been reflected nationally. In 1995 the nationwide population of incarcerated people in state and federal prisons stood at 1,085,022. By 2004, less than ten years later, that figure has more than doubled to about 2.3 million inmates. And, once again, that rapid growth has occurred without major incident, public outcry, or environmental impact consideration.

In my opinion, pleasant prison appearance and conditions are responsible for this public tolerance, and even embrace, of contemporary prisons, which has resulted in the historic and unprecedented growth of prisons (scope and number) and inmate populations. This growth has been broad and rapid enough to be considered revolutionary in terms of impact on the nation's sociopolitical landscape and the very nature of our democracy.

The Bureau of Justice Statistics reported that as of December 31, 2004, there were about 2.3 million inmates in state and federal lockups, 5 million people on parole or probation, 13 million people in a state or federal lockup during the one-year period between 2003 and 2004, and 760,000 people working as prison guards.*

To better comprehend the revolutionary consequences of these statistics, consider that the 13 million people who have been in state or federal lockup in 2004 represent the total population of the following eleven states: Wyoming, Vermont, North Dakota, Alaska, Utah, New Hampshire, Maine, New Mexico, West Virginia, Idaho, and Montana. Therefore, while Americans have been distracted by concerns over the war in Iraq, the war on terror, and same-sex marriage, the silent and steady incarceration revolution has politically and socially disenfranchised (through incarceration) the equivalent of every man, woman, and child in eleven of

---

* See the Department of Justice's website, http://www.ojp.usdoj.gov/bjs/correct.htm.

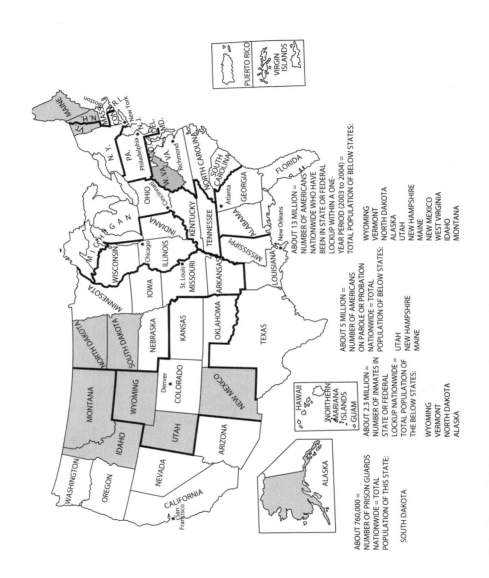

ABOUT 13 MILLION =
NUMBER OF AMERICANS
NATIONWIDE WHO HAVE
BEEN IN STATE OR FEDERAL
LOCKUP WITHIN A ONE-
YEAR PERIOD (2003 to 2004) =
TOTAL POPULATION OF BELOW STATES:

WYOMING
VERMONT
NORTH DAKOTA
ALASKA
UTAH
NEW HAMPSHIRE
MAINE
NEW MEXICO
WEST VIRGINIA
IDAHO
MONTANA

ABOUT 5 MILLION =
NUMBER OF AMERICANS
ON PAROLE OR PROBATION
NATIONWIDE = TOTAL
POPULATION OF BELOW STATES:

UTAH
NEW HAMPSHIRE
MAINE

ABOUT 2.3 MILLION =
NUMBER OF INMATES IN
STATE OR FEDERAL
LOCKUP NATIONWIDE =
TOTAL POPULATION OF
THE BELOW STATES:

WYOMING
VERMONT
NORTH DAKOTA
ALASKA

ABOUT 760,000 =
NUMBER OF PRISON GUARDS
NATIONWIDE = TOTAL
POPULATION OF THIS STATE:

SOUTH DAKOTA

our fifty states. This revolution has also partially disenfranchised 5 million Americans who are on parole or probation. Moreover, 760,000 prison guards have been dedicated to doing nothing other than keeping people disenfranchised. In these terms, the growth and impact of the incarceration revolution suddenly becomes evident.

Between 1994 (when Albion was opened) and 2004, the number of inmates, in Pennsylvania and nationwide, increased by more than 50 percent. Therefore, by 2014, the incarceration revolution promises to disenfranchise, through incarceration, at least an additional 6 million Americans while employing 325,000 more prison guards to keep these people removed from the benefits of the Constitution and full citizenship.

As the number of our states goes "black" (i.e., their population equals the increase in the number of incarcerated, and therefore disenfranchised, Americans), our nation slips closer to becoming an apartheid nation. This condition is similar to the sociopolitical climate that existed when Doc Joe was first hired into the Pennsylvania Bureau of Corrections and when Jim Crow and segregation were the hallmarks of our laws and society.

If this revolution is allowed to continue, like it or not, we will eventually be forced to experience a sociopolitical shift that moves us from a Constitutional Democracy and places you in a Constitutional Apartheid. Then our quality of life will entirely depend on whether we are a member of the decreasing number of free states or of the growing number of states gone black.

CONTEMPORARY PRISON LIFE

To understand day-to-day life in a contemporary prison, consider this typical day in my life:

6:00 AM

A very loud bell sounds, the lights in my cell turn on automatically, and a loudspeaker announces: "Count time. All inmates stand for count." My cellmate and I get out of bed, stand by the cell door, and wait for two prison guards to pass and count us. Once the guards have passed, we make our beds (failure to do so is a misconduct), take turns using the sink and toilet, and prepare for the start of our day.

6:30–7:00 AM

The loudspeaker announces: "Breakfast line. Five on the door." This means that I have five minutes to press a call button located near the threshold of the cell door. This will cause my cell door to be unlocked. My cellmate leaves the cell, locking the door behind him. I stay in the cell to use the toilet. Then I use the cell's hot tap water to make a cup of instant coffee.

About twenty minutes later, my cellmate returns to the cell from breakfast, and we both remain locked in the cell, awaiting the next line movement. There isn't enough room in the cell for both of us to move around so we each sit or lay on our bunks (I have the bottom bunk) and watch/listen to the news on the TV/radio.

8:00 AM

The loudspeaker announces: "Work lines. Education lines." My cellmate and I have five minutes to hit the call button and leave the cell to go to work or school. My cellmate goes to work while I stay in the cell waiting for line movements that will allow me to go through my morning workday routine.

8:15 AM

The loudspeaker announces: "Yard out." At this time, I have five minutes to hit the call button to open my cell so that I can go to the yard. Instead, I choose to stay in my cell so later I can take a morning shower. If I go to the yard, I will have to wait until the afternoon to shower and since I work in the afternoon, I will not be able to shower. On workdays, instead of yard, I take a morning shower and then enjoy the luxury and solitude of an empty cell.

9:00 AM

The loudspeaker announces: "Half-time move for yard." At this time, men in the yard can return to their cells while men in their cells can go to the yard. The block guard will only open my cell for a five-minute window ("five on the door") during line movements. I hit my call button to get my cell opened so that I can take a shower. Wearing a bathrobe and slippers, I walk the few feet to one of eight stalled showers on the tier. After showering, I return to my cell, get dressed and, since I'm a morning person, I write or read with the radio on; usually I listen to National Public Radio. Inmates are not allowed to use the dayroom in the morning except on weekends. This is to encourage inmates to leave their cells and go to work, school, or the yard.

10:00 AM

The loudspeaker announces: "Yard in." Everyone in the yard returns to their cells. I use this opportunity to press my call button so that I can go out of my cell and make a fifteen-minute phone call to my family. (There are four wall-mounted pay phones on the pod.) After the call, I return to my cell.

11:15 AM

My cellmate returns from work, and we both wait to go to lunch.

12:00 Noon

The loudspeaker announces: "Main line out." We have five minutes to hit the call button and leave the cell for lunch. I join the one-hundred-plus other inmates on the pod who leave their cells to go to to eat. The design of the block requires us to exit the block in a single column of men. Once out of the unit, the column thickens as inmates pour onto a concrete walkway. I move with the herd along the walkway that leads to a larger perpendicular concrete walkway, extending to my left and right. I turn left at the intersection, along with the herd, being careful not to collide with other men walking in the opposite direction to return to their block after finishing their meal. Blocks are called to meal lines one at a time so that when one block of men is leaving the chow hall, another block of men is called to eat. I eventually enter my assigned cafeteria and go through a food service line, at the end of which I am handed a preplated tray of food and a beverage. I am assigned a seat at a four-man table. I have about seven minutes to eat before the guards order me to finish eating and return to my block.

12:30 PM

I'm back in my cell with my cellmate, a bell sounds, and the loudspeaker announces: "Count time. All inmates stand for count." The lights in my cell are turned on, and my cellmate and I stand up in front of the cell door until two guards go by to count us. I then read or take a nap while waiting for count to clear.

1:00 PM

The loudspeaker announces: "Count is clear."

1:05 PM

The loudspeaker announces: "Work lines. Education lines." We have five minutes to hit the call button. We both go to work. We join the herd of inmates exiting the unit. I walk the maze of concrete walkways to my assigned job in the library.

2:00 PM

At work a loudspeaker announces: "Line movement." Men in the library have five minutes to return to their cells, or they can stay until the next line movement, which will be on the hour. Also, eligible inmates in their cells have five minutes to come to the library. Inmates are allowed to attend the regular library one time per week (per assigned day and time) and the law library twice per week (per approved written request).

3:00 PM

The loudspeaker announces: "Line movement." Inmates in the library have five minutes to return to their blocks or stay until the library closes.

3:15 PM

The loudspeaker announces: "All inmates return to your block." The library is closed, and I have five minutes to return to my cell.

4:00 PM

The loudspeaker announces: "Count time. All inmates stand for count." The lights go on in my cell, and my cellmate and I stand by the cell door until two guards pass to count us. We then return to our bunks to read or watch TV until the evening meal.

4:30 PM

The loudspeaker announces: "Count is clear."

5:00 PM

The loudspeaker announces: "Main line out." My cellmate and I go to chow with the rest of the block. We return to our cell at about 5:20 PM.

6:00 PM

The loudspeaker announces: "Work lines. Education lines." I have five minutes to leave the cell and go to my job assignment. My cellmate has the cell to himself. On weekends I will be able to stay in my cell, use the dayroom, or in spring and summer months, go to the night yard when Yard lines are called.

7:00 PM

The loudspeaker in the library announces: "Line movement." Men in the library have five minutes to return to their cells or stay until the library closes. Eligible men in their cells have five minutes to come to the library.

8:00 PM

The loudspeaker announces: "All inmates return to their block." The library is closed and I return to my cell. I can stay in my cell, play chess in the dayroom, take a shower, or use the phone. I usually use the phone and then play chess.

8:40 PM

The loudspeaker announces: "Lockup for count." I have to return to my cell within the next five minutes.

9:00 PM

The loudspeaker announces: "Count time. All inmates stand for count." The lights in my cell go on, and my cellmate and I stand in front of the cell door until two guards pass to count us.

11:00 PM, 2:00 AM, 4:00 AM

The "security lights" in my cell go on for nonstanding count. It is a half-light, but it is bright enough to allow me to read. The lights turn off about fifteen minutes later. It interrupts my sleep, even though I wear a towel over my face.

6:00 AM

A bell sounds and the loudspeaker announces: "Count time. All inmates stand for count." I get to do everything all over again.

PRISON GHOST TOWNS

Like most contemporary prisons, Albion fragments and meters my time out of the cell to enslave me to line movements that are methodically announced by bells or loudspeakers. A generous estimate of my daily out-of-cell time is less than seven hours. The rest of the time, I am in my cell waiting for count or line movements. My life consists of constantly trying to go or return from somewhere within the five minutes of allowed movement time. This routine of keeping in synch with mass herd movement, leaves me too busy to cause a disturbance or plan some mischief.

Combined with a warehousing philosophy, controlled line movement erodes efforts at rehabilitation. This is because classroom, chapel, and all other treatment service times are also fragmented into one-hour portions. Thus, when counts are late, which is often the case, the classroom sessions scheduled immediately after count are cancelled because they are too short to be of any value.

Considering that classrooms are only accessible three and a half hours in the morning, two and a half hours in the afternoon, and two hours in the evening (eight hours total), losing three hours of classroom time due to late counts means losing one third of available classroom time. Five hours per day of classroom time for an inmate population of 2,300 is simply inadequate.

This erosion of classroom time also discourages inmate enrollment in educational programs and frustrates teachers who, like me, must spend much of their day waiting for count to clear rather than teaching. This frustration results in absenteeism and an increase in social distance between inmates and teachers. In the end, neither students nor teachers feel that participation in educational programs is of any meaningful value.

In 2003, I charted, for a four-month period, classroom cancellations. There were ten one-hour classroom sessions scheduled weekdays between 8:00 AM and 8:00 PM. During that time, 43 percent of classroom time was canceled because of teacher absenteeism. This did not take into consideration sessions canceled due to late counts, which I would estimate to be an additional 10 percent. Thus over this four month period, fully 53 percent of education classes were cancelled.

Elevating controlled line movements over treatment programs has resulted in shrinking the availability of such programs in most contemporary prisons. In addition, while Albion's walkways were packed with inmates going to or from the yard, commissary, or chow, classrooms in the overcrowded prison remained eerily empty, silent, and still—a sterile ghost town in the hollow of human activity. The same was true of the large and beautiful interfaith chapel.

The reigning warehousing philosophy, combined with a firm belief in "nothing works," has allowed all of a prison's resources to be directed toward keeping inmates going and coming with destinations being much less important than the movement itself. In the end, all inmate destinations in a contemporary prison are really to nowhere. This might not make a difference to you, unless you knew that tens of thousands of taxpayer dollars per inmate per year were being used to route inmates around fully staffed but empty classrooms and chapels, to hurry them to nowhere until they are finally hurried out to the free world.

SNITCHES, SNIPERS, AND EAR HUSTLERS

Another consequence of Albion's combination of warehousing and controlled movement is limited inmate social interaction. Inmate masses are continuously segmented into smaller groupings, going to separate locations: blocks, yards, dining halls, classrooms, and soforth. Each inmate, his own path to take, must always separate himself from the larger group. This constant fragmentation produces a dominance of self-interest over social integration.

Self-interested inmates are prone to developing antisocial behavior, since focusing only on individual concerns erodes one's ability to participate in cohesive or cooperative group activity. In short, Albion was teaching inmates to be selfish. As a consequence, the social distance between inmates was as great as it was between staff and inmates.

Prison security officials actively increase the social distance between inmates to discourage planning of group disturbances or uprisings. To this end, informants are openly recruited and rewarded for providing any information regarding rule infraction—no matter how petty—or past crimes. Rewarding and elevating this behavior attracts many practitioners, which in turn keeps inmates distrustful of each other.

In fact, the federal government has enacted a statute referred to as "Rule 35," which permits the downward modification of court-imposed sentences in cases where an inmate provides law enforcement with information that leads to the prosecution of new criminal activity. There is no limit on how great a reduction in sentence an informant might receive for information. It's strictly supply and demand. As a result, being "Rule 35d" (or "35d") has become part of the federal inmate argot, referring to being informed on by an inmate seeking a sentence reduction.

Federal Rules of Criminal Procedure, Rule 35

United States Code Annotated Federal Rules of Criminal Procedure for the United States District Courts
VII. Post-Conviction Procedures

Rule 35. Correcting or Reducing a Sentence
  (a) Correcting Clear Error. Within 7 days after sentencing, the court may correct a sentence that resulted from arithmetical, technical, or other clear error.
  (b) Reducing a Sentence for Substantial Assistance.

(1) In General. Upon the government's motion made within one year of sentencing, the court may reduce a sentence if:

   (A) the defendant, after sentencing, provided substantial assistance in investigating or prosecuting another person; and

   (B) reducing the sentence accords with the Sentencing Commission's guidelines and policy statements.

(2) Later Motion. Upon the government's motion made more than one year after sentencing, the court may reduce a sentence if the defendant's substantial assistance involved:

   (A) information not known to the defendant until one year or more after sentencing;

   (B) information provided by the defendant to the government within one year of sentencing, which did not become useful to the government until more than one year after sentencing; or

   (C) information the usefulness of which could not reasonably have been anticipated by the defendant until more than one year after sentencing and which was promptly provided to the government after its usefulness was reasonably apparent to the defendant.

(3) Evaluating Substantial Assistance. In evaluating whether the defendant has provided substantial assistance, the court may consider the defendant's presentence assistance.

(4) Below Statutory Minimum. When acting under Rule 35 (b), the court may reduce the sentence to a level below the minimum sentence established by statute.

Albion's security department relies almost exclusively on an abundance of informant information. The appetite for such information has resulted in a collection of reports from friends, enemies, and strangers about almost every inmate in the prison. It is the responsibility of individual security officials to decide which reports merit belief and action.

Therefore, at any given time, most inmates in Albion are subject to disciplinary action based entirely on a security official's decision to believe an informant's report. Of course, inmates are very aware of this vulnerability—that's the point of it—and this knowledge increases the already wide social distance between inmates.

Case in point: When I arrived at Albion, two security officers, whom I had never met, nevertheless resented me because I had published a book and previously filed conditions of confinement suits (they eventually confessed this to me). There is always a percentage of prison staff who are so hostile to inmates that they maliciously target those who dare complain about any aspect of prison conditions.

One day, an inmate was caught with colored pencils, stolen from an art class. The thief noticed my name mentioned in the misconduct report, as part of a list of men assigned to that art class session. My name appeared first, so the thief, being an experienced informant, offered to strike a deal: for a reduced sentence, he would implicate me by confessing that I had stolen and then sold him the pencils in exchange for a lenient punishment. Whether the security guards actually directed the thief to make a false statement against me is speculation. What is certain is that based on the thief's statement, I was found guilty of stealing the pencils and threatening the informant for "snitching on me." I was sanctioned to ninety days in the hole while the thief received only thirty days.

I was in the hole even though the thief had sworn that I had stolen the pencils at a time when I was on a visit, so his story was demonstrably false. The security officers knew the misconduct hearing system at Albion was entirely dispositional with no truth-finding component. This meant that once I was issued the misconduct, the hearing examiner's purpose was limited to deciding the disposition—that is, the degree of punishment. At the hearing level, innocence is of no consequence. On appeal, prison managers would be left to decide whether to release me.

Gloating, the two guards privately confessed to me that they had decided to use the informant's lies to punish me for being so "arrogant." It was a blessing that they were too lazy to investigate my whereabouts on the day in question or else the informant might have given a statement that I could not have so easily disproved.

On appeal to the superintendent, I was released and fully exonerated after serving twenty days in the hole. I filed a formal prison complaint and, eventually, a federal law suit against the two officers. As a result of my prison complaint, I was reimbursed one hundred dollars for property I lost when I was sent to the hole. Nothing happened to the security guards because they were just following "procedures." However, they increased their determination to get even with me for complaining about their misbehavior.

Eventually, the two security officers succeeded in having me transferred to a maximum security prison based on their unsupported claim that I posed a threat to the institution. I spent another ten days in the hole on my receipt in the super-max facility. No misconduct report had been filed to justify my transfer, so there was nothing for me to appeal. Later, as a result of my federal lawsuit, I received a copy of the "secret" memo used to transfer me. It contained nothing but unsupported allegations of "possible" misconduct.

As a result of my transfer to a super-max prison, my privileges were greatly restricted and my record of adjustment was burdened. Over the course of three years and soon after a judge decided to allow my federal suit to trial, I was suddenly transferred to a medium security prison. All my privileges and security levels were reinstated to Albion levels. This is what vindication looks and feels like in contemporary warehouse prisons where—only when necessary—justice is treated as an accommodation you must be willing and able to fight for.

Institutional dependence on informant testimony has turned prisons into training grounds for predatory informants who sell true or false information for benefits, revenge, or just plain fun. The lexicon of informing has been increased to accommodate its refinements: "Snitches" are now garden-variety informants who report misconduct that they have personally been made aware of or are actually a part of; "snipers" are informants who carefully watch group or individual activities from a distance to detect misconduct that they can use to "rule 35" someone; and "ear hustlers" are informants who, unnoticed, place themselves within listening distance of groups or individuals to hear about misconduct they can use to rule 35 someone.

The fear of being targeted by prison informants has replaced the fear of predatory violence. The anti-social and selfish behavior typified by informants, as well as the mistrust it breeds, travels with a convict when he or she is finally released to the free world. Thus, contemporary ex-cons are totally unprepared for life in a cooperative society where, ideally, anti-social behavior is punished and not rewarded.

WHEN SPECIAL NEEDS AREN'T SPECIAL ANYMORE: SOME STORIES FROM INSIDE

There has been a sea change in the composition of contemporary prison populations As a result, the very definition of a criminal has changed. Traditionally, career criminals were those who committed crimes to financially enrich themselves, and it was these for-profit criminals who filled American prisons. Today, the vast majority of convicts committed criminal acts as a result of mental illness, drug addiction, anti-social behavior, or parole violations. Only a small minority of convicts committed crimes for financial profit.

Despite this core change in the nature of prison populations, modern prisons still operate primarily to punish and discourage for-profit criminals. What benefit is gained by using prisons to punish and discourage mentally ill or hopelessly addicted inmates from profiting from crime if attempting to profit from crime is not what landed them in prison?

He was an old man in his late sixties, palsied left arm, diabetic, and afflicted with a host of age-related illnesses acquired as payment for a lifetime of drug and alcohol abuse. A decade and a half earlier, I'd met him when we were both struggling to survive Western. He had been a forceful and abrasive man whom I disliked and avoided. However, while he still had a lot of attitude, the ravages of a misspent life had rendered his aggressiveness pathetic.

Actually, his weathered, bent, and crippled body is a fate that has befallen or awaits many inmates in today's warehousing prisons. Including me! This impending reality had me deeply affected by our chance meeting in Albion and, so, despite our past dislike for each other, I decided to listen to what he had to say and to help if I could.

"These guys keep messing with me, Vic," he carped as we sat in the library. I was amused by his familiarity, which conveniently ignored past differences.

"Who's messing with you?" I asked, curious to learn who would bother an old and disabled man who was so obviously helpless and harmless.

"Medical and the guards. I can't get no medical care. And when I try, the guards stay on me and won't let me get to medical," he answered, looking around as if he worried that someone might be watching or listening.

"Look. You got to help me. You got them to do the right thing in Western. I carry the court's decision with me everywhere. Boy, that was something what you did there. I've been down going on thirty years, and I ain't ever seen nothing like it in my life," he chuckled. From inside his coat pocket, he pulled a worn photocopy of the seventy plus page court decision in *Tillery v. Owens*. I noted his sudden change in focus and mood.

"You know me. I ain't ever been good with writing or the law. Will you help get these people to give me my medical care?" he asked.

If he was really having problems getting medical care, I wanted to help him. I instructed him to return during his next scheduled library session and to bring whatever documentation he had regarding his medical issues.

"So you going to help me? I keep all my papers. I remember that from what you did at Western. That was something. I even got a judge writing me, trying to help me. But I don't know what I'm supposed to do. I get all confused and frustrated. I'll bring everything with me next week. Good looking-out," he stated, as he abruptly turned to walk out of the library, still looking furtively around.

The following week, the old man returned to the library with a folder full of old, wrinkled, and creased documents. They looked like he had quickly thrown them together while escaping a fire. He had pulled the thick collection of papers from an inside coat pocket, fashioned by tearing a slit in the lining. His coat bulged from the many other things stashed in his makeshift carryall.

I reviewed his records and learned that he was classified as a "special needs" inmate. This meant that prison officials had determined that he had serious mental issues. Albion had been designed with a Special Needs Unit that was one pod of Housing Block, dedicated to housing inmates whose medical and/or mental condition demanded close supervision. The SNU was, physically, the closest pod to the medical and psychology departments. Also, the Unit Team members (prison staff assigned to manage the pod) were given special training for dealing with special needs inmates.

Unfortunately, the SNU was filled, and the waiting list for assignment to the pod was extremely long. Special needs inmates comprise one of the largest growing population segments in contemporary prisons. Between one-third and one-half of prison populations are designated special needs inmates. In fact, contemporary prisons have become the largest mental health service providers in the nation.

I also learned that the old man was within two years of his max date—meaning the date he would have to be released from prison because he had served his total sentence. This was a problem because the health care services at Albion had been privatized, and the service provider was reluctant to fund expensive medical treatment if the inmate was soon to be released from the prison, when he would be able to have a public health care provider foot the bill for costly medical procedures. As a result, Albion's medical care policy was to approve operations or other expensive medical treatments only in life-threatening cases.

This policy and practice is legally questionable, since non-life-threatening medical conditions, left untreated, can become deadly. However, since the majority of inmates are illiterate, most convict patients are not able to formally challenge application of the policy; the few who do often eventually receive the needed medical care. Therefore, the policy and practice is actually a procedural hurdle meant to reduce costs by discouraging demands for medical care.

One of the medical documents in his possession reported that he would benefit from an operation that would relieve chronic pain by improving the worsening condition of his crippled arm. Nevertheless, the old man could not get the medical department to schedule him for the operation. The old man had even written to a federal judge, seeking judicial assistance in getting medical care. The judge had responded by instructing him to file a lawsuit so the court could help officially. The judge then sent a letter to the superintendent, inquiring about the old man's medical concerns.

Even though his condition and need for medical care were clearly documented, the old man could not "access" the required medical care because of his inability to overcome the procedural hurtles constructed by the private health care provider. The old man simply did not know what to do next. He explained that the letters and grievances he had initiated in the past were the work of jailhouse lawyers who later abandoned him when he could no longer pay them. Also, though he was literate, the progression of his mental illness had left him confused and frustrated, so he tended to ramble about unrelated things in the middle of a conversation.

To make matters worse, an obscure document that he had forgotten to mention revealed that he had been diagnosed as suffering from an early onset of Alzheimer's disease. To a convict, such an illness would place him beyond the ability to overcome any of the many procedural hurdles particular to contemporary prisons and meant to limit inmate access to treatment programs and services, including medical care. Like an animal in the wild that has lost all its teeth, the old man was surrounded by nourishment that he simply could not eat.

After putting his files in order, I helped him fill out an inmate request slip to the medical department, asking to be examined by a doctor to determine the causes of his multiple ailments. The request slip carbon-copied the judge and superintendent. The simple act of carbon copying the request attached an urgency born of the threat of accountability.

The prison's nurse manager responded to his request, stating that there was nothing more they could do for him. I then helped the old man file a formal grievance in which he specifically asked to be examined by a specialist to assess his need for an operation on his crippled arm. The judge was carbon-copied while the superintendent would automatically receive a copy of the formal grievance.

That's when things began to happen. The old man was suddenly transferred to the SNU (Special Needs Unit). He was then interviewed by the nurse manager. One day when I was at Medical, tending to my own needs, I had occasion to speak to the nurse manager on the old man's behalf. The nurse was very hostile to me and ordered me out of the area. She seemed mad that the old man was getting so much attention.

A few days later, a friend informed me that the old man had been locked up in the hole for being in an unauthorized area. It seems that the old man had been having a problem remembering that he had moved to the SNU and, on occasion, he would appear at his previous cell assignment when he returned from the yard. The guards treated it as a breach in security. As was the practice, the misconduct hearing examiner simply imposed punishment.

That same day, I happened to encounter the superintendent on the walks, and I explained to him what had happened to the old man and how he suffered from Alzheimer's, which rendered his actions a result of illness, not rule breaking. The superintendent promised to look into the matter and, if he actually were diagnosed with the disease, he would have him released.

The next day, the old man was released from the hole and appeared in the library. He was frustrated, angry, and confused. He had a letter from the judge that included a copy of a letter that the judge had sent to the superintendent, inquiring about his medical care.

"We gonna get them now, ain't we?" he asked.

"We're going to try and get you the medical care you need," I answered.

The old man then quickly turned away and walked out of the library, mumbling. The stay in the hole had worsened his condition. The next day, I was informed that the old man had been locked up again for arriving at his old cell assignment. The guard who had issued the first misconduct had issued this one, probably because he felt that the old man had manipulated his release from the hole the first time. Of course, the misconduct hearing examiner once again simply assigned punishment and sent the old man back to the hole.

This time, the superintendent saw me on the walks and asked me how the old man was doing. I informed him that he had been returned to the hole for, again, reporting to his old cell assignment. Frustrated and a little angry, the superintendent promised that he would have the old man released immediately.

"This prison isn't designed to deal with men in his condition. We punish rule breaking. Corrections officers are not trained to distinguish between mental illness and misconduct. Oftentimes, they treat both the same," he explained in a pensive, almost apologetic, tone.

"There must be something you can do because he'll just end up in the hole again," I remarked.

"I'll make sure all staff are aware of his condition, but as he gets worse, it may not help. I'll tell you what. They have just opened up a special medical needs prison. There is a long waiting list, but I'll try to get him transferred there as soon as possible. Until then, I'll contact medical and ask them to monitor him closely," the superintendent assured.

The next day I spoke with the old man's treating psychologist. She had worked as a mental health service provider before being hired by the prison, and she was much more helpful and forthcoming than the nurse manager. The psychologist explained that not only was this an issue of a private medical provider trying to save money, but the old man's mental health issues made him a very difficult person to treat in a prison. Also, because he was a sex offender, the truth was, many of the prison staff were reluctant to care for him.

"Bottom line: while his medical and mental health needs are genuine, the prison simply isn't able to effectively treat all of its special needs inmates. So, priorities have to be set and, for one reason or another, he wasn't considered a priority. Actually, he's better off than most of the others going through the same problems, because they don't have you helping them. The silver lining here is that many of these men would be worse off if they were on the streets," the psychologist reasoned.

A few weeks later, the old man was transferred to the special medical care prison. This certainly was a victory for him but cold comfort to the ever-growing population of special needs inmates whose primary treatment is mistreatment by staff and inmates or simply being confined in the hole.

The Return of Debtors' Prison

One of the purposes of our founding Constitution was to abolish the hated British practice of imprisoning debtors for not paying their debts. Now, through the vehicle of contemporary prisons, this long dead practice is finding a second life in America.

The technology and information revolutions have made it possible for criminal justice bureaucracies to easily tax convicts for restitution, court costs, and fines. Albion's accounting department possesses state-of-the-art computer software that allows a single database manager to electronically bill, invoice, track, and manage the accounts of every inmate in the prison. This capability has encouraged vote-seeking legislators to enact new laws requiring automatic monthly deductions from inmate monetary accounts as the payment for a growing number of inmate obligations.

In the past, these obligations were paid by convicts on release from prison when they would be able to get a job and earn a living wage. Completing these financial obligations was ensured by including the debt payment as a condition of continued parole. Today, things are very different. This is how it works.

All money received by an inmate must be deposited in his prison account. The account is managed as a running debt/credit voucher.

An inmate makes deposits to his account through earned wages, gifts (from friends and family), and any other source of income. The vast majority of deposits to inmate accounts come from inmate wages and gifts from family members.

When a sentencing court requires an inmate to pay restitution, costs, or fines (almost every inmate today must make these payments), the prison accounting department will automatically deduct 20 percent of any money that the inmate receives each and every month and then send the deducted funds to the sentencing court. If an inmate files a federal conditions of confinement suit, he must now pay $350 in filing fees, which are deducted from his inmate account using the same monthly deduction schedule used to collect payment for the inmate's sentencing obligations. If the inmate has child support obligations, again, money is automatically deducted from his account every month to satisfy that debt. The law caps such deductions at 50 percent of inmates' gross monthly receipts and forbids deductions from accounts possessing less than $10.

For those inmates fortunate enough to have a job, the average monthly wage is about $35. Those who do not work receive idle pay, totaling about $12 per month, which allows the purchase of cosmetics and toiletry items that the prison is normally required to provide to every inmate.

The vast majority of mandatory deductions from inmates' accounts are made from prison wages. Prison wages are paid with tax revenues received by prisons from the general fund. Therefore, most deductions from inmate accounts are merely paper transfers of tax revenue credits from one governmental agency to another.

The next most common deposit to inmate accounts comes from gifts. If family members want to send an inmate money to buy a pair of shoes, they must send between 20 percent and 50 percent more than the cost of the shoes to offset the prison's automatic monthly deductions from the inmate's account. This, in fact, constitutes a tax on convicts' family members who wish to maintain family ties. Such a tax erodes, even destroys, inmates' connections to family members who cannot afford to pay the extra tax.

Thus, while the stated purpose behind making automatic deductions from inmate accounts is to hold criminals accountable for their debt to society, in truth, the practice burdens taxpayers and convicts' families who are the ones paying for the inmates' debts through the imposition of hidden taxes.

Secondary consequences of these deductions include keeping inmates impoverished and thereby increasing thievery in prisons, preventing inmates from filing conditions of confinement suits, and erosion of the rehabilitation processes due to the anger and frustration created by induced convict poverty.

Despite the negative consequences, the practice of making automatic deductions from inmates' accounts has grown a great deal since they began in the late 1990s. Private health care providers charge inmates' accounts four dollars for each sick-call visit or prescription (which chills access to medical care). Collect and prepaid calls made by inmates are taxed up to 50 percent by prison officials (which greatly increase the cost of calls and erode family ties). Even prison commissaries, which have now been privatized, charge inmates for a cost-of-doing-business tax that they must pay the hosting prison (greatly increasing the cost of commissary items and the likelihood of prison thievery).

In a warehouse prison model, rehabilitation is only a peace-keeping accommodation, so taxing convicts' families and taxpayers to create a stream of discretionary income makes sense. After all, if prisons can't make inmates law-abiding, then at least they can render them profitable to the prison.

Also, maintaining the illusion that inmates are paying for their own incarceration is important to politicians who use this white lie to win votes during election cycles. As explained, inmates only pay for their incarceration through their increased poverty. It is taxpayers and convicts' family members who are actually paying the cost of keeping inmates poor. That means that these taxpayers and convicts' families are actually involuntarily subsidizing politicians' election advertisements.

One day, a fellow convict came to me with a problem that rather poignantly reflected the priorities of our debtors' prisons.

"They paroled me but they won't let me go. Can you help me?" the frustrated man asked.

"Why won't they release you?" I asked.

"They say I have to pay sixty dollars to the Parole Board for administrative fees before I can be released," he answered.

"You don't have the money on your books?" I asked.

"Look. I've been in prison for ten years, and I live off prison wages. When I was approved for parole, I was immediately discharged from my job and placed on idle pay like the rules say. I only had ten dollars in my account. If I have to pay this sixty dollars from my idle pay, it will take almost a year. I am not allowed to work, and I'll need some of my idle pay to buy soap and shit," he explained.

"Don't you have anyone sending you money?" I asked.

"Man. That money dried up years ago. My people can't afford to send me nothing. Plus, I've been out of touch with them, because it costs too much to call them. No one in my family is good with letters, so they don't write me," he responded.

"Why didn't you save up for this stuff before?" I asked.

"I was living off prison wages. By the time the prison took out their cut [deduction] and I paid for cable, I only had enough money to buy stuff to wash my ass with. I've always been broke. Can you help me?" he asked.

From the Associated Press
9/11/99

by Ben Dobbin

Days before breaking out of jail in April, a disconsolate Ralph "Bucky" Phillips [a suspect in the killing of a police officer] sent his parole lawyer a thank-you note that hinted at an ominous turn in his life.

"I'm just not cut out for the life you folks live. I tried it, it didn't work," Phillips wrote, nearing the end of a 90-day sentence for a parole violation and fearing that his sentence was going to be extended—for months, if not years.

A petty criminal for most of his life, he'd only left prison in November after 13 years for burglary and larceny. Out of the past 23 years, he spent 20 in state prisons.

I couldn't help him. The man ended up spending another entire year in prison because that's how long it took him to pay the sixty dollars through idle wages. During that year, he had to beg for things from his friends. Because we were in a super-max prison at the time, it cost taxpayers an additional fifty thousand dollars to house him for that extra year, just to recover the sixty dollars that they could have collected from him while he was on parole. In addition, there were thousands of inmates in the same predicament all over the state.

Debtors' prisons didn't work in Britain or Colonial America because they prevented the jailed debtors from becoming free and earning the money to pay their debts. More important, it created a great deal of anger and resentment in the large and growing population of imprisoned debtors who felt that they were being mistreated by the government. Modern prisons are reliving history by ignoring the fact that Americans successfully fought a revolution to end an unfair practice that is being resurrected in our prisons today.

PERFORMANCE OF ALBION AND ITS FIVE SISTERS

Albion is the most comfortable, best designed, most structured, and most attractive prison that I have ever lived in. It looks and feels like it can actually work as a rehabilitative prison, but in fact it is the least effective prison of all. It is a dysfunctional, mean-spirited facility that callously steeps you in despair while it lavishes you with physical comfort.

Albion provides the inmate a sterile environment with faceless bells and voices precisely controlling time and movement for no apparent purpose other than order. It is a place where everyone is suspicious of each other and superficial friendliness is all that can exist. It is a place where perception is the only reality that matters and where induced poverty is used to generate illusory wealth.

In addition, it is a place of great violence but not in the same way that Graterford or Western were violent. The violence in Albion is subtle and more controlled but just as threatening. It is a violence deeply rooted in hatred for the government, society, and anyone else believed to be responsible for the unfairness, meanness, and despair openly served up to Albion's involuntary residents.

One psychologist, who conducted a long-term offenders group that I participated in, discussed with me her worries about the emergence of a prison gang recently discovered operating in the prison. Albion had only been in operation for five years and had never experienced prison gang activity before.

"I am concerned that gang activity will bring Graterford-style violence into the prison," she confided.

"I don't think you have to worry about that," I speculated.

"What makes you say that? You've been in these older prisons and have seen firsthand the violence that gangs bring into a prison," she responded in surprise.

"This prison is too comfortable and safe for gang violence," I explained.

"What are you saying? You don't believe there is a gang problem? I'm telling you, they have locked up gang members who admit to being in a gang," she insisted.

"There may be a gang here, but it can't be the same as the Graterford or Western gangs," I said.

"What do you mean?" she asked, curiously.

"Well, in Graterford and Western, gangs were created by inmates to protect themselves from other inmates. Gang violence in Graterford reflects the violence that made it necessary. Here, there are no rival gangs and no serious threats of violence between inmates. There are a lot of random rapes and fights but no organized predatory violence that would require inmates to form and join a violent prison gang. This prison is just too safe, comfortable, and over-staffed for that," I clarified.

"So why is there a gang if they aren't going to start trouble?" she asked, challenging my evaluation.

"They are here to make trouble, but if there are no other inmate gangs posing a threat, then the only trouble they can hope to cause is for prison staff which, in my opinion, is the "gang" those inmate gang members most need protection from," I explained. My point was that Albion was creating its own angry and bitter antagonists who could hope to do nothing in unison except resist the imposed order of the prison.

Certainly, a lone and inept prison gang can not disturb Albion's order and security. But as prison gangs rise and fall in the soup of Albion's inmate population, evolutionary forces will eventually lead to the development of a gang that specializes in the successful disruption of prison operations. Confined to a prison, the inevitable consequences of the tension between indifferent prison staff and antisocial prison populations are of no moment to free-world citizens. But the clash between prison order and convict dysfunction will eventually spill into the free world as 95 percent of all convicts are finally returned to an unsuspecting society. And, as antisocial warehouse prison populations continue to grow, more and more of their convicts will spill into the free world to spread their learned fondness for disorder; not as members of prison gangs but as agents of crime waves or domestic terrorism challenging the peace and order of our nation.

To fully grasp the ineffectiveness of contemporary warehouse prisons, consider this. When I was first incarcerated in Graterford, the population of Pennsylvania stood at about twelve million. There were eight state prisons and about eight thousand state inmates. The annual prison budget was well below $100 million. Also, keep in mind that Pennsylvania's prison system is purely punitive in that it does not offer good time, earned time, or any other kind of time credit for good behavior. If a convict receives a five- to ten-year prison sentence, he/she will have to serve at least five years. Consequently, Pennsylvania inmates serve more time in prison than any other inmates in the nation.

Now, let's look at Pennsylvania today. The state's population still stands at about twelve million, so the same taxpayer base that supported the prison system in 1980 is supporting it today. However, there are now almost thirty state prisons, forty-five thousand inmates, and it cost $1.3 billion this year to fund the prison system.

What did taxpayers get for the five-fold increase in inmate population, fourteen-fold increase in prison budgets, and more than three-fold increase in the number of prisons? They have gained an ever-expanding prison system that continues to grow at a rate much greater than the state's civilian population. A recidivism rate that is higher now than it was in 1980 when there was only a fraction of the inmates and prisons in Pennsylvania. Most important, the citizens of Pennsylvania have received no significant decrease in the overall crime rate. If anything, the Pennsylvania experience reveals that the more a state allows prisons to grow and drift away from attempting to rehabilitate inmates, then the more will crime rates and the need for prisons continue to grow.

Conclusion
The Runaway Train

EDITORS' NOTE

Victor Hassine's apt analogy of the prison as a runaway train suggests that the problems facing American prisons will inevitably lead to cataclysm. Impending doom has been a recurring theme of prison reform movements. For nearly three centuries, American prisons have confronted one crisis after another yet have continued relatively unchanged. To be sure, many of the system components that we take for granted today—for example, probation and parole—are products of these crises. Hassine believes that the challenges facing American prisons today may be more profound than any past crisis.

For several decades, our prison system was growing steadily, sometimes wildly. This rate of growth has slowed and, in some cases, declined slightly. Nevertheless, the absolute number of convicts remains remarkably high (over two million), and poses daunting challenges to prison managers. Hassine is right when he says that our prison system is functionally out of control. How control might be reestablished is an open and intriguing question that we, as free citizens, should address. Hassine's image of contemporary prisons growing day by day, eventually becoming a train so long that it becomes a wall dividing America into a land of the haves and the have notes, the free and the unfree, leaves us with the sobering question: Can we continue our prison binge and remain true to our most cherished ideals?

O vercrowding is the harbinger of cataclysmic change in our nation's prison system. That change is so profound that it is transforming the very structure and operation of the entire system, not just individual prisons. On the one hand, it is giving birth to a renegade bureaucracy obsessed with maintaining its own uncertain existence in the struggle to retain control over the penal system. On the other hand, it is creating a terrified population of inmates who have lost all sense of security and live like "moment dwellers" with no thought of the future.

To better understand the nature and extent of this transformation, consider the analogy of a runaway train. Imagine you're a passenger on a train. As you travel along, you sense that your train is moving faster than usual. This does not alarm you, but you stop reading your newspaper, take a look at your watch, then peer out a window. You notice the countryside whizzing past you at an increasing rate. Suddenly you see the train speed past the station where you were supposed to get off.

Now you are alarmed. But a voice over the loudspeaker apologizes for the inconvenience, assures everyone that everything is under control, and promises the train will stop at the next station. The train continues to accelerate.

Soon, the train hurtles past yet another station. You begin to realize that something is seriously wrong. You try to find a conductor or anyone in authority, but you get caught in a crush of passengers who have decided to do the same thing. Again you hear the loudspeaker voice, but because of all the confusion you can't make out what it is saying. In any event, you no longer trust any announcements. The train plunges forward out of control, faster and faster.

The crowd, the uncertainty, and the noise cause panic. It is at this point that the train has been transformed from a vehicle of mass transit to a machine that spreads pandemonium among passengers, who now face an uncertain future.

As panic and confusion rise, desperation sets in. No one cares anymore about their jobs, their schedules, or their futures. Everyone is thinking about right now and how they are going to survive this madness. Every human intuition has surrendered to the primitive instincts of "survival of the fittest." The passengers are no longer passengers, and the train is no longer a train.

Now imagine that you are the train engineer. You were the first to realize the train's acceleration problem. Because you are a trained expert, you felt certain you would be able to fix any mechanical problem. You radio the next station and inform them of the problem, then you pull out your repair manual and go about trying to fix the engine. But the train continues to accelerate and refuses to respond to any of your efforts. At this point you begin to worry.

As you work feverishly to control the train, you hear passengers banging on your engineer's door. The frustration of your failed efforts, the loud din of the uncooperative engine, and the panicking cries of passengers combine to unnerve you. You angrily take a moment to bark over the loudspeaker, "Everything is under control—please remain in your seats." But the screams and banging intensify as the train continues to accelerate beyond your control. You need help but you know you're not going to get any.

Despite your desperate and futile efforts, you realize that the longer you fail to slow your train, the more problems you'll be forced to fix. Weaknesses in design and construction of the train have caused additional mechanical failures. You find yourself reacting to a multitude of new emergencies that give you little or no opportunity to address the original problem. You know that unless this acceleration is stopped, collision or derailment is imminent.

At this point, you are no longer a trained professional concerned only with train schedules and engine maintenance. You have become a reactionary crisis-control manager who no longer cares where the train is headed. Your main goal now is to avert a catastrophe, and you have to keep those hysterical passengers from interfering with what you're trying to do. Meanwhile, the train races faster and faster.

Now imagine that you are a commuter on a train station platform. All of a sudden you see a train speed past you. You catch a glimpse of passengers banging on the passing windows. You notice that their faces show hysteria and that some of them are holding up signs, which you can't make out because the train is out of control, a runaway.

What you have seen causes you some fear and anxiety until you hear an authoritative voice over a loudspeaker apologizing for the inconvenience and announcing that everything is well under control. You are instructed to wait calmly until your train arrives. Though a bit perplexed, you are at least relieved that *you* will be able to reach your destination on time and in one piece.

The message of this parable is clear. I am one of those hysterical passengers on the runaway train, and this book is a sign that I'm waving at my window, hoping against hope that someone outside the train can read it and get help to us before a catastrophe destroys us all. Prison administrators are the frantic engineers trying to keep me and the other hysterical passengers out of their way while they work to bring the runaway train back under control.

And you, my readers, are the people calmly standing in the station as we tear by. You live in a normal world with all of its normal worries, such as whether your train will be on time or whether you will be late for work. A brief glimpse of our frantic faces may disturb your normal world for a moment. Will you assume that everything is really all right and go back to reading your newspapers? Or will you to try to get help to those passengers who, in the final analysis, are fellow human beings on the train of life?

And what if that train eventually grows so large that it never passes you by but instead the cars keep coming, one after another, day after day, week after week, month after month, year after year, leaving you standing on the platform with nowhere to go. Imagine new passenger cars, some converted into luxury units. Each car is still crowded but, from the outside, some of the cars look comfortable and spacious with reflective glass windows, adding a contemporary touch. And still they keep coming, a continuous chain of captive passengers.

When you stand back for a moment, you see that the train now looks like a wall. And that wall, you realize, is a dividing line between those on the "right" and the "wrong" side of the tracks—the haves and have nots, the contended and the discontented. There is you and there is me; there are the "free" and the "unfree." Things may stay this way indefinitely, since there are more free citizens than captive ones, but then again this bald line of social demarcation may make some of us very, very uneasy. We live in a free society, we like to think, but this train blocks our view. We look up and see nothing but prison, and find it hard to lose ourselves in our morning paper. Will we dismantle this train—or at least some of its endless cars—or will we simply find another way to go about our lives, content to be on our side of the tracks.

Prisons and Prison Reform
Hassine's Book in Perspective
Robert Johnson
Ania Dobrzanska

Many prisoners have written books about their experiences behind bars. As criminologists with a special interest in prisons, we have read a fair sample of those books. None offers more insight into the daily routines and social dynamics of contemporary American prisons than Victor Hassine's *Life Without Parole*. Reading this book is like actually being there, behind bars, wandering through the cellblocks of a men's maximum-security prison; an incredible experience that will make a lasting impact on students and the public alike. In our view, this book is highly credible and has much to contribute to the social science literature on prison life. More than just a good read, it is a serious work of scientific value.

VICTOR HASSINE, PRISONS HE HAS LIVED IN, AND EXTERNAL VALIDITY

Social scientists are always concerned about whether their observations are idiosyncratic or can be generalized to other persons, settings, and situations. Normally, researchers have only sufficient resources to survey a handful among the throng of individuals who share the particular characteristics under study. In scientific jargon, this is a problem of external validity. Is one's sample representative of some larger population (see Babbie 1992; Denzin 1989)?

External validity is a particularly taxing problem in life-histories research, where one individual in one setting tries to speak for many persons in different places (Denzin 1989). Although a number of famous studies in criminology are life histories of one offender (e.g., Shaw 1930; Sutherland 1937) or small groups of offenders (e.g., Ianni 1972; Whyte 1943), some scholars dismiss most life-history research as biased.

On the surface of things, the demand for external validity would seem to pose an insurmountable problem of interpretation in the case of Victor Hassine and Graterford Prison, which serves as the focus for many of the chapters in this book. When Hassine first arrived at Graterford, he was a "square john," prison slang for a middle-class, law-abiding inmate who usually identifies more with the staff than with other inmates. Few square johns end up in maximum-security prisons, though most who do are murderers. The square-john killer is a rare breed in maximum security, sharing nothing more than an address with the lower-class career criminals confined in prison. Even more unusual, Hassine is a Jewish immigrant from Egypt who holds a law degree. This combination of factors makes him a unique prisoner.

Graterford is more representative of American prisons than Hassine is of American prisoners, but there are still problems in generalizing from Graterford to other correctional settings. Graterford is an infamous "big house" penitentiary. Until the recent construction of "super-max" prisons in Pennsylvania, which impose a regime of solitary confinement, Graterford was the last stop for the state's most dangerous male felons. There are no other prisons like Graterford in Pennsylvania. For comparable institutions, one must consider such notorious places as Attica Prison in New York, Stateville Penitentiary in Illinois, Kansas State Penitentiary in Lansing, Huntsville Prison in Texas, Washington State Penitentiary in Walla Walla, or the federal penitentiaries in Marion, Illinois, and Leavenworth, Kansas. Gangs, drugs, violence, rape, and corruption are much more common in these penitentiaries than in other types of prisons, which tend to have fewer menacing inmates and more modern, manageable physical plants.

In Graterford, therefore, Hassine was a unique prisoner confined in an unusual setting. Normally, this combination would create an external validity nightmare. In Life Without Parole, however, Hassine writes more about fellow inmates in ordinary prison situations than about his own experiences at Graterford. His focus on observation rather than introspection converts a potential methodological catastrophe into a genuine success. Moreover, in this latest edition, Hassine has extended his analysis of prisons to include several other institutions with different histories, social climates, and management styles. We examine prisons with roots in the nineteenth century and prisons built near the turn of the twenty-first century. With Hassine, meet a range of situations and people in a range of penal institutions described by a man who has himself evolved over twenty-five years of incarceration. Hassine has, in our view, produced a very robust piece of ethnography as well as an original insider view of prison history.

Anyone familiar with prisons will immediately recognize the cross-section of humanity on the cellblocks and yards Hassine describes: the contorted face and broken gait of Chaser, strung out on psychotropics; the slumping, defeated Albert Brown as he shuffles outside his deserted cell; the scheming, manipulative Clarence, plotting to trick the program review committee; the drunken, bellowing Hammerhead, guzzling hooch as he runs from the hacks; the pathetic old man who struggles through the mundane details of every day prison life, starting with the pursuit of breakfast. The situations described by Hassine are everyday occurrences in countless prisons: The swag men brazenly hawking sandwiches to their customers, the gruesome tasks of the meat-wagon crews loading victims of violence and drug overdoses onto their gurneys, the inmate's dilemma of confronting a burglar caught ransacking his cell, and the punk's quandary—whether to submit or fight a hulking strong-arm rapist.

Hassine gives the reader a panoramic view of modern prison life rather than a retrospective self-portrait. His book captures the atmosphere of crushing boredom, numbing routine, mindless amusement, and occasional gripping fear that almost every inmate experiences at one time or another in every American prison.

DEPRIVATION, IMPORTATION, OR TRANSACTION? THOUGHTS ON PRISON ADJUSTMENT IN A CHANGING WORLD

An inmate subculture marked by distinctive norms, values, attitudes, beliefs, and language, flourishes in prison (see Carroll [1974] 1988, 1977; Clemmer 1940; Goffman 1961; Irwin [1970] 1987; Irwin and Cressey 1962; Jacobs 1977; Sykes 1958; most recently, with a cross-cultural focus, Crewe 2005 and Einat 2005). Strong evidence of this prisoner subculture is found in chapter 1 ("How I Became a Convict"), especially when Hassine notes how jailhouse slang unifies inmates into one big clan, in chapter 5 ("The Underground Economy") and chapter 23 ("In Search of the Convict Code"), where he examines the inmate code of conduct in Graterford and other prisons he has lived in.

Scholars debate the origins of this subculture. Those who support the deprivation model argue that the pains of imprisonment—including the loss of liberty, material goods, and services; heterosexual relationships; autonomy; and personal security—contribute to the formation of an inmate society with well-defined prisoner roles (see Clemmer 1940; Goffman 1961; in particular, Sykes 1958). Hassine recalls how he received his first misconduct charge in Graterford because he missed one of life's simple pleasures: a fresh-cooked hamburger. He purchased ten pounds of frozen ground beef from a swag man, a convict who specializes in providing goods and services to prisoners desperate for the material comforts of the outside world. Deprivation theorists argue that complex inmate societies, of which swag men are only a small part, have an indigenous origin (Sykes 1958). In other words, they claim that the hardships of confinement lead to the development of a criminogenic subculture found only within prisons.

Proponents of the importation model argue that the inmate subculture is not solely a response to the isolation and deprivations of imprisonment but is instead brought into the prison from the streets (see Carroll [1974] 1988, 1977; Jacobs 1977; in particular, Irwin [1970] 1987; Irwin and Cressey 1962; most recently, Crewe 2005 and Einat 2005). For example, Irwin and Cressey (1962) argued that prison subcultures and prisoner roles are composites of various criminal and conventional street identities imported into prison. As one example, Hassine is a square john to the other convicts because of the law-abiding, middle-class values and conventional identity he carried with him from the outside world. The consensus among many correctional scholars is that the importation model is the superior explanation for the inmate subcultures found in modern American prisons (Wright 1994; for a different view, see Hunt, Riegal, Morales, and Waldorf 1993). One important source of evidence on this point is that prison societies change as free world societies change; so, too, does the meaning of 'doing time' change as prison sentencing guidelines (an external force) change the obstacles inmates must circumvent to gain release (see Crewe 2005).

Of course, one can never fully separate what offenders import into the prison from what the prison encourages or even demands in terms of adjustment. A balanced assessment suggests that inmates bring to prison a frame of reference from the outside world, and that frame of reference must in turn be adapted to meet the particular challenges of adjustment that arise in particular prisons at particular points in time. As prisons have changed over time, partly in response to changes in prison populations and in prison management strategies (see Toch 2005), so have the adjustment challenges posed by confinement. In particular, with the notable exception of "super-max" prisons, penal institutions have become less "total," to quote Erving Goffman (1961). This means that more of the free world has been imported into the prison along with prisoners, who themselves come from a wider range of subcultures than was the case in earlier times. The ready availability of television in prisons these days keeps some aspects of popular culture alive on otherwise isolated prison tiers (see Johnson, 2005). Toch suggests that we conceptualize prison adjustment as a "transaction" of persons and environments, with the defining influences moving in both directions; that is, people shaping environments and, in turn, environments shaping people (see Toch 1992).

In the 1960s and early 1970s, correctional reforms and federal court decisions reduced some of the pains of imprisonment, making it easier for prisoners to retain their street identities and lifestyles (Carroll [1974] 1988, 1977; Jacobs 1977). Carroll and Jacobs note that the liberalization of visitation, telephone, and mail privileges, the permission to wear street clothes and hairstyles, to decorate their cells, and to bring television sets and radios into prisons all enabled inmates to maintain closer contact with the outside world and hence better preserve their preprison street personalities. United States Supreme Court decisions extended the freedom of religion to prisoners (in *Cooper v. Pate* 1964), virtually abolished the censoring of inmate mail by prison officials (in *Procunier v. Martinez* 1974), and extended limited constitutional protections to inmates (in *Wolff v. McDonnell* 1974), further reducing the isolation of prisoners from society. It seemed at the time that prisons were on a trajectory that would lead to more and more liberal reforms and, it was supposed, more decent and even empowering prison regimes that would more closely resemble life in the free world. Under these conditions, importation seemed to some scholars to be the only reasonable way to understand prison adjustment.

Regrettably, some of these liberal reforms have been eroded in recent years. People on the scene—ethnographers like John Irwin (2004)—chart the return of a more expressly punitive, warehousing approach to prisons (see also Irwin and Owen 2005). Others remind us that prisons have been a growth industry in recent decades. More than half of all the prisons in the United States have been built within the past twenty years (Tonry and Petersilia 1999). America, once commonly referred to as the "land of the free" is now the "land of the kept." The paradox of our time is that we live in a nation that sees itself as a bastion of human freedom, yet we operate a penal system that denies the very freedom we claim to value, and does so on a massive scale. These days we build more prisons than schools. It should come as no surprise that "the United States has a higher per capita incarceration rate than any other industrialized democracy" (Petersilia 2003).

These and other changes appear to support the deprivation model of imprisonment. If prisons are more common and more depriving, won't widespread deprivations determine the contours of prison life? We would say no. The point of a transactional perspective is that change is to be expected and must always be accommodated in some fashion. Nothing is set in stone, so to speak, not even our prisons. The free world is always changing, and at a pace that far outstrips changes within prisons. If any general point might be made, it is that isolated institutions like prisons, no matter how open they try to become, are going to be increasingly out of touch with life on the outside. On the outside, rapid change is the norm, not the exception. Communications technologies allow free citizens to be in almost constant touch with one another; as a result of all this interaction, social complexity increases, and social change occurs at an increasingly rapid rate. It is said that technology has made the free world a global village. If so, prisoners are banished from that village, held in a kind of suspended animation in remote enclaves, then released into a world that is increasingly unrecognizable to them (Johnson 2005).

Although Hassine describes the deprivations of imprisonment and the importation of values and norms, *Life Without Parole* offers strong support for the transactional model, the model more in touch with the changing nature of prisons and the larger society in which they are embedded. Hassine observes that in the early 1980s, the ghetto evils of decaying American inner cities were compressed into Graterford. Almost overnight, gang bangers, drug addicts and dealers, the homeless, the mentally ill, and juvenile offenders poured into the penitentiary, disrupting prison life and routines. Almost overnight, confinement to the walled ghetto that was Graterford disrupted the routines that comprised the daily life of these various groups when they lived in the streets. Mutual, though not necessarily balanced, accommodations took place between the institution and its inhabitants. The violent, addictive, acquisitive, disorganized lifestyles of the new inmates (the "Pepsi Generation" in current prison slang; Fong, Vogel, and Buentello 1996; Hunt et al. 1993), though comparatively muted in prison, especially offended the Old Heads, who longed for the good old days when the outside world was kept outside and prisons were more self-contained. Changes continue as Hassine works his way through the Pennsylvania prison system; these changes, in turn, reflect differences in prison type, social climate, changing societal attitudes about crime and punishment, and of course changes in Hassine himself as he ages and matures behind bars, and as a result brings a wealth of prison wisdom to each new setting and situation that presents itself.

Correctional practitioners and researchers now recognize that the imposing prison walls that surround institutions are surprisingly permeable. That gang culture survives even the virtual solitary confinement conditions imposed in super-max prisons reminds us that prisons are living environments, that people adapt to those condition to meet at least some of their needs, and that we as citizens (including correctional professionals) must live with these realities. It is also telling that street culture influences today's prisons, just as prisons have influenced street culture, and will continue to do so by influencing those inmates who will one day return to the streets. With the growing appeal of MTV and rap music, which feature a distinctive mix of prison and street culture, we may see a fusion of prison and free-world values and lifestyles that would have been unimaginable in earlier times. It may be that we will one day come to think of slum streets and prison tiers as environments that have been cast off from the larger society, allowed to evolve—or devolve—at their own pace, falling further and further out of touch with the life and culture of the free world. This is a grim scenario for corrections, but is the logical extension of the notion that prisons are essentially human warehouses for expendable people.

THE PENAL HARM MOVEMENT

Some scholars claim that conservative politicians are spearheading a penal harm movement in America today, with the intention of increasing the misery associated with punishment (Clear 1994; Cullen 1995; Simon 1993; Tonry 1995) and, we would add, increasing the social isolation of offenders. Whether politicians intend to harm prisoners or believe they are meting out hard justice to hardened offenders, we cannot say. It is apparent, however, that prison reforms of recent years have made doing time harder still, and this can certainly be said to inflict harm on offenders, intended or not (Johnson 2002; Irwin and Owen 2005). This trend can be seen in the recent popularity of mandatory sentencing laws, including those that mandate "three-strikes-and-you're-out" (requiring life sentences for third-felony convictions), the war on drugs, the restriction or abolition of parole, and the reappearance of chain gangs in several jurisdictions.

Stiffer sentencing policies have sent massive numbers of poor, black, drug-addicted, inner-city offenders to Graterford and other American prisons during the last two decades. Prison administrators must manage prisons filled beyond capacity with devalued people—diseased, drug-addicted, illiterate inmates. There has also been a growth in the population of mentally ill prisoners; in some circles, prisons are called "our other asylums" because they now serve as storage settings of last resort for people we used to put into treatment-oriented facilities (Earley 2006). Increasingly, administrators must do their often thankless jobs under the pressure of budget freezes imposed by state legislatures.

Life Without Parole details the practical effect of the penal harm movement on the lives of inmates (see in particular chapter 4, "Prison Violence"). By the mid-1980s and continuing through the mid-1990s, prison officials had apparently lost control of Graterford to rival inmate gangs, cellblocks filled with drugs, violence, and corruption. Assigned to the meat wagon crew, Hassine served as a medic on the front line of the penal harm battleground. Although he argues (in chapter 5, "The Underground Economy") that the confrontation between Double D and Rocky replaced disorganized, tribal gang violence with a united "Kingdom of Inmates," recent events suggest that this period of relative tranquillity in Graterford was short-lived (see Appendix A, "A State Tries to Rein In a Prison Awash in Drugs").

The penal harm movement has almost certainly increased the suffering of most inmates in America. In chapter 19 ("Prison Overcrowding"), Hassine offers a personal account of the suffering he had experienced as a result of double celling. In some prisons, inmates are now triple and even quadruple celled, sometimes even required to sleep barracks-style in warehouses, gymnasiums, or auditoriums. Hassine argues in chapter 21 ("Prison Rape") that these conditions have contributed to an increase in the frequency of prison rape. Life for Hassine has been less dramatically stressful in recent years, when he was housed in modern, podular prisons like Albion; he and other inmates are safer but life is also more disconcerting, because modern institutions such as Albion look so normal, even inviting, to outsiders. Victor feels great frustration in such settings—empty time hangs heavy there—but he senses that others think he has it easy.

In an attempt some years ago to articulate a new ideology for punishment, the eminent correctional scholar John Irwin sensibly argued:

> Those convicted of serious crimes must be punished and imprisoned—knowing that imprisonment itself is very punitive, we need not punish above and beyond imprisonment. This means that we need not and must not degrade, provoke, nor excessively deprive the human beings we have placed in prison. (1980, 248)

By promoting prison overcrowding and related evils like prison rape, by allowing empty time to be seen as normal, even generous, the penal harm movement has extended degradation, provocation, and deprivation well beyond the act of confinement to the daily experience of prison life.

A WORD ON STAFF

Staff, especially line correctional officers, take a different view of recent changes in prisons. For them, the rapid growth of prisons translates not into human warehousing but into a difficult work environment. To keep up with the rapid prison growth in prisons, correctional managers are facing tremendous pressure to recruit, hire, train and retain quality staff to run these facilities in a professional manner. Recruitment is a difficult task because corrections is a challenging field marked by litany of difficulties including a poor public image. People don't grow up wanting to be correctional officers; at least, not many young people set their sights on corrections as their field of choice.

Finding good employees is never easy, and adding to this challenge, retaining good staff members is difficult as well. Lack of proper recognition, poor career prospects, low pay, burdensome hours and shift work, stress and burnout, poorly qualified supervisors, undesirable location of corrections facilities, a shortage of qualified applicants, and low morale are all reasons why staff retention is a problem in many systems. Moreover, even on a good day, work in corrections can be stressful; corrections is not by and large a dangerous professional (policing is much more dangerous), but the risk of danger always seems high because officers are typically outnumbered by offenders. As you read Hassine's book, imagine yourself as an officer in his world. Imagine yourself surrounded by offenders who have a very low opinion of you—even Hassine, an educated man, by and large holds officers in low esteem. Imagine how the tougher convicts view staff. Officers feel vulnerable, and who can blame them.

THE PENOLOGY OF DESPAIR

Criminal justice theorists and philosophers of punishment debate the appropriate rationales for criminal justice processing. In a famous conceptualization of criminal procedure, Packer (1968) distinguishes between the crime control and the due process models of criminal justice operation. The crime control model emphasizes the efficiency of convictions, the presumption of guilt, and the validity of the coercive power of the state over the offender. Due process emphasizes the reliability of convictions, the presumption of innocence, and the strict protection of individual rights through the limitation of state power. Philosophers of punishment examine the relative merits of retribution (matching the severity of punishments to the seriousness of crimes), rehabilitation (implementing treatment strategies and programs to reform individual offenders and prevent future crimes), deterrence (using threatened or actual punishments to convince persons not to commit future crimes), and incapacitation (preventing crime in the larger society through the use of punishment to remove criminals from society) as the rationales for correctional policies and programs.

Some recent commentators claim that these older models and rationales have little relevance to the current operations of prisons. Rutherford (1993) contends that bureaucratic expediency guides correctional thinking today. In this context, corrections amounts to cold efficiency in the management of what is essentially a human warehouse. Feeley and Simon (1992) refer to this administrative approach as the new penology. These authors argue that bureaucratic expediency is a practical response to the immediate pressures of overcrowding, violence, and disorganization in prisons. Central to the management of these human warehouses, Hassine suggests, is the manipulation of fear (chapter 24, "A Hitchhiker's Guide to Prisons, Part I"). A well-run prison, he argues, can reach beyond fear, offering the stability necessary for offenders to work on personal rehabilitation and preparation for their return to the free world.

Well-run prisons remain the exception, not the norm, however. Hence, fear rules in most prisons most of the time. Hassine's runaway train analogy (chapter 27, "Conclusion") offers a disturbing image of current correctional operations. He believes that the problems in many modern prisons have become so grave that prison administrators are simply crisis-control managers whose primary goal is to avert catastrophe in a crisis-ridden bureaucracy. Overcrowded cellblocks ruled by gangs and filled with drugs and violence force prisoners and staff alike to be concerned only about how they are going to survive this madness. Where controls are better, the prison experience is marked by isolated, empty time; indeed, an increase in cell time (physical isolation) and a reduction in open group recreation (social isolation) are the main ingredients in the newer, safer, high security, bureaucratically-run prisons (see chapters 24 and 25), the extreme case of which is the super-max institution where prisoners spend up to twenty-three hours a day in isolation cells. The implication is that correctional policy has rapidly shifted from variations of crime control, due process, retribution, rehabilitation, deterrence, and incapacitation to mere survival.

Paradoxically, a focus on the primitive goal of survival has occurred during a time when our understanding of the change process has grown substantially (Lin 2000). We know how to run decent prisons, at least in principle (Johnson 2002). There is also a growing consensus that prisons must be held accountable for the living conditions they impose; the energy devoted to implementing the Prison Rape Elimination Act makes it clear that correctional professionals want to run safe, decent prisons (Owen and Wells 2006). It is of urgent importance that we as a nation reconsider the policies that have increased the harms inflicted on prisoners, and which impose a considerable burden on staff as well. Prisons should be safe, certainly, but they should also hold out the prospect of growth and change, which is to say, corrections or rehabilitation. If we cannot promote reform for captives like Victor Hassine, then we must at least do so for their captors, who want nothing more than to manage decent, constructive prisons in our name.

REFERENCES

Babbie, Earl. *The Practice of Social Research,* 6th ed. Belmont, CA: Wadsworth, 1992.

Carroll, Leo. *Hacks, Blacks, and Cons: Race Relations in a Maximum Security Prison.* 1974. Reprint Prospect Heights, IL: Waveland, 1988.

———. "Race and Three Forms of Prisoner Power: Confrontation, Censoriousness, and the Corruption of Authority." In *Contemporary Corrections: Social Control and Conflict,* edited by C. Ronald Huff, 40–53. Beverly Hills, CA: Sage, 1977.

Clear, Todd R. *Harm in American Penology: Offenders, Victims, and Their Communities.* Albany, NY: State University of New York Press, 1994.

Clemmer, Donald. 1940. *The Prison Community.* New York: Holt, Rinehart and Winston, 1994.

Crewe, Ben. "Codes and Conventions: The Terms and Conditions of Contemporary Inmate Values." In *The Effects of Imprisonment,* edited by Alison Leibling and Shadd Maruna, 177–208. Devon, England: Willan Publishing, 2005.

Cullen, Francis T. "Assessing the Penal Harm Movement." *Journal of Research in Crime and Delinquency* 32 (1995): 338–58.

Denzin, Norman K. *The Research Act,* 3rd ed. Englewood Cliffs, NJ: Prentice-Hall, 1989.

Earley, Pete. *Crazy: A Father's Search Through America's Mental Health Madness.* New York: Putnam, 2006.

Einat, Tomer. "'Soldiers,' 'Sausages' and 'deep sea diving': Language, Culture and Coping in Israeli Prisons." In *The Effects of Imprisonment,* edited by Alison Leibling and Shadd Maruna, 285–305. Devon, England: Wilian Publishing, 2005.

Feeley, Malcolm M., and Jonathan Simon. "The New Penology: Notes on the Emerging Strategy of Corrections and Its Implications." *Criminology* 30 (1992): 449–74.

Fong, Robert S., Ronald E. Vogel, and Salvador Buentello. "Prison Gang Dynamics: A Look Inside the Texas Department of Corrections." In *Corrections, Dilemmas and Directions,* edited by Peter J. Benekos and Alida V. Merlo, 57–77. Cincinnati, OH: Anderson, 1992.

———. "Prison Gang Dynamics: A Research Update." In *Gangs: A Criminal Justice Approach,* edited by J. Mitchell Miller and Jeffrey P. Rush, 105–28. Cincinnati, OH: Anderson, 1996.

Goffman, Erving. *Asylums: Essays on the Social Situation of Mental Patients and Other Inmates.* Garden City, NY: Anchor, 1961.

Hunt, Geoffrey, Stephanie Riegal, Tomas Morales, and Dan Waldorf. "Changes in Prison Culture: Prison Gangs and the Case of the Pepsi Generation." *Social Problems* 40 (1993): 398–410.

Ianni, Francis A. J. *A Family Business: Kinship and Social Control in Organized Crime.* New York: Russell Sage Foundation, 1972.

Irwin, John. *The Felon.* 1970. Reprint Berkeley: University of California Press, 1987.

———. *Prisons in Turmoil.* Boston: Little, Brown, 1980.

———. *The Warehousing Prison: Disposal of the New Dangerous Class.* Los Angeles, CA: Roxbury Publishing, 2005.

Irwin, John, and Donald R. Cressey. "Thieves, Convicts, and the Inmate Culture." *Social Problems* 10 (1962): 142–55.

Irwin, John and Barbara Owen. "Harm and the Contemporary Prison." In *The Effects of Imprisonment,* edited by Alison Leibling and Shadd Maruna, 94-117. Devon, England: Willan Publishing, 2005.

Jackson, George. *Soledad Brother.* New York: Bantam, 1970.

Jacobs, James B. *Stateville: The Penitentiary in Mass Society.* Chicago: University of Chicago Press, 1977.

Johnson, Robert. *Hard Time: Understanding and Reforming the Prison.* Belmont, CA: Wadsworth, 2002.

———. "Brave New Prisons: The Growing Social Isolation of Modern Penal Institutions." In *The Effects of Imprisonment,* edited by Alison Leibling and Shadd Maruna, 255–284. Devon, England: Willan Publishing, 2005.

Lin, A. C. *Reform in the Making: The Implementation of Social Policy in Prison.* Princeton, NJ: Princeton University Press, 2000.

Owen, Barbara and James Wells. *Staff Perspectives: Sexual Violence in Adult Prisons and Jails—Trends from Focus Group Interviews.* Prison Rape Elimination Act Report, June 2006, Volume 1:24. Prepared under Cooperative Agreement Number 05S18GJ10 by the National Institute of Corrections and The Moss Group, 2006.

Packer, Herbert L. *The Limits of the Criminal Sanction.* Stanford, CA: Stanford University Press, 1968.

Petersilia, J. *When Prisoners Come Home.* New York: Oxford University Press, 2003.

Rutherford, Andrew. *Criminal Justice and the Pursuit of Decency.* Oxford, England: Oxford University Press, 1993.

Shaw, Clifford R. *The Jack-Roller: A Delinquent Boy's Own Story.* Chicago: University of Chicago Press, 1930.

Simon, Jonathan. *Poor Discipline: Parole and the Social Control of the Underclass, 1890–1990.* Chicago: University of Chicago Press, 1993.

Sutherland, Edwin H. *The Professional Thief.* Chicago: University of Chicago Press, 1937.

Sykes, Gresham M. *The Society of Captives: A Study of a Maximum Security Prison.* Princeton, NJ: Princeton University Press, 1958.

Toch, Hans. *Living in Prison: The Ecology of Survival.* Washington, DC: American Psychological Association, 1992.

———. "Reinventing Prisons." In *The Effects of Imprisonment,* edited by Alison Leibling and Shadd Maruna, 465–473. Devon, England: Willan Publishing, 2005.

Tonry, Michael. *Malign Neglect: Race, Crime, and Punishment in America.* New York: Oxford University Press, 1995.

Tonry, M. and J. Petersilia. *Prisons.* Chicago: University of Chicago Press, 1990.

Whyte, William Foote. *Streetcorner Society.* Chicago: University of Chicago Press, 1943.

Wright, Richard A. *In Defense of Prisons.* Westport, CT: Greenwood, 1994.

CASES

Cooper v. Pate, 378 U.S. 546 (1964).

Procunier v. Martinez, 416 U.S. 396 (1974).

Wolff v. McDonnell, 418 U.S. 539 (1974).

Appendix A

EDITORS' NOTE

During the editing of the first edition of this book, the State Correctional Institution at Graterford experienced a system-wide breakdown, a derailment. Hundreds of corrections officers and specialists who had never before been inside Graterford were brought in to help fix the problem. What these outsiders discovered when they explored Graterford for the first time was the "Kingdom of Inmates" that Victor Hassine accurately described in this book—and that they subsequently reported on in The New York Times *article reprinted below.*

A State Tries to Rein In a Prison Awash in Drugs

Matthew Purdy

GRATERFORD, Pa., October 26—In February, the Pennsylvania authorities paroled Robert Simon, despite his being a convicted killer and known prison drug user who had killed another inmate in self-defense.

Three months later, back on the street, Mr. Simon was accused of another killing, this time the shooting of a New Jersey police officer who had stopped him and a fellow motorcycle gang member in Gloucester County for a traffic violation.

When the authorities in Pennsylvania began looking into why Mr. Simon was set free, the trail led back to the state prison here, where officials say the case is another sign of the widespread drug trade, mismanagement, and possible corruption at the crowded maximum-security prison outside of Philadelphia.

In the view of state corrections officials, it was as if the prison had fallen into enemy hands. Last Monday, 650 state troopers and corrections officers from other prisons were deployed in a nighttime surprise assault on Graterford. During the next seventy-two hours, they searched all 3,500* inmates, the prison's staff, and its 1,700-acre grounds, looking for drugs and weapons. As a result, nine ranking officers at the prison retired or were transferred, and twenty-one inmates suspected of drug trafficking were moved to other prisons.

The shakedown, in which about 200 homemade weapons and more than sixty caches of drugs were seized, was unusual in scope. But the extreme action was an indication of the frustration many corrections officials and politicians feel at the constant battle to keep drugs out of prisons, especially as tougher laws are sending drug-addicted criminals away for longer sentences.

The question that prompted the raid—"Who runs the prison?" in the words of Martin F. Horn, Pennsylvania's Corrections Commissioner—is a common one for prison administrators. Corrections officials across the country say controlling prisons is becoming more difficult because of increasing inmate populations, harder-core prisoners, and tighter budgets. Earlier this month, inmates were ordered confined to their cells at federal prisons after uprisings at five sites.

The drug economy in prisons not only threatens peace among inmates but also dangles temptation before guards. In the last year at the federal prison in Atlanta, for example, several employees have been arrested on drug charges and there has been a spate of violence, including the first killing of a corrections officer at the prison since 1987.

(On Friday, federal prosecutors announced the indictments of four corrections officers, four inmates, and two others on charges of trying to smuggle marijuana, cocaine, and heroin into the Atlanta prison.)

"In large systems, it's almost a truism that you're going to have some drug trafficking," said a former Texas prison official and a consultant on prison conditions, Steve Martin. "But when it seeps into your security staff you have serious problems."

Governor Tom Ridge of Pennsylvania, who approved the search of Graterford, said, "The first thing we need to do is control the prisons, and we weren't in control of that one."

Officials said that in Mr. Simon's case a complete record of his prison misdeeds was not in his file when the parole decision was made. Inmates told a recent State Senate hearing that it was common practice

---

*Editors' Note: At the time of the publication of the first edition of this book, the actual number of inmates at Graterford was over 4,000. When this article originally appeared, a portion of the prison had been shut down for repairs and emptied of inmates, considerably reducing this figure.

among prisoners at Graterford to avoid punishment for infractions and to cover up evidence of drug use by paying officers to alter records.

At the hearing, an inmate who was a clerk at Graterford from 1992 to this January, Jonathan Brown, told the State Senate Judiciary Committee about officers' selling furloughs and other privileges, and about drug trafficking among officers. He said Mr. Simon paid officers to cover up his disciplinary infractions, though the allegations have not been proved and are under investigation.

"The fact that he was allegedly selling and using dope was not in his file," said the committee chairman, Senator Stewart J. Greenleaf.

Mr. Simon's case was just more evidence of trouble at Graterford, one of the largest state prisons in the country. Since 1989, thirteen staff members have been arrested on charges of trying to smuggle drugs, eleven inmates have died of drug overdoses, and about 20 percent of the urine tests done on prisoners each month show signs of drug use.

In March, three inmates were found in a cell, all with hypodermic needles and all unconscious from drug overdoses, Mr. Horn said. They recovered, and one took another nonfatal overdose the next night.

Calling the drug trade in prison "enormously frustrating," Mr. Horn said it "gives the lie to everything we're trying to do in terms of rehabilitation."

The search had been planned since April by Mr. Horn and his staff without the knowledge of Graterford officials. In the raid, officers with drug-sniffing dogs removed inmates from their cells one at a time, searching the cells, strip-searching the inmates, and then moving to the next cell.

Officials say they might have found more drugs, but many inmates flushed them down toilets after hearing about the search.

"I suspect all of the bass and trout in the streams connected to that sewage system are jumping far out of the water," Mr. Ridge said.

Mr. Horn was realistic about the search's effect. "The minute we walk away from here, the inmates are going to start trying to figure out how to get drugs," he said.

Although few deny that Graterford has a drug problem, some prisoner advocates say the search, with all of its drama, had political motivations. The Simon case, which led to an overhaul of the state parole board, came less than a year after the release of a Pennsylvania inmate, Reginald McFadden, who went on to kill and rape on Long Island and in Rockland County, New York.

In last year's election, Mr. Ridge criticized his opponent, Lieutenant Governor Mark S. Single, for voting in favor of the McFadden parole as a member of the parole board.

Drug use at Graterford is both long-running and well-known.

"There was a period of time at Graterford that I smoked a joint when I woke up, at lunch, at dinner, and when I went to bed," said Kenneth Tervalon, 49, who was released in 1993 and says he has stopped using drugs.

Although just 10 percent of Pennsylvania's state prisoners are at Graterford, the prison accounts for 25 percent of inmate attacks on staff members and a third of inmate drug infractions, said Mr. Horn, who headed the parole system in New York State before becoming Commissioner in March.

Donald T. Vaughn, the superintendent at Graterford, said the drug problem was caused largely by its proximity to Philadelphia, which is thirty miles to the southeast. The drug market behind Graterford's thirty-foot wall mirrors the city's.

Mr. Vaughn acknowledges that his staff might not have provided the "intense supervision" required for the prison. He said he had asked the corrections department for help in the past but had not yet received it.

Mr. Horn said he would leave Mr. Vaughn in charge.

With 85 percent of the inmates from Philadelphia or neighboring counties, there are frequent crowds in the visiting room, a key entry point of drugs in most prisons. Drugs packed in small balloons are passed mouth-to-mouth when inmates kiss female visitors, and inmates swallow them and pass them later. Although visitors are searched before coming in, they have been known to hide drugs in babies' diapers or in their own body cavities.

Inmates and others say Graterford has a more casual atmosphere than other prisons, which may contribute to the drug problem.

Prisoners are allowed to walk down the halls freely, not in straight lines under close supervision as is required in other prisons. And the number of volunteer workers—almost 400—gives inmates many chances to make contact with people from the outside.

"If you don't want to go to work, you just go out to the yard," said Steven Blackburn, an inmate for twelve years there until 1991. "Compared to a lot of other institutions around the state, Graterford is still considered loose."

Whatever that buys in inmate peace, it has its downside. On August 4, an inmate serving a life sentence for murder hid on a bread truck leaving the prison. He was recaptured eighteen days later, but his escape was made possible because no one reported that he failed to show up for his job that day or that he was in the delivery area without authorization, Mr. Horn said.

Some inmates have been allowed to acquire enormous power.... A gang leader in Philadelphia has led Graterford's Muslim movement, officials said, controlling part of the prison's drug trade.

A prison guard, Lieutenant Cynthia Link, said that when the lights in the prison's mosque suddenly went out one night two years ago, the 100 inmates ignored her order to leave. Finally, one of them said, "Ms. Link, these people aren't going to move until [the gang leader] tells them to."

"I said, 'Well, go get [him], tell him I need him,'" Lieutenant Link recounted. He came, told the prisoners to leave, and they did.

Appendix B

EDITORS' NOTE

Shortly after the publication of the first edition of Life Without Parole, *Julia Cass wrote an article about Victor Hassine in* The Philadelphia Inquirer. *Cass offers salient details about the crime allegedly committed by Hassine and about his subsequent trial. She also briefly discusses how the First Edition was received by academics, Pennsylvania correctional officials, and prison inmates. These points remain valid today.*

Struggle to Survive: View from Behind Bars

Julia Cass

BELLEFONTE, Pa.—In the 1970s, Victor Hassine toured Camp Hill state prison with classmates in a criminal justice course at Dickinson College. The sight of caged men horrified and fascinated him, but the thing he would remember for years afterward was the pool table, sitting in the center of an "honor" block for well-behaved inmates. "Jeez ...those guys must be having a blast," Hassine recalls joking to his friends. "I was incredibly naive."

Not anymore. Sixteen years into a life sentence for a 1980 Bucks County murder, Hassine is so well-acquainted with prison life—in particular, the chaotic world of Graterford—that he could write a textbook. And he has.

Published this summer and headed for college courses on penology and criminal justice, *Life Without Parole: Living in Prison Today* details Hassine's painful adjustment to incarceration. But the primary object of his lesson is that today's big prisons are "runaway trains," where both inmates and staff are struggling to survive.

EXAMPLE A: GRATERFORD

Convicted of hiring a hit man in a drug deal gone sour, Hassine spent the first five years of his sentence, from 1981 to 1986, in the state's largest maximum-security prison—the "Kingdom of Inmates," he calls it.

Going in, he had expected rigid structure. What he found, he said, was mayhem.

"Fights, stabbings and weapons were commonplace," said Hassine, 41, in an interview at Rockview state prison here, where he has been since 1989. "Prison gangs robbed with impunity. Staff smuggled in contraband. Enforcement of rules was arbitrary. It wasn't what anybody would want in a prison—or on the planet."

Hassine's book reinforces the picture that has emerged in the last year of a turbulent Graterford. In May 1995, there was the Robert "Madman" Simon scandal. Paroled from behind its walls, with the recommendation of Graterford staff, Simon then allegedly killed a New Jersey state trooper. At the legislative hearings that followed, witnesses described Graterford as violent, drug-ridden, and out of control.

Last October, state prison officials staged a massive drug and weapons raid. They transferred some staff and inmates and reduced the number of volunteers entering the prison for such programs as literacy tutoring, Bible studies and gardening.

Last spring, ten Graterford inmates were indicted for making $2 million in illegal credit card purchases from prison telephones. So officials installed a new system restricting inmates' calls.

Hassine considers such attempts to regain control as superficial and misguided. "[Administrators have] done nothing to reduce the number of men jammed in there, and they've cut back on positive programs," he said. Instead, "what they're doing is poking a stick at the inmates."

Neither Graterford officials nor state prisons Commissioner Martin Horn had read the book and could comment, according to their representatives.

The book, however, has gotten favorable reviews in professional journals and praise from academics at schools, including the University of Scranton and Troy State University in Alabama, where it will be used.

Hassine's work is welcome because "most of the good prisoner-written books now are 20 years old, and so much has changed since then—overcrowding, budget freezes, the lean-and-mean movement, the gang bangers," said Richard A. Wright, a criminal justice professor at [Arkansas State University].

The book's harshest critics appear to be Graterford inmates. Hassine has heard they fear it will be used by state officials as reason to further tighten the reins.

"That was not my purpose," he said, "but I also think the men at Graterford should talk about what's really happening."

In Hassine's analysis, Graterford authorities began losing control in the early '80s, the beginning of a surge in the inmate population. During his confinement there, the number of men swelled from 1,900 to 2,600—750 per cell block, with a handful of guards.

The population has since grown to about 3,600.

Among the newcomers, he says, was a more aggressive and fatalistic breed of social misfit. There were the mentally ill, who commanded much of the staff's attention; the drug addicts, who would do anything to get high; and the juveniles, who became targets for rape and created havoc to attract "parental" attention.

The "older heads," Hassine says, were dismayed at the young inmates who cared more about making themselves comfortable in prison—by getting drugs and other contraband and forming gangs—than about working on their appeals and parole applications and otherwise trying to get out.

"Most of these guys have already been in and out of juvenile facilities," Hassine said, "and they've been told, 'This is your life.'"

At one point, Graterford ran out of room in the "hole"—the disciplinary unit for troublemakers and inmates who want to be protected from them. "When things got so bad that inmates couldn't even commit themselves to protective custody," Hassine said, "the population knew they had to fend for themselves."

Gangs proliferated, both for predation and protection, and guards, afraid for their own lives, usually looked the other way.

For Hassine, one of the defining moments in this inmate ascendancy came in 1983, in the "Super Bowl Sunday Chicken Riot."

First one inmate, then many more, defied the prison rules by openly bringing their chicken dinners from the C-Block dining hall to their cells to eat while watching the game.

Along the way, they fought off the guards who tried to stop them. Only when the game was over, and the chicken bones were picked clean, did prison officials move to discipline some of them.

During those years, too, Graterford's underground economy grew and thrived. If he wanted his laundry done, Hassine says, he would pay an inmate laundry worker with cigarettes to have it picked up, cleaned, and delivered. If he tried to send his laundry through the authorized system, he probably would not have gotten it back.

He also had at his disposal "swag men" to deliver freshly cooked food, smuggled from the kitchen, to his cell; and drugs and homemade hooch if he wanted them.

Hassine finds irony in the illegal commerce: It may have saved Graterford from becoming even more violent, for the inmates had a financial stake in some measure of peace.

An Egyptian Jew whose parents immigrated to Trenton when he was a child, Hassine took refuge in the prison's synagogue, where he helped establish halfway houses for inmates gaining release. "When you met volunteers from the outside, you were encouraged, you had a name, and whatever good values ... you had were reinforced."

But for inmates not involved in such activities, there was a different lesson.

"Prison is a crude communism," Hassine said. "You're told, 'You're no different than anybody else.' Ambition is discouraged. They want you to do X, not less than X, but also not more than X."

Hassine's book does not detail his murder case or raise the issue of whether he deserves to be behind bars—although he has elsewhere maintained his innocence.

According to trial testimony, Hassine and his partner in a Morrisville meat market hired an acquaintance to murder a man who had gotten into a dispute with the partner over diluted drugs sold surreptitiously at the market. The hit man only wounded the intended victim but killed another man, James Puerale, who happened to be present.

The prosecutor sought the death penalty, but the jury sentenced Hassine and his partner to life in prison. In Pennsylvania, that means life without parole unless the governor commutes the sentence.

While Hassine may never escape the system, he has moved around inside it.

From Graterford, he landed in Western State Penitentiary in Pittsburgh. There, an inmate smashed his skull with a barbell, causing nerve damage that makes his left eye appear smaller than his right.

Hassine, who has a degree from New York School of Law, was a plaintiff in two lawsuits against Graterford and Western State, alleging conditions so bad they constituted cruel and unusual punishment. The inmates ultimately lost the Graterford case, although prison officials agreed to make some physical improvements. A federal judge found conditions in the Pittsburgh prison unconstitutional and ordered many changes.

Compared with Graterford and Western State, Hassine says, Rockview is calmer and more structured. He credits the preponderance of "short-timers"—inmates who are about to go home—and the warden's emphasis on education.

There, about five years ago, Hassine began writing as "a catharsis." In 1993, Thomas J. Bernard, a criminologist at nearby Pennsylvania State University, came to speak to a group of inmates, and Hassine got his card and mailed him some essays. He asked Bernard to share them with his students so they would get a more realistic view of prison life.

In Hassine's material, Bernard saw a book. "Unlike a lot of prison writing, Victor's wasn't self-serving," Bernard said. "With all the resources we are committing to prisons, I thought it would be useful to have a book that just describes what contemporary prisons are like."

Bernard showed Hassine's writings to the editor of Roxbury Publishing Co. in Los Angeles. He, too, saw a book.

Last year, Mumia Abu-Jamal, convicted of killing a Philadelphia police officer, was disciplined for writing his book, *Life From Death Row*. State prison officials said he violated the rule barring inmates from "engaging in a business or profession." A department spokesman said Hassine, unlike Abu-Jamal, isn't receiving payment. His royalties are going to the organization, Families of Murder Victims.

Hassine continues to write.

"Outsiders debate whether prisons should punish or rehabilitate," he said, "but the truth inside is: *There is no goal.* . . . It's strictly survival and crisis-control."

From *The Philadelphia Inquirer,* August 12, 1996. Copyright © 1996 by *The Philadelphia Inquirer. The Philadelphia Inquirer* has not endorsed any point of view, any person, any enterprise, any services or products, any approach in dealing with tasks or situations, any officials or employees. Reprinted by permission.